Chris Paulis

THE END

A Readers' Guide
to Revelation

by A. D. Bauer

First Edition 1997

Copyright © 1997 Square Halo Books
P.O. Box 18954, Baltimore, MD 21206

ISBN 0-9658798-0-1

Library of Congress 97-091783

Scripture taken from the HOLY BIBLE: NEW INTERNATIONAL VERSION®.
NIV® Copyright © 1973, 1978, 1984 by International Bible Society.
Used by permission of Zondervan Publishing House.

Illustrated, designed, and otherwise prepared
to the point of printing by Ned Bustard.

Printed in the United States of America by Forrey & Hacker, Inc.

THE END

A Readers' Guide
to Revelation

by A. D. Bauer

Jeremiah 5:30f
A horrible and shocking thing
has happened in the land:
The prophets prophesy lies,
the priests rule by their own authority,
and my people love it this way.
But what will you do in the end?

This book is dedicated with much love to Diana, Suzannah and Chara who allowed me the time out of our family schedule to write it. It is also dedicated to Maya and William who expressed interest and encouraged me in my writing. My family's support of this project made the time consuming and difficult task of researching, writing and editing this book much easier.

Many thanks to all the people who helped in various ways to bring this book together. Special thanks to Kevin Jones and Mary Grace O'Rourke whose editorial contributions made the final product clearer and more readable. Also, special thanks to Ned Bustard, whose illustrations and other contributions have inspired me.

Foreword

Why another book about Revelation? A further rehashing of the traditional eschatological positions and the traditional interpretations is not needed. Many commentaries and reference books cover the traditional approaches to Revelation quite adequately. When I first came to the study of Revelation it was not with the thought of expounding on it, but with fear and trepidation. I had to prepare for a class I was scheduled to teach, in which the topic of eschatology was to be covered. I had delayed as long as possible in scheduling this course, not knowing what I was going to do with Revelation. I read commentaries and reference materials but still was not confident that I could offer a coherent interpretation of the book.

I began intensively studying Revelation and some related biblical passages with an approach I have used on other parts of Scripture. This approach is not particularly innovative, although it is used less frequently today than it was in the past. My approach was to allow Scripture to interpret Scripture by finding common themes associated with a particular phrase or type of imagery. As I examined the phrase "the Day of the Lord" and imagery in which the earth was shaken, the heavenly bodies changed and catastrophes occurred, I saw patterns develop. Old Testament passages that described God's judgment of nations using imagery of cataclysmic disasters on earth and in the heavens, were fulfilled without the sun being darkened or the stars falling from heaven. From this came my understanding of the use of extreme language in Scripture to depict judgment. Other insights came from consistently applying a meaning, derived from Scripture, to symbols that were repeated in Revelation.

I still had no intention of writing a book, but I felt more comfortable with my understanding of the message of Revelation and I was able to approach the course with greater confidence. Friends with whom I shared my insights were very supportive, commenting that, from what I shared, they were better able to understand Revelation. Surprisingly, the same response came from my students who, at the end of the class, asked when I was going to get my material published.

Another impetus to publishing this work is that the time of the end is certainly much nearer now than it was when Revelation was written. Some have recently interpreted Revelation in such a way that they have proposed dates when the Lord would return. It does not appear to me that the date and time of the Lord's return can be known. However, the Lord is returning. By understanding the message of Revelation the church should be encouraged to patiently endure.

I offer this then as a reader's guide to Revelation. It is my hope that the reader will be helped as much as I have been by this approach to Revelation.

Introduction

How to Use This Book

People from all backgrounds and religious convictions want to read and understand the book of Revelation. However, most of those who decide to read Revelation for the first time find that their good intentions and efforts result in confusion and frustration. The symbols are baffling. The story line appears to be disjointed. Many of the faithful people who read the book have no idea what John was trying to say. For some this experience is so humbling that they never bother with Revelation again. Others ask their pastors to explain how the book should be interpreted. The problem is that even many scholarly pastors do not know how to interpret Revelation.

There are some who claim to understand Revelation. Often these "experts" present an analysis of Revelation filled with jargon and complicated explanations. A review of their supporting texts reveals that many verses are interpreted inconsistently with their context. If their view was correct, neither an interested modern reader nor a first century Christian would ever have discovered the meaning of the text.

The premise of this book is that Revelation was designed to be understood by the people in the churches to whom it was addressed. As such, it is also understandable for Christians today. That is not to say that it is easy to understand. Revelation is a complex book that requires the reader to have a broad knowledge of the Scriptures. Those unfamiliar with the Scriptures would be better off studying Revelation after they have built a foundational knowledge of God's word that will give them the background they need.

An important key to understanding Revelation is to be familiar with Old and New Testament passages that provide the background for the images in Revelation. Some symbols are defined in biblical passages outside Revelation. John defines other symbols as he describes what he saw. To aid the reader in defining the symbols used in Revelation, the third section is a glossary of most of the images in Revelation.

It is also important to understand the relationship between Old Testament and New Testament eschatological passages (passages about the return of Christ and the final judgment.) This is necessary in order to form a complete picture of what the Scriptures teach. There are themes repeated throughout Scripture that refer to the final judgment and the return of Christ. What is the significance of the use of extreme language (the sun darkened and the stars falling from the sky) in the Old and New Testaments? What is the meaning of phrases like "the day of the Lord" that have Old Testament roots? The first section of this book answers these questions so that the use of extreme language and key phrases in Revelation can be understood.

Even using the method of interpretation presented in this book, understanding Revelation is not easy. However, helpful insights are available for anyone who takes the time to examine and compare all of the relevant texts.

The first section of this book provides a brief overview of rules for interpreting Revelation. It also examines some of the most important texts outside Revelation. While some might be tempted to go first to the sections that interpret Revelation, such an approach is not recommended. Without the background of the first section, the information in the second and third sections will be less helpful. When reading the overview of texts outside Revelation, it is recommended that you have the Bible opened to those sections. This will allow you to verify the information provided. It would be even better to read the entire passage in your Bible before reading the overview of the background texts.

The second section is an interpretive summary of Revelation that offers my approach to understanding the book. It explains how the symbols and related biblical texts provide insights into the meaning of the vision. It is not a commentary, nor is it in commentary format. It is an orderly progression through Revelation with interpretations of passages presented and the reasons for the interpretations explained. To help you in evaluating the information presented, symbols and terminology defined in the third section are highlighted. This will allow you to look up how that phrase or symbol is used in Scripture and the reasons why it has been assigned a particular meaning.

The third section is a glossary of terms and phrases found in Revelation. It also includes a few terms or phrases popular in discussions of the end of the world but not found in Revelation. Section three helps you see where the term or phrase comes from, how it is used throughout Scripture and particularly, how it is used in Revelation. Section three lists every place in Revelation that the term or phrase appears. In each definition, symbols or terms found elsewhere in the third section are highlighted the first time that they appear.

This is a reader's guide to Revelation. It will be of greatest help to you if you refer to your Bible to look up passages discussed. As you read the biblical text you can verify the context of the verses and the accuracy of the comments. Additionally, the biblical text may discuss in greater detail ideas of interest to you.

You may not agree with every interpretive point made within the book. I have tried to be accurate and complete, however, infallibility is a quality of God not shared by me. The purpose of this book is not to form a universal consensus but to make Revelation more accessible for study as an encouragement to the church.

Revelation 1:3 Blessed is the one who reads the words of this prophesy, and blessed are those who hear it and take to heart what is written in it, because the time is near.

SECTION ONE

Principles of Interpretation

For Passages Related to the Return of Christ

Before discussing how the book of Revelation should be interpreted, it will be helpful to define a pair of terms with which the reader may not be familiar. These words are widely used and are important in the study of the theology of the second coming of Christ.

ESCHATOLOGY refers to the doctrine of the last or final things. It is the study of topics that include death, judgment, heaven and hell. Eschatology is not concerned solely with the book of Revelation. Biblical passages providing information about the last things, such as the return of Christ and the end of the world, are found throughout Scripture. A strong eschatological position can reconcile passages from many books, including Revelation, so that there is congruity among passages.

HERMENEUTICS is the science of interpretation that, in theology, focuses on the principles of biblical interpretation. Within Christianity, there are many groups whose interpretations of Scriptural passages differ. Usually, the differences in how passages are interpreted are based on the rules applied. Different rules produce different results, so passages are interpreted in ways that lead to different conclusions.

Some people think that biblical interpretation is simply a matter of common sense. For many passages this is true. However, many difficult passages in Revelation use imagery based on texts from other parts of Scripture. The interpreter must consider the meaning of images that appear elsewhere in Scripture. It is also important that passages quoting or referring to other biblical texts be understood in light of the meaning of those background texts. What appears on the surface of a text may be misleading to those who do not know the meaning of the images or the background.

Additionally, many people have never considered what principles of interpretation should be used to interpret biblical passages. Everyone has some set of rules for interpreting Scripture. It is crucial that the rules, for an issue as important as biblical interpretation, be carefully considered before they are applied to a particular set of texts. This is the reason that hermeneutics is the first consideration in preparing to read Revelation. Some of the principles of interpretation proposed below are identical with those that apply to other biblical passages. Others are unique to passages with eschatological content.

Most of the principles of interpretation that follow are not new. The purpose in presenting them is to explain the rules used throughout this book. Some will disagree with the principles or with how they are applied. What is most important is that the issue of principles of interpretation be considered. Each person must decide if the principles proposed make sense. The principles presented are helpful if they stimulate thought about how Revelation is to be interpreted.

Internal Consistency

Images appearing elsewhere in Scripture, especially in apocalyptic texts, should be presumed to have similar content to those within Revelation. The term apocalyptic refers to writings, sometimes making extensive use of imagery, which describe the end of the world. The New Testament writers were very familiar with the Old Testament. The apocalyptic material in Revelation often stands on the foundation of apocalyptic images from the Old and New Testaments. That is not to say that John wrote with certain images in mind. He wrote down what he saw in his vision. But God communicated through the vision so that John was able to understand much of what he saw, based on God's use of images from the Old and New Testament Scriptures.

Sometimes it appears that John supplemented the description of what he saw using images from other Old and New Testament passages. He used the additional images to clarify the meaning of the text. For example, in Revelation 11 the two witnesses are also called two lampstands and two olive trees. The identity of the witnesses would have been obscure if John had not used the lampstand and olive tree images. Often it is the lack of sufficient knowledge of the Old and New Testaments that makes passages in Revelation appear more difficult to understand than they really are.

While John did sometimes supplement the description of what he saw, normally the images that John recorded from his vision were exactly what he saw. God used images from other parts of Scripture to clarify the meaning of the vision to the church. After all, God's purpose in inspiring Scripture is to communicate truth to his people. No one could take Revelation to heart (Rev. 1:3) if its meaning were beyond comprehension. Therefore, it must be difficult but not impossible to understand. The images have meaning and help the reader interpret passages that are more difficult.

Revelation's use of images from other biblical texts obscures its meaning to those outside the church. Images from Scripture can clarify the meaning for believers while hiding the meaning from those who are not familiar with the Scriptures. Jesus told his disciples that the knowledge of the secrets of the kingdom were given to them but not to all the people (Matthew 13:11.) When Jesus spoke in parables many would not understand his meaning (Matthew 13:13f.) The images in the parables were understood by those who had ears to hear. Through the images, the meaning of the parables was hidden from those who were outsiders. In the same way, the images in Revelation can reveal truth or hide it. The reader must be very familiar with the Old and New Testament Scriptures to understand the meaning of the images in Revelation. The book will remain a mystery to the biblical novice.

Prior Definition

If the meaning of an image is defined within apocalyptic material the same image has the same meaning throughout the document. For example, there is an image of seven lampstands in Revelation 1 that is defined as seven churches. When lampstands are used symbolically in Revelation 11:4, it should be assumed that they are also churches. It is this element of consistency that makes apocalyptic material understandable.

Scholarly documents or textbooks tend to define terms the first time they appear. In Revelation, images are sometimes defined after they have been used several times. Images that appear at the beginning of Revelation are sometimes not defined until near the end. In such cases, knowledge of the whole book is necessary to interpret symbols found at the beginning of the book. John assumes that an image in Revelation needs no definition when he does not provide the definition. Either the image exists elsewhere in Scripture or its meaning can be understood from the context.

Extreme Language

Extreme language is a term applied throughout this book to those passages found both in the Old and New Testaments that describe a devastating series of signs in the heavens and on earth. These events can include earthquakes, thunder and lightning, hailstorms, and dramatic changes in the sun, moon, and stars.

Do the many passages using extreme language intend for the description of events to be taken literally or is the language symbolic? The interpretation of extreme language in the New Testament should be consistent with its use throughout the Old Testament where it refers to historical events. For example, in Revelation 6:12-14 the sun is darkened, the moon is turned blood red, and the stars fall to the earth. Similar language appears in Matthew 24:29, and Mark 13:24f, and there is a reference to it in Luke 21:25. The language in the New Testament passages is similar to that used to describe the destruction prophesied in Isaiah 13:9-13, concerning the Lord's overthrow of Babylon.

> *Isaiah 13:10* The stars of heaven and their constellations will not show their light. The rising sun will be darkened and the moon will not give its light.

There is no indication in historical records that the signs in the heavens described in Isaiah 13 literally occurred immediately prior to Babylon's destruction. Likewise, in Isaiah 34:4 extreme language is used of God's destruction of all the nations, but especially of Edom.

> *Isaiah 34:9,10* Edom's streams will be turned into pitch, her dust into burning sulphur; her land will become burning pitch! It will not be quenched night and day; its smoke will rise forever. From generation to generation it will lie desolate; no one will ever pass through it again.

Edom was judged and destroyed, but the land has not been turned into burning pitch. Ezekiel 32:7f uses similar language of God's judgment on Egypt.

> *Ezekiel 32:7,8* When I snuff you out, I will cover the heavens and darken their stars; I will cover the sun with a cloud, and the moon will not give its light. All the shining lights in the heavens I will darken over you; I will bring darkness over your land, declares the Sovereign Lord.

Egypt has been judged and destroyed, but the events in the heavens that were described did not literally occur. The judgments pronounced in all these passages occurred without the literal darkening of the heavens or the literal burning of the land. From this it can be concluded that the language was not intended to be taken literally. Its purpose is to describe the extreme chaos that results from the destruction of a nation or world power.

Some interpreters believe these passages have not been fulfilled because the signs were not literally fulfilled. They theorize that the nations will be reestablished and literally destroyed as described in the prophesies. It is difficult to believe that these nations will be reestablished. It is also difficult to believe that the prophets were not talking about the nations that existed during their own time. The context supports the idea that the text is speaking of the destruction that has already occurred. Regarding the Babylonians God says:

> *Isaiah 13:17* See I will stir up against them the Medes, who do not care for silver and have no delight in gold.

History tells us that the Medes and Persians conquered the Babylonians. The context of Ezekiel's prophesy also supports its fulfillment at the time it was made. Ezekiel prophesied after Babylon captured Jerusalem. Speaking to Egypt which failed to help Israel against Babylon he says:

> *Ezekiel 32:11* " 'For this is what the Sovereign Lord says: " 'The sword of the king of Babylon will come against you.

History tells us that Babylon conquered Egypt after capturing Jerusalem. The judgment of these nations has already come just as the prophesy stated. Therefore, it is reasonable to assert that the literal ful-fillment of the extreme language in the prophesy was not intended.

The purpose of extreme language is to communicate the devastating nature of God's judgment. God's judgment on nations has been so severe that it would seem to those judged as though the sun was darkened and the stars were falling from the sky. This does not mean that the Old Testament images cannot literally come true at the end of human histo-ry. It is prophesied in several places in the Old Testament, and in Revelation, that there will be a great earthquake at the very end (Ezekiel 38:19, Zech. 14:3-5, Rev. 6:12, 11:13,19, 16:18.) There is every reason to believe that there will be an earthquake at the end of history. The possible literal fulfillment of some extreme language at the end of human history does not diminish its significance as language that throughout Scripture symbolizes judgment by the Lord.

Extreme language in the Old Testament regularly appears in the same context with passages that mention the Day of the Lord. A further discussion of extreme language and its connection with the Day of the Lord appears in the Apocalyptic Terminology section.

Consider to Whom the Book is Addressed

Passages containing apocalyptic material were understood by the peo-ple to whom they were sent. New Testament passages were written for an audience who would directly benefit from the teaching. It is also rele-vant for modern Christians, and that is part of what makes Scripture unique. Paul's epistles are named for the churches and individuals to whom the letters were written. The gospels are a blessing to all who read them because of their record of the life and death of our Lord. They are also written to particular audiences. Luke's gospel is addressed to an individual named Theophilus. Theophilus shared his letter with the rest of the church so that all believers benefit from Luke. The other gospels are not directly addressed to any individual or church but they were writ-ten for regional churches. They provide encouragement for the situa-tions that existed within those regional churches. For example, Mark wrote his gospel for the Christians in Rome and Italy. He writes that Jesus "was with the wild animals and angels attended him" as part of the description of the temptation of Jesus in the wilderness (Mark 1:13.) Mark included the description of Jesus facing wild animals to encourage

Roman believers when they or their loved ones faced wild animals in the Colosseum.

When a book is addressed to a specific church, the material within the book, is first applicable to the situation in that church. For example, the Corinthian church had a problem with divisions and lack of love. Paul's first letter addresses those problems and offers solutions. Modern churches can be troubled by divisions and can learn from the Corinthian letter how to show love. Christians receive benefits from reading the epistles because the problems they face are similar to those in the early church. The letter must first be read as a document written to a particular church's situation. The modern church benefits because God is able to expand the impact of His Word beyond the original target audience.

Some have wanted to treat Revelation as though it were a letter addressed to the modern church. While some prophetic elements have not been fulfilled and will be fulfilled in the future, the book must belong primarily to the seven churches. John wrote Revelation for the seven churches and it deals with particular situations they faced. As with the Corinthian letters and Paul's other letters, the modern reader is reading someone else's mail. It is to God's glory that "someone else's mail" is profitable to the church of the twentieth and twenty-first centuries for teaching, rebuking, correcting, and training in righteousness (II Tim. 3:16.)

Passages within Revelation that pertain to the end of the world and the second coming can be distinguished from those that do not. Frequently, texts describing the culmination of human history directly refer to the judgment at the end of the world or to Christ's return. These texts typically include extreme language tied to a judgment theme, or a description of the coming of the Lord and the fear experienced by his enemies. Some texts also describe the ascension of the church into heaven or a song of celebration that the Lord is reigning. The faithful in the seven churches are connected to the end of the world by being promised things that those who endure until the end receive (e.g., to eat from the tree of life, or to sit with Jesus on his throne.) It cannot be assumed that because a text is in Revelation it automatically has something to do with the end of the world.

Old Testament Fulfillment

One difficulty in interpreting Old Testament passages that may pertain to the end of the world is in knowing exactly which passages have been fulfilled and which await fulfillment. Old Testament prophesies that refer to God's judgment on Israel and other nations should be largely if not entirely fulfilled. This is particularly true when the nation prophesied against was later destroyed by a competing nation or empire. It is not always clear how a passage was fulfilled. Nevertheless, the limited knowledge of modern scholars should not be the basis for proposing that extensive portions of the Old Testament require fulfillment in the future. There are many passages in the New Testament that discuss the end of the world. It is therefore unnecessary to build an eschatology based largely on Old Testament passages that may have already been fulfilled.

Material describing how God will judge particular nations that no longer exist has been fulfilled. Some are comfortable proposing the reconstruction of ancient kingdoms. However, it seems that such a reconstruction would itself require a separate prophesy, if that were what the text was describing.

Some Old Testament texts clearly refer to the final judgment, God descending with his holy ones or the ultimate purification and vindication of Israel. Some of these passages include a description of how local nations which no longer exist acted against the people of God. However, the primary focus of those passages is God's judgment of the nations of the world, the purification of Israel and the establishment of an idealized world blessed by God. These texts do have eschatological relevance and should be used with New Testament eschatological passages to build a fully developed theology of the end of the world. Typically, images or teachings from relevant Old Testament texts are used in Revelation.

Consider the Context of the Passage

As with any passage of Scripture, the context of the passage is the meaning of the passage. Almost any meaning can be derived from reading a short section of Scripture in isolation. For any interpretation to be valid, it has to be consistent with the meaning of the surrounding passages. Some interpreters have strung together a series of passages to prove a particular eschatological view. The verses tied together and in isolation from other texts can be convincing. However, a comparison of the meaning of those passages with their context discredits the interpretation.

Do Not Presume to Know More Than Jesus

Jesus clearly stated that he did not know the day or hour of his return (Matt 24:36.) If he who was the perfect Son of God did not know, it is presumptive for anyone to suggest that he does know.

It should be understood that Jesus had several advantages that are not available to the modern biblical scholar. Jesus was unfallen and without sin, so he could understand the Scriptures as God's word better than anyone else. He would not have the blind spots fallen men have because of their sins. Jesus, as a prophet of God, was able to know things others did not. If it had been God's intention to communicate the day and time of Christ's return, God would have given that information to Jesus. Jesus would have handled that information with wisdom and discretion superior to any modern man. Jesus' knowledge of the Old Testament and of texts in the New Testament that come from his teaching would have to be superior to that of any interpreter today. Jesus would have understood the information contained in those portions of the New Testament where he is quoted or where the Old Testament is quoted or referred to. There are few biblical texts that could contain information with which Jesus might not have been familiar during his earthly ministry. Those few texts do not appear to provide detailed chronological information that would allow anyone to determine the day or hour of Jesus' return. Portions of Paul's writings, the other epistles, and Revelation contain very little that is not derived from the Old Testament or Jesus' teaching.

References to Time in Revelation

Most references to time in Revelation are symbolic and do not give an exact chronology of events. References to time can be symbolic when the length of time is a large number rounded to the nearest one thousand or when the period is indefinite (as in time, times, and half a time.) They also can be recognized as symbolic when they come from biblical passages outside Revelation where they are used symbolically (again, as in time, times, and half a time.) They are symbolic when the same unit of time in different forms (as in 1,260 days and forty-two months) is connected to symbolic references to time (see Rev. 12:6,14 where time, times, and half a time is equated with 1,260 days.) The handling of references to time in eschatological texts elsewhere in Scripture is a clue to how they should be handled in Revelation.

The significance of references to time in Daniel helps one understand how similar symbols should be handled in Revelation. In Daniel there are several references to time. Some are symbolic and have been interpreted that way by the church throughout history. Others have no obvious symbolic significance and so are more likely to be intended to be understood literally.

Daniel uses the phrase time, times, and half a time in two of his visions. Where it appears, it refers to two different periods. In Daniel 7:25, time, times, and half a time describes the period during which the saints are handed over to the Man of Lawlessness. Since his reign is likely to be less than seven years (as will be explained later), the time, times, and half a time is a very short period. However, in Daniel 12:7, time, times, and half a time describes the period from Daniel's vision until the end of human history. See the article on Time, Times, and Half a Time in Section 3 for an in depth explanation. It should be expected that since Daniel uses the phrase to describe two different periods, the intent must be to describe an indefinite period. This suggests that the intent in Revelation also will be to describe a period of unknown length.

Daniel also writes of seventy 'sevens' or 'weeks' in Daniel 9:24-27 that are not literal weeks. Within the first sixty-nine 'sevens' (consisting of seven 'sevens' and sixty-two 'sevens') the Anointed One (the Messiah) comes. The seven 'sevens' come first, then the sixty-two 'sevens', and after the sixty-two 'sevens' the Messiah is cut off. This occurred almost five hundred years after the decree to rebuild Jerusalem. After the Messiah is cut off, the people of the ruler who will come (the Man of Lawlessness, note Daniel 9:27) destroy the city and the sanctuary.

The decree to rebuild the city occurred as prophesied in Daniel 9:25 and the city was rebuilt. Later, the Romans destroyed the city and sanctuary in 70 AD. Consequently, it is necessary that the Messiah must have come before 70 AD. The only figure to have come and made any credible claim to being Messiah prior to 70 AD is Jesus.

Interestingly, each 'seven' or 'week' appears to represent seven years (one year for each 'day' in the 'week'.) The decree to rebuild Jerusalem was announced approximately 493 BC. There were approximately 483 years (sixty-nine 'weeks' times seven years) from the decree to rebuild Jerusalem to the birth of Jesus (which occurred approximately 10 BC.)

This pattern suggests that the final 'seven' or 'week' (Dan 9:27), during which the Man of Lawlessness reigns, will be approximately seven years. The Man of Lawlessness and his reign are covered in the discussion of passages from Daniel and in the in Section 3.

The primary point of this observation is that the 'sevens' and 'weeks' are references to time that represent an indefinite period leading up to the birth of the Messiah. No Old Testament scholar or bible student was able to provide a definitive chronology of this event until after it had occurred. Having observed the pattern of the first sixty-nine 'weeks', the modern Bible student can apply the lessons learned to the portion of the prophesy awaiting fulfillment.

There are three other references to time in Daniel's visions (Daniel 8:14, 12:11,12.) The number of days are not multiples of any symbolic number (7, 12, or 1000) and are not equivalent to numbers found elsewhere in Scripture that are used symbolically. It is therefore most reasonable to interpret them literally.

In Revelation, the purpose of John's vision is not to tell when everything will happen. Jesus' promise that all these things will come soon provides sufficient warning that believers should be ready when the Lord returns. The important issue is not when things will happen, but what things will happen. This is why the references to time in Revelation are almost all symbolic. As symbols, they do not define specific dates and times, but do describe a series of interconnected events. This allows the believer to see that God planned all events, and they are in his hands. This assurance will help the church, as it faces persecution, to endure patiently until the end.

It should be assumed that references to time are symbolic when the section in which they appear contains a significant amount of imagery and is part of a vision. The references to time based on Daniel should be taken as literally as he meant them. References to time that can be shown to be non-literal in Daniel should be interpreted similarly in Revelation.

Dating Revelation

While there are some minor disagreements about the dating of other books in the New Testament, the issue is nowhere more critical than in Revelation. The date Revelation was written determines how some passages are interpreted. In several places Jerusalem and the temple are mentioned. The primary issue is whether Revelation was written before the fall of Jerusalem or after its destruction in 70 AD.

Two schools of thought surround the dating of Revelation. Some have proposed an early date for Revelation, suggesting that it was written during the reign of Nero (54-68 AD.) Some have dated Revelation as early as 48 AD, but most proponents of the early date maintain that Revelation was written between 64-68 AD. Recently, scholars have increasingly supported the early date.

The alternative to the early dating of Revelation suggests it was written during the reign of Domitian (81-96 AD.) For the proponents of this later view, John's vision occurred about 95 AD. It is possible that John could have written during this time because Irenaeus, a church father, states that John lived until the reign of Trajan (98-117 AD.) The later date has been the dominant view among biblical scholars.

Those who hold to the later date point to Irenaeus and Clement for support because they are believed to have recorded that John wrote Revelation during Domitian's reign. While there is not time in a short work such as this to cover the issues adequately, an overview of the arguments is helpful. [1] Irenaeus has traditionally been translated as saying that the book of Revelation was written toward the end of Domitian's reign. However, many scholars since Wetstein in 1751 have asserted that Irenaeus was actually speaking of John, saying "for he was seen ... almost in our generation toward the end of the reign of Domitian." While it is not necessary to take a position in this debate, it should be noted that Irenaeus' statement does not provide the absolute support that proponents of the later date have sometimes asserted.

Clement of Alexandria is quoted by a number of scholars as supporting the later date. The portion that pertains to this discussion is as follows:

When after the death of the tyrant he (John) removed from the island of Patmos to Ephesus, he used to journey by request to the neighboring districts of the Gentiles, in some places to appoint bishops, in others to regulate whole churches, in others to set among the clergy some one man, it may be, of those indicated by the Spirit. [2]

If it is assumed that the tyrant is Domitian, the text is a strong support for the later date. However, Domitian's name is not mentioned. A case can easily be made for either Domitian or Nero as the tyrant referred to in this text. In considering which might be preferred, it should be remembered that if Domitian were the tyrant, John's work described in the quotation would begin in 96 AD when he would have been in his mid-eighties or older. While it might be possible for him to travel and work in this way at such an advanced age, it is more likely that he would have performed these duties if he left Patmos in 68 or 69 AD.

Another document that aids in determining the date Revelation was written is the "Shepherd of Hermas." The Shepherd of Hermas was a devotional writing popular early in the church's history. Some in the early church proposed that the Shepherd of Hermas should be included in the New Testament. Many scholars have detected similarities in the imagery used in the Shepherd of Hermas which lead them to conclude that its author was familiar with John's Revelation. The Muratorian Canon (180 AD) teaches that the Shepherd of Hermas was written by the brother of Pius I, about 140-150 AD. However, Origin attributes it to the Hermas greeted by Paul in Romans 16:14. Both Origin and Irenaeus quote from it as Scripture which would be unlikely if Irenaeus was aware that it had been written after the apostolic period. [3]

Another argument presented to support an earlier date is that Hermas is told to send one of two books he writes to Clement who "was to send it to foreign cities, for this is his duty." If Clement's duty is to send out documents, he is acting as a secretary. It would be unlikely that he would perform this kind of task after his elevation to bishop in 90 AD. If the Shepherd of Hermas was written before Clement was made bishop, and if Hermas was aware of Revelation, Revelation must be dated significantly earlier than 90 AD.

In addition to the external evidence above, an important witness to the dating of Revelation will be the book itself. Several arguments based on internal evidence lend strength to the earlier dating of Revelation.

It has been observed by some scholars that the idiom of Revelation reflects a younger John than the one who wrote the Gospel of John.

Persecution and conflict with Jewish synagogues suggest the earlier rather than the later dating of Revelation. In fact, the way that persecution is handled by the book implies that there has been no significant experience of this kind of persecution by the church. If Revelation was written at the end of Domitian's reign, it could be expected that a church that had already survived the Neronian persecution and the lesser persecutions of several subsequent emperors would not have to be warned about the need for patient endurance.

Finally, it seems strange for John to measure the temple (Rev. 11) if it had been destroyed more than twenty years earlier. If John was measuring a temple that was already gone, it could be expected that he would say something about its demise or restoration. If he was counting worshippers in a former temple, the significance of those worshippers should be mentioned, but it is not.

Based on the above evidence, this text assumes the earlier date for Revelation.

Apocalyptic Terminology

There are two phrases used in conjunction with eschatological language that need to be understood within their Old Testament and New Testament contexts if the reader is going to develop a consistent eschatological view.

Day of the Lord

One of the first places where the day of the Lord is mentioned is in Isaiah 2. In response to superstition (vs. 6) and idolatry (vs. 8), the passage states that the Lord alone will be exalted on that day (vs. 11.) The Lord has a day in store (vs. 12) and the Lord alone will be exalted in that day (vs. 17.) There is a use of extreme language in verses 19 and 21 where the Lord rises to shake the earth. From the language of this chapter, the reader begins to see the meaning of the Day of the Lord. It is a day of judgment. Not necessarily "the" day of final judgment as shall be seen from some of the other passages. This is a day when the Lord will judge a people, typically resulting in their destruction.

In Isaiah 13, the chapter begins by stating that this is a prophesy regarding Babylon. Verse 6 warns that the day of the Lord is near and it will mean destruction. Verses 9-13 sound like a great eschatological passage of the final judgment. But the remaining verses are consistent with the context. They warn of what God's judgment against Babylon will be like. In Isaiah 13, the destruction is temporal and an act of judgment on an evil nation that God has used to judge Israel.

Before moving to the next passage, some mention should be made of the extreme language used in connection with passages referring to the Day of the Lord. Extreme language appears both in eschatological passages and in passages dealing with God's intervention for judgment. As previously noted, in Isaiah 2 there are two descriptions of the earth shaking. In Isaiah 13 the stars and the constellations will not show their light, the rising sun will be darkened, the moon will not give its light (vs. 10.) The heavens will tremble and the earth will shake (vs. 13.) If a literal approach was to be used in interpreting these passages, they could only be speaking of the final judgment. It would be difficult to justify spot references to the end of the world within passages whose context has already been defined as addressing God's judgment on a specific nation. It is more consistent with the meaning of the text within its context to view this as a use of exalted and symbolic language to describe the magnitude of God's judgment.

The destruction of a world power by the Lord would be a terribly difficult thing to live through. In the world today, the relatively peaceful fragmentation of the Soviet Union provides a lesser illustration of this point. The loss of the Soviet empire has been unpleasant for those who formerly ruled. The loss has been even more difficult for world empires that have been suddenly and violently overthrown. For those who have built their lives on material things and personal power, the violent destruction of their nation and their loss of status and goods would be as if their world had been shaken and their lights put out.

Other examples of this language referring to God's judgment appear in Isaiah 34:4,9f, Ezekiel 32:7,8, Amos 8:9, and Joel 2:2,10,30. There is not a single instance where the extreme language of an Old Testament passage was fulfilled literally. This is true in spite of the fulfillment of the destruction of the nations mentioned in the prophesies. There is a pattern of Old Testament prophesies using extreme language, in a context where that language is tied to the Day of the Lord. This is understandable because the Day of the Lord refers to a day of judgment, and the extreme language accompanying it illustrates the devastating nature of that judgment.

The passages listed above clearly depict the Day of the Lord as a day of judgment. In Joel, the Day of the Lord is a day of judgment and destruction. Joel 1:15 warns that the day of the Lord is near; it will come like destruction from the Almighty. In Joel 2:1f, the day of the Lord is close at hand, a day of darkness and gloom, a day of clouds and blackness. With the warning of the Day of the Lord comes extreme language in Joel 2:10 where, the earth shakes, the sky trembles, the sun, and moon are darkened, and the stars no longer shine. Then in Joel 2:11, the prophet warns that the day of the Lord is great; it is dreadful. Who can endure it? Clearly the Lord, in context, is speaking of Israel's judgment that will result in her destruction. The day of judgment is temporal, it is not the final judgment. The extreme language of the passage reflects the extreme impact on Israel.

Additionally, Joel 2:30f, a passage that Peter said was fulfilled in Pentecost, describes wonders in the heavens and on earth…The sun will be turned to darkness and the moon to blood. There is perhaps a partial fulfillment of these signs fifty days before Pentecost when the sun was darkened during the crucifixion. Yet, at that time the moon was not turned to blood and during Pentecost there is no indication that any of these things literally took place. Peter connects Joel's prophesy with the events at Pentecost not because the heavenly signs appeared, but because the Holy Spirit fell on the people of God. The imagery of the signs in the heavens is a warning of judgment and of how important this event at Pentecost is. The coming of the Spirit at Pentecost is an act of judgment. It validates the new church, and with the Scriptures condemns those who refuse to believe in Christ.

Joel's prophesy includes both a threat and a warning. The threat is that the day of the Lord is coming against unfaithful Israel at the time Joel is writing. The warning is to the nations of the world. They should beware of the day of the Lord that will occur at the end of history. At that time, God will bless Israel and judge the nations (compare Joel 1:15, 2:1 and Joel 3:1,2,9-16.)

In the New Testament, there are many places where the terms "day of the Lord" or "the day of our Lord Jesus Christ" appear. The content is similar in that it refers to judgment by God, but in most places the text does not use extreme language. Why is that? The description of the day of the Lord in the Old Testament typically refers to God's judgment which will have a devastating effect on Israel or on some other nation. In the New Testament, the Day of the Lord refers to God's final judgment which believers look forward to with anticipation. Where extreme language appears in the New Testament, it addresses God's judgment of those who do not believe in him. For them, his return and judgment will be as though their world had been shaken and turned upside down.

The term, "day of the Lord," continues to be used concerning judgment throughout the New Testament. In I Corinthians 1:8, Paul promises that he (the Lord) will keep you strong to the end, so that you will be blameless on the day of our Lord Jesus Christ. This verse is in a context where Paul has already mentioned waiting for the Lord Jesus Christ to be revealed (the second coming). It might be thought "the day" could refer to the day of Christ's return only. However, both the Old Testament usage of Day of the Lord and the idea of being blameless suggest that it is a day of judgment as well as the day of Christ's return.

In I Corinthians 5:5, Paul orders a man to be handed over to the Satan, so that his sinful nature may be destroyed and his spirit saved on the day of the Lord. This is another clear reference to the day of the Lord as a day of final judgment. The church hands this man over so that he will be saved from condemnation at the final judgment.

In II Corinthians 1:14, Paul includes the phrase, . . . as we will boast of you on the day of the Lord. Again the reference is to the final judgment. Paul will boast of them when the powerful working of the grace of God is exhibited in them when they are evaluated at the judgment. He will not boast of them at the return of Christ. It is at the judgment that their godliness will be shown to have brought glory to God.

In I Thessalonians 5:2ff, Paul writes that the day of the Lord will come like a thief in the night . . . destruction will come on them suddenly. This is another clear description of the judgment. For those who are unprepared to meet the Lord, the day comes as a thief and destroys them. But verse 4 continues, "you are not in darkness so that this day should surprise you like a thief." The point Paul is making has nothing to do with the date and time of Christ's return. It is a warning that Christ's return will surprise some who have not prepared themselves to face the judgment. They will be destroyed.

In II Thessalonians 2:2ff, Paul quiets the fears of the Thessalonians who wonder if the day of the Lord may have already come. It may seem strange that they would anticipate the judgment and does seem to more naturally connect the Day of the Lord to the return of Christ. However, here and elsewhere, there is no great differentiation between the return of Christ and the final judgment. The many passages that speak of the return of Christ usually mention the final judgment within the same context. Nowhere in Scripture is it suggested that Christ returns, followed by a series of intervening events over some period, after which comes the final judgment. Christ will come and judge the nations (Jude 14.)

There are many examples of this connection between Christ's coming and judging at the same time. Two of the more obvious passages that do not require much interpretive work are:

> *Matthew 25:31,32* When the Son of Man comes in his glory, and all the angels with him, he will sit on his throne in heavenly glory. All the nations will be gathered before him, and he will separate the people one from another as a shepherd separates the sheep from the goats. (Note the end of this passage, verse 46.)

> *II Thessalonians 1:7b,8,9* This will happen when the Lord Jesus is revealed from heaven in blazing fire with his powerful angels. He will punish those who do not know God and do not obey the gospel of our Lord Jesus. They will be punished with everlasting destruction and shut out from the presence of the Lord and from the majesty of his power on the day he comes to be glorified in his holy people and to be marveled at among those who have believed.

For the believers in Thessalonica, there is nothing to fear from the judgment and everything to gain from the Lord's presence.

In II Peter 3:10, is found the exception that proves the rule. Peter warns that the day of the Lord will come as a thief in the night. The heavens will disappear with a roar, and the elements will be destroyed by fire. This passage uses extreme language but in this one case, the context supports the taking of this language literally. It should be taken literally because it is not like the other uses of extreme language in the Old or

New Testaments. It is not describing a disaster for God's people who have become unfaithful, nor the destruction of a national power. It is describing the events surrounding the final judgment. In verse 7, Peter has already said that the present heavens and earth are reserved for fire, being kept for the day of judgment. In light of verse 7, it is not surprising that his description of the coming of the Day of the Lord (the day of judgment) includes the destruction of the heavens and earth with fire.

When extreme language appears in Revelation, it is always a symbol of judgment. It may be literally fulfilled but it may be as symbolic as it was in the Old Testament. Sometimes, extreme language anticipates the presentation of a series of judgments, some of which are not directly related to the final judgment. An example of this occurs in Revelation 8:5 where, in preparation for the sounding of the seven trumpets, a censer with fire from the altar is cast to earth and there are peals of thunder, rumblings, flashes of lightning, and an earthquake. This extreme language prepares the reader for the seven trumpets which are seven judgments.

The Coming of the Lord

The Coming of the Lord is a phrase referring to the second coming. The return of the Lord is discussed in a number of different passages and is examined from a variety of perspectives. Several crucial points are made in the passages: the time of his return is unknown and unknowable, the coming is noisy, visible, and unmistakable, and his coming results in the final judgment.

In Matthew 24:30,31, the return of Jesus is described. The Lord will come with his angels to gather his elect and leave the non-elect. He will appear in the sky and will be seen by all people. Here and elsewhere the return of Christ is noisy, visible, and final.

Some interpreters have suggested two returns of Christ, a secret one and a visible one. The passages that depict the Lord's return in the clearest of terms describe this return as visible. It should be noted that in the discussion of I Thessalonians 4:15-18 that follows, a serious objection will be raised to the idea of a silent rapture that would remove believers but permit the world to continue on. Paul's assertion that he could be included among those who depart in the "noisy" return of Christ makes it difficult for anyone to hold to a silent rapture preceding the visible return of Christ.

In Matthew 24:36-44, Jesus points out that no one knows when he will come, not angels, nor the Son (vs. 36.) Because the time cannot be known, Jesus cautions that they (and we) are to be ready "because the Son of Man will come at an hour when you do not expect him" (vs. 44.) The significance of this section is that no one knows when the Lord is coming and so all of God's people should be prepared at all times. To handle the text properly, it is necessary that verses 36-41 of Matthew 24 not be read in isolation from the verses earlier in the chapter. The one taken and the other left of verses 40 and 41 are a reference to the angels described in verse 31 who gather his elect from the four winds. When they gather the Lord's elect, they leave the non-elect behind. Those who are prepared go with the Lord to heaven, while the unprepared are left for the destruction. This taking of some and leaving others who face destruction is seen in Matthew 24:31,40,41,50,51.

In Matthew 25:31ff, the coming of the Son of Man is in glory with his angels and results in the separation of the sheep and the goats, i.e., judgment. This text describes such a close connection between the return of Christ and the judgment that they are not two things but one. The one leads naturally to the second and there is no break or separation between them.

In I Thessalonians 4:15-18, Paul speaks of those who are still alive, who are left until the coming of the Lord, not preceding those who are asleep. The primary point being made here is that those who die in the Lord before his return will participate in that return. Within this text is a strong argument against any view proposing a silent rapture and two returns of Christ. Paul includes himself with those who could still be alive when the Lord returns. He does this by saying,

> *I Thessalonians 4:15* "According to the Lord's own word, we tell you that we who are still alive, who are left until the coming of the Lord, will certainly not precede those who have fallen asleep."

By saying we who are still alive, he includes himself as one who could be present when the Lord returns. The return of the Lord he is expecting is described in verses 16 and 17. The coming of the Lord he is waiting for is with a loud command, with the voice of the archangel (indicating that there are angels present), and with the trumpet call of God. Then, we who are still alive and are left will be caught up in the air with the Lord. This is a "noisy" return of Christ and is like the return described in Matthew 24. If Paul expected Christ to return in this noisy manner for him, then either there is one return of Christ and it is noisy, visible, and final or, Paul is wrong in what he teaches the Thessalonians in Scripture.

Those who hold to a silent rapture will either have to assert that the return of Christ which includes the loud command, the voice of the archangel, and the trumpet call of God is not visible and noisy or they will have to say Paul was mistaken. Neither option is plausible. It appears that the trumpet call of God in I Thessalonians 4:16 is the same trumpet call seen in Matthew 24:31. If the same return is being described, it is clear from Matthew 24:30 that it is a visible return. Obviously, anyone who holds to the inerrancy of Scripture will not assert that Paul was mistaken in what he taught in Scripture.

In II Thessalonians 1:7-10, Paul describes the return of the Lord. The Lord Jesus will be revealed from heaven in blazing fire with his powerful angels. This is followed by judgment "on the day he comes to be glorified."

Again it must be asked, why would Paul emphasize for the Thessalonians a return of Christ in which they would never participate, if there was to be a silent rapture of believers before the final return of Christ? The church has been expecting Christ's return from its inception and all members of the church have hoped that they would be living when Christ returned. In II Thessalonians 2, Paul calms the Thessalonians who feared that the Lord may have already come, and reminds them of the signs that must precede the return of Christ.

If Paul, who felt qualified to write about the return of Christ, had been aware of a silent rapture that would remove the church, it would be expected that he would emphasize that silent rapture as the church's hope. But he does not. In fact, Paul emphasizes that Christ's noisy and visible return at the end of human history is the hope for the Thessalonians and for him as well.

II Thessalonians 1:6-8 God is just: He will pay back trouble to those who trouble you and give relief to you who are troubled, and to us as well. This will happen when the Lord Jesus is revealed from heaven in blazing fire with his powerful angels. He will punish those who do not know God and do not obey the gospel of our Lord Jesus.

The relief and hope for both the Thessalonians and for Paul is not an invisible rapture. Rather their hope is in the visible return of Christ with angels followed by the punishment of the wicked.

In verses 14f, Jude ties together the return of Christ with the final judgment.

> ... See the Lord is coming with thousands upon thousands of his holy ones (angels) to judge everyone, ...

Several common features appear in these passages. There is only one coming of Jesus and it is visible and noisy. It is an appearing of the Lord accompanied with a tremendous number of angels. The coming of the Lord includes separating the people of God from the enemies of God and this separation is performed by the angels. The coming of the Lord results in the judgment of all people. Its purpose is the glorification of God and it accomplishes that purpose.

Important Eschatological Passages
Outside of the Book of Revelation

Before attempting to understand the book of Revelation, it is important to review other passages in the Old and New Testaments describing the end of the world and the return of Jesus Christ. By learning what these passages teach, it becomes possible to apply their witness to the additional information provided in Revelation.

Old Testament Passages

Before any Old Testament passage is examined, it must first be determined that the passage has some relationship to the material in Revelation. How can this be determined? Different people will use different criteria. The criteria used in this book are as follows:

1. Passages are more likely to have some application to the material in Revelation if parts of those passages are quoted from or alluded to in Revelation.

2. Passages should be considered that have similar themes to those in Revelation. This is particularly true when passages in the Old Testament refer to the return of God with angels to earth or to the final judgment.

3. No individual verses will be considered in isolation. Rather, larger passages will be studied that are at least one chapter in length. This will prevent the use of an individual verse in a manner inconsistent with the context of the chapter or chapters that surround it.

Using these criteria, a number of passages have been identified that must be studied before moving on to Revelation. These passages provide necessary background information that will assist the reader in understanding Revelation.

Isaiah 24-29

Isaiah chapters 24 through 29 describe God's devastation of the earth and the final restoration of Israel. Several passages appear to be explicitly describing the final judgment and the end of the world. Portions of this section of Isaiah are also quoted in Revelation concerning the end of time.

Isaiah 24:1-13 describes the destruction of the earth. The reason for the destruction of the earth is that it has been defiled by its people (Isaiah 24:5.) The burning up of the earth's inhabitants (Isaiah 24:6) bears a strong resemblance to the sun's scorching of people in Revelation 16:8f. The description of the earth which is completely laid waste, plundered, devastated, and defiled by its people, is universal in scope, suggesting the end of the world.

Verses 14-18a portray the contrast between the revival of the people of God (Isaiah 24:14-16a) and the treachery and betrayal of those who lead the peoples of the earth into destruction. This text presents a contrast similar to that pictured in Revelation between the revival of the church at the end of history (Rev. 11:11 - The interpretation will be provided in Section 2) and the destruction of the nations that occurs at the end (Rev. 11:13-19.)

Isaiah 24:18b-23 is a description of final judgment including both extreme language and a reference to "that day" (the Day of the Lord.)

> The floodgates of the heavens are opened, the foundations of the earth shake. The earth is broken up, the earth is split asunder, the earth is thoroughly shaken. The earth reels like a drunkard, it sways like a hut in the wind; so heavy upon it is the guilt of its rebellion that it falls —never to rise again. In that day the Lord will punish the powers in the heavens above and the kings on the earth below. They will be herded together like prisoners bound in a dungeon; they will be shut up in prison and be punished after many days. The moon will be abashed, the sun ashamed; for the Lord Almighty will reign on Mount Zion and in Jerusalem, and before its elders, gloriously.

The earthquake in verses 18b-20 is similar in scope to the earthquake described in Ezekiel 38:19f, Zechariah 14:3-5, and Revelation 16:18f. In this text as in others, the earthquake appears both as extreme language to represent judgment and in a literal sense because there will be a great earthquake at the end (see the article on Earthquake in Section 3.)

The "that day" in verse 21 is a day of judgment as are all references to the Day of the Lord. It is not a judgment of a few nations but is a judgment of the "powers in the heavens above and the kings on the earth below." This combined with the extreme language of verse 23 and the description of the Lord Almighty reigning in Jerusalem is a clear reference to the end of time.

Isaiah 25 and 26 express praise to the Lord who reigns in Zion. Several elements in that reign are described in terms that in other texts apply to the end of human history.

> *Isaiah 25:8* he (the Lord Almighty) will swallow up death forever. The Sovereign Lord will wipe away the tears from all faces; he will remove the disgrace of his people from all the earth. The Lord has spoken.

> *Isaiah 26:11* O Lord, your hand is lifted high, but they do not see it. Let them see your zeal for your people and be put to shame; let the fire reserved for your enemies consume them.

> *Isaiah 26:19-21* But your dead will live; their bodies will rise. You who dwell in the dust, wake up and shout for joy. Your dew is like

the dew of the morning; the earth will give birth to her dead. Go, my people, enter your rooms and shut the doors behind you; hide yourselves for a little while until his wrath has passed by. See, the Lord is coming out of his dwelling to punish the people of the earth for their sins. The earth will disclose the blood shed upon her; she will conceal her slain no longer.

The themes presented in these texts—death swallowed up, the Lord wiping away tears, the resurrection of the dead and the punishment of sins—appear in many other biblical passages concerning the end of the world.

Isaiah 27 describes the Day of the Lord. The text makes repeated references to "that day" (Isaiah 27:1,2,12,13) in which the wicked are judged and God's people are gathered to his holy mountain.

The Lord slaying Leviathan the serpent (Isaiah 27:1.) represents the judgment of Satan. This act of judgment is in contrast to Isaiah 27:2-5 where the Lord protects and nurtures a fruitful vineyard representing his people. Those not of the vineyard are offered the alternatives of making peace with the Lord and having him as a refuge, or facing him in battle.

In Isaiah 27:6-9, God reminds Israel that while she has been disciplined, she has not been destroyed as have other nations. This discipline makes Israel fruitful, atoning for her guilt, and removing her sin.

Isaiah 27:10-13 concludes by comparing the current situation of alienation from God to "that day" when the Israelites will be gathered one by one. The gathering is reminiscent of the gathering of the faithful by the angels at the return of Christ. The sounding of the great trumpet reminds the reader of the loud trumpet call of Matthew 24:31 and I Thessalonians 4:16. In that day all God's people will worship him on the holy mountain in Jerusalem.

In Isaiah 28 and 29, the prophecy goes on to address the tribe of Ephraim. There are a number of elements in these chapters referring to the end of human history. Isaiah 28:5 mentions "that day" in a context where six verses earlier "that day" was the occasion for the gathering of the faithful one by one and the sounding of a great trumpet.

God speaks against those who think worshipping him involves keeping a set of rules (Isaiah 28:10, 29:13.) If they are so enamored with rules, the word of the Lord to them will become a set of rules (Isaiah 28:13.)

The alternative to rule keeping is trusting in the precious cornerstone (Isaiah 28:16.) This passage is used in the New Testament to refer to Jesus Christ who is the believer's cornerstone (Romans 9:33, I Peter 2:6.)

Isaiah warns of a destruction against the whole land (Isaiah 28:22.) He describes the destruction in chapter 29 where Jerusalem (Ariel) is besieged by hordes of all the nations. Jerusalem will be brought low, but then the Lord Almighty will come with thunder, and earthquake, and great noise. This description is similar to the attack on Jerusalem and the return of the Lord in Zechariah 14. It is a description of the loud and visible return of Christ at the end of history.

Isaiah 29:22-24 describes Israel when it is restored in the new Jerusalem. Israel will keep God's name holy and stand in awe of him. The wayward gain understanding and the complainers accept instruction. There is no mention of the new Jerusalem until later in the book, but idealized behavior on the part of Israel is typical of Israel in the new Jerusalem.

Ezekiel 38, 39

Ezekiel chapters 38 and 39 contain a prophecy against Gog and Magog that is referred to in Revelation 20:8 at Satan's gathering of the nations for battle. The reference to Gog and Magog in Revelation 20 is designed to clarify that Revelation 20 and Ezekiel 38 and 39 describe the same events. Ezekiel 37 leads into this section with a description of the restoration of Israel that includes the making of an everlasting covenant of peace, and God's sanctuary among them forever. This is clearly a promise to be fulfilled in the new Jerusalem at the end.

Gog was a chief ruler of Meshech and Tubal, and Magog is thought to be the country where he lived. What makes Gog such a fearful figure is that he comes with an army described as hordes and a cloud covering the land. This army is gathered from many nations. Persia, Cush, and Put are mentioned as being included among the nations who participate in this gathering.

The description of the inhabitants of the holy land in Ezekiel 38 fits the reestablishment of national Israel that has occurred during the twentieth century.

Ezekiel 38:8f After many days you (Gog) will be called to arms. In future years you will invade a land that has recovered from war, whose people were gathered from many nations to the mountains of Israel, which had long been desolate. They had been brought out from the nations, and now all of them live in safety. You and all your troops and the many nations with you will go up, advancing like a storm; you will be like a cloud covering the land.

Gog represents the Man of Lawlessness who gathers the nations to attack Israel. In Revelation 20:8, Gog and Magog are connected with the release of Satan and the gathering of the nations for battle. Those who are gathered are "like the sand on the seashore." The horde of people gathered by the Man of Lawlessness surround "the camp of God's people, the city he loves" (Jerusalem), and attack it. Beginning in Ezekiel 38:18, many passages similar to the descriptions of the end are found in Revelation and elsewhere. When Gog (the Man of Lawlessness) attacks Israel:

Ezekiel 38:19 In my zeal and fiery wrath I (God) declare that at that time there shall be a great earthquake in the land of Israel (see Zech. 14:4f, Rev. 6:12, 11:13, 16:18.)

Ezekiel 38:21f Every man's sword will be against his brother (see Zech. 14:13.) I will execute judgment upon him with plague and bloodshed; I will pour down torrents of rain, hailstones and burning sulphur on him and on his troops and the many nations with him (see Daniel 8:25, Rev. 11:19, 16:21, 20:9.)

Ezekiel 39:4-6 On the mountains of Israel you will fall, you and all your troops and the nations with you. I will give you as food to all kinds of carrion birds and to the wild animals. You will fall in the open field, for I have spoken, declares the Sovereign Lord. I will send fire on Magog and on those who live in safety in the coastlands, and they will know that I am the Lord (see Rev. 19:17-21, 20:9.)

Ezekiel 39:17-20 Son of man, this is what the Sovereign Lord says: Call out to every kind of bird and all the wild animals: 'Assemble and come together from all around to the sacrifice I am preparing for you, the great sacrifice on the mountains of Israel. There you will eat flesh and drink blood. You will eat the flesh of mighty men and drink the blood of the princes of the earth as if they were rams and lambs, goats and bulls—all of them fattened animals from Bashan. At the sacrifice I am preparing for you, you will eat fat till you are glutted and drink blood till you are drunk.   At my table you will eat your fill of horses and riders,mighty men and soldiers of every kind,' declares the Sovereign Lord (see Rev. 19:17-21.)

The descriptions of animals eating the corpses and drinking their blood discredits the view that some have held, based on Zechariah 14:12, that God destroys the nations who gather to attack Israel through nuclear weapons. Such weapons would destroy not only the enemies, but would kill the birds and animals who are called to consume the corpses. For no reason would God need to use modern human technology to destroy his opponents.

At the conclusion of Ezekiel 39, God promises to pour out his Spirit on the house of Israel. This is consistent with Romans 11:25f, where Paul asserts that after the full number of the Gentiles have come in, all Israel will be saved.

Daniel 7:1-8:27

This section consists of two visions, both of which trouble Daniel greatly. The two visions describe the same thing but they look at history from different perspectives.

In Daniel 7 four beasts represent four kingdoms. The first is a lion with wings, representing Babylon. Its wings are torn off and it stands like a man, and the heart of a man is given to it. This represents Nebuchadnezzar who was made mad by God and then restored to sanity (Daniel 4.) Because of this, he wrote a song of praise to God (Daniel 4:35f), reflecting a change of heart that can only be regeneration. Only a man of faith could write:

> *Daniel 4:37* "Now I, Nebuchadnezzar, praise and exalt and glorify the King of heaven, because everything he does is right and all his ways are just. And those who walk in pride he is able to humble."

The second beast looked like a bear and represents the Medes and the Persians. This beast is to eat its fill of flesh representing the bloody wars this empire fought. The third looked like a leopard and had four wings and four heads. It represents the Greek empire of Alexander the Great. The four wings and four heads represent the division of Alexander's kingdom into four parts; Syria, ruled by Seleucus; Egypt, ruled by Ptolemy; Greece; and Asia Minor. The fourth beast represents the Roman empire and the civilization that grew from it. It has ten horns representing ten kings. After the kings have finished their reigns, another king who is different from them will reign. He will speak against the Most High, wage war against the saints and defeat them. It is at the time of final judgment that he will be destroyed and thrown into the blazing fire (Daniel 7:9-11.) The final judgment, destruction of the boastful horn, and the coming of the Son of Man with the clouds of heaven appear to occur in close proximity. Based on a comparison with II Thessalonians 2 and Revelation 13-19, the horn that speaks boastfully must be the Man of Lawlessness who is destroyed by the coming of the Lord at the very end of human history. His destruction results in the everlasting kingdom of the saints (Daniel 7:27.) While the conclusion means victory for the people of God, this vision troubled Daniel because of the wickedness it revealed.

In chapter 8, Daniel sees a vision describing the time of the end (Daniel 8:17) in the distant future (Daniel 8:26). A ram representing Media and Persia is replaced with a goat representing Greece under Alexander the Great. The description of these two kingdoms is accurate in outlining Greece's supplanting of the Persian empire and the division of Alexander's kingdom into four parts.

In verse 23, the interpretation of the vision is focused on the end of the reign of the four parts of Alexander's kingdom when a king will destroy the holy people and stand against the Prince of princes. Many interpreters have struggled to fit this king into the time immediately before the Roman empire. Such efforts have not succeeded because they have overlooked the clue provided that this vision concerns the time of the end (Daniel 8:17.)

The clue clarifies that the king in Daniel 8:9-12, 23-25, is again the Man of Lawlessness from II Thessalonians 2 and Revelation 13-19. There is a similarity to II Thessalonians 2:3 which says that the day of the Lord will not come until "the rebellion" occurs and the man of Lawlessness is revealed. Likewise, Daniel 8:12 speaks of a rebellion and in verse 23 the king arises when "rebels have become completely wicked." Daniel and II Thessalonians are speaking of the same rebellion. The Man of Lawlessness sets himself up to be as great as the Prince of the host, the saints are given over to him, he will prosper in everything he does, and the truth is thrown to the ground. He destroys the mighty men and the holy people, suggesting that during his reign the holy people, the church, is destroyed. This interpretation is offered only after great reflection and careful consideration. The reader is urged to consider the entire argument for this position, including the proposed interpretation of Revelation 11 before dismissing it. Support for this view is found in Daniel 7:21, 12:7 and Revelation 11:7 which also teach that the Man of Lawlessness will destroy the people of God (see the discussion of Revelation 11 in Section 2 for a clarification of the nature of this destruction.)

The man of Lawlessness will become strong but not by his own power. His power must come from another source as it does in Revelation 13:2,14,15, where the beast out of the earth exercises the authority of the beast out of the sea that comes from Satan. He will be destroyed, but not by human power. So he must be destroyed by God. In both II Thessalonians 2 and in Revelation 19, the Man of Lawlessness is destroyed by the coming of the Lord Jesus Christ.

Daniel records the question, (Daniel 8:13) "How long will it take for the vision to be fulfilled—the vision concerning the daily sacrifice, the rebellion that causes desolation, and the surrender of the sanctuary and of the host that will be trampled underfoot?" The answer (Daniel 8:14) is that it will take 2,300 days before the sanctuary is reconsecrated. This period does not appear to be symbolic. It is not a multiple of 7, 12 or 1000, and is not equivalent to any other symbolic number in Daniel or Revelation. The question being asked is how long the reign of the small horn (the Man of Lawlessness) will be. The answer may be precise or it may be rounded to the nearest 100 but regardless, his reign will be less than six and a half years. The Man of Lawlessness could expect to reign seven years based on what is written in Daniel 9:27 (he reigns for one 'week' or 'seven' which in the first sixty-nine 'weeks' was seven years per 'week'.) His time has been cut short for the sake of the elect (Matthew 24:22) and his reign will be less than six and a half years.

Again Daniel was appalled by the vision because he saw evil prospering at the end until the Lord intervenes.

Daniel 9:20-27

This passage is a source of great controversy. The seventy 'sevens' or 'weeks' have been interpreted in many ways, but the seventy 'weeks' has to be the period from the time of the decree to rebuild Jerusalem until the very end. The starting point is explicitly stated in Daniel 9:25. The conclusion of the period is clear because the seventy 'weeks' are decreed "to bring in everlasting righteousness."

It is important to begin with the context of the first nineteen verses. Daniel understood from Jeremiah that the desolation of Jerusalem would last seventy years. In Jeremiah 25, God prophecies that the king of Babylon will make Judah and the surrounding nations a wasteland for seventy years. When the seventy years are fulfilled, Babylon will be made desolate forever.

Daniel prays to God for "the men of Judah and people of Jerusalem and all Israel." The prayer is a prayer of confession of Israel's sins that have resulted in her judgment. Daniel reminds God that Israel and Jerusalem are "your people" and "your city." As a result of this prayer, the angel Gabriel brings a message regarding Jerusalem and Israel.

From the context where Daniel has been praying for national Israel and where he speaks of "my people Israel", it is clear that the seventy 'sevens' apply to national Israel. (The next vision in Daniel 10-12 will use "your people" in a different way. If the meaning of "your people" was not redefined, it would be expected that the meaning would remain the same throughout Daniel. The change in meaning is required because the term is redefined in Daniel 12.) In this passage, Daniel defines the term when he speaks of "my people Israel."

Beginning in verse 20 the meaning of the passage is relatively clear. From the issuing of the decree to rebuild Jerusalem until the Anointed One comes, there are seven 'weeks' and sixty-two 'weeks'. Christians have applied a formula of one year per day for the sixty-nine 'weeks' or 483 years and have found that Jesus is born about the time that the Messiah would be expected. This formula is reasonable because the sixty-nine weeks must occur within a limited timeframe. The Messiah must be born after the decree to rebuild Jerusalem and before the destruction of the city and sanctuary described in Daniel 9:26. This destruction took place in 70 AD when Rome beseiged and destroyed Jerusalem and the temple.

The seven 'weeks' represent the period from the decree to rebuild Jerusalem until the building of the temple is completed. With the formula of one day per year, the temple would have been rebuilt about forty-nine years after the decree to rebuild it. In John 2:20, the Jews tell Jesus that it took forty-six years to rebuild the temple. It is reasonable that from pronouncement of the decree three years would have passed before the work on the temple began. It would have taken some time for word of the decree to reach Jerusalem. Once the decree reached Jerusalem it would take more time to gather the necessary building materials and to have architects design the building.

The sixty-two 'weeks' represent the period from the completion of the rebuilding of Jerusalem until the coming of the Messiah. The Anointed One is the Messiah, since that is what the word 'Messiah' means. After the sixty-two 'weeks' (which has already been preceded by seven 'weeks'), the Anointed One will be cut off and will have nothing. This is a timely fit with the circumstances surrounding Jesus' life and death. Jesus is born approximately 483 years after the decree to rebuild Jerusalem and when he died he left no descendants or inheritance. After the Messiah is cut off, the text says the people of the ruler who will come will destroy the city and the sanctuary. This destruction of Jerusalem, occurring after the Anointed One is "cut off", limits when the Messiah can come. Regardless of the theory, the Messiah must come after the decree to rebuild Jerusalem and before the next destruction of Jerusalem and its temple. Given these limitations, Jesus is the only man who can be the Messiah prophesied by Daniel. He is the only significant Jewish religious figure who lives within the timeframe provided by Daniel and he fulfills the prophecy of being cut off and having nothing.

The people of the ruler who will come destroy the city and the sanctuary. This indicates that the ruler who will come, who puts an end to sacrifice and offering and sets up the abomination that causes desolation, will come out of Italy. The Romans were the people who destroyed the city and the sanctuary. Therefore, the ruler who will come must originate from Rome or in the modern setting, from Italy.

The "he" who confirms a covenant with many for one 'week' is the Man of Lawlessness. The description of the Man of Lawlessness in

II Thessalonians 2 matches the descriptions in Daniel 8 and 11 where he sets up the abomination that causes desolation. In Daniel 9 he establishes a covenant community in opposition to God's covenant people.

The final 'seven' or 'week' of Daniel 9:27 is the time of the Man of Lawlessness. If each of the sixty-nine 'weeks' or 'sevens' represent seven years, as it appears they do from the previous discussion, the reign of the Man of Lawlessness should last seven years. According to Daniel 8:14 it will be shortened to 2,300 days (or less than six and a half years.) The period is abbreviated in fulfillment of the promise of Jesus that the days of the Man of Lawlessness would be shortened for the sake of the elect (Matthew 24:22.)

Between the end of the sixty-two 'weeks' and the beginning of the final 'week' is the time of the Gentiles, which is not included in Daniel's vision because it is describing only the seventy 'weeks' for "your people and your holy city." The seventy 'weeks' apply to Israel only. The seventieth 'week' of the Man of Lawlessness belongs to Israel because it is during this time that the hardening of Israel ends. The period of hardening, during the time of the Gentiles (Romans 11:25f), is not included in Daniel's chronology.

In the middle of the 'week' of the Man of Lawlessness, he puts an end to sacrifice and offering. This is not a reference to a rebuilt temple where sacrifice and offering have been reinstituted. Such a temple and practices would be a farce because the sacrificial system has been fulfilled and replaced by the once-for-all-time sacrifice of the Lamb of God, Jesus. If it is impossible for the blood of bulls and goats to take away sin (Hebrews 10:4), what purpose could be served by the reestablishment of the temple? Instead, it is a reference to the ending of true worship. In Daniel's time this would have involved the daily sacrifice and offerings, but it now represents gathering for worship, the preaching of the gospel of Jesus Christ, and the proper observance of the sacraments. This directly corresponds to the three and a half days of Revelation 11:7-9 during which the two witnesses lay dead. This three and a half day period during which the two witnesses are dead and refused burial is the period from the middle of the final week until the end. (See the sixth trumpet in Revelation 11 in Section 2 for clarification.)

The Man of Lawlessness also sets up an abomination that causes desolation. The abomination that causes desolation is not described with any greater detail. The abomination is set up on a wing of the temple. The interpreter will need to wait until the reign of the Man of Lawlessness to see what kind of abomination is set up. A vivid description of the end decreed for the Man of Lawlessness and his followers is found in Zechariah 14:12-15.

> This is the plague with which the Lord will strike all the nations that fought against Jerusalem: Their flesh will rot while they are still standing on their feet, their eyes will rot in their sockets, and their tongues will rot in their mouths. On that day men will be stricken by the Lord with a great panic. Each man will seize the hand of another, and they will attack each other. Judah too will fight at Jerusalem. The wealth of all the surrounding nations will be collected—great quantities of gold and silver and clothing. A similar plague will strike the horses and mules, the camels and donkeys, and all the animals in those camps.

Daniel 10:1-12:13

In this section there is another prophecy about the Man of Lawlessness, following prophecies about the conquests of nations. Once again Daniel was troubled by the vision that he saw. On understanding the vision, he was unable to eat or care for himself because he was in mourning for three weeks (Daniel 10:2f.)

The description of the vision and its meaning begins in Daniel 11, but chapter 10 contains important background material that is critical to understanding the vision. The figure who Daniel sees in chapter 10 is similar to the description of Jesus in Revelation 1 both in physical attributes and in his dress. Both figures have golden belts (Revelation - sash), blazing eyes, shining faces, gleaming feet/legs, and a loud voice.

The Christ figure in Daniel 10 tells Daniel that he has come to explain what will happen to "your people" in the future. Since the "your people" of Daniel 9 is defined as Israel many interpreters believe the meaning is the same in Daniel 10. Lacking any redefinition of the term, that is the most natural way of understanding the phrase. However, the text does redefine this term so that it does not refer to national Israel. Many interpreters, by presupposing that "your people" is Israel, understand this vision as referring exclusively to Israel. The text will not allow such an interpretation. In Daniel 12, the one who explains what will happen redefines who "your people" is in this vision.

> *Daniel 12:1* "At that time Michael, the great prince who protects your people, will arise. There will be a time of distress such as has not happened from the beginning of nations until then. But at that time your people—everyone whose name is found written in the book—will be delivered.

The "your people" of this vision is everyone whose name is written in "the book" (i.e., the book of life.) In Revelation "the book" is defined as the book of life (Revelation 3:5, 20:12, 21:27.) Likewise, in the Old Testament, "the book" refers to the book of life. When Israel sins with the golden calf, Moses asks God to forgive them or to blot his name from God's book (Exodus 32:32.) In Psalm 69:28, David calls on God to blot the names of his enemies from the book of life.

The vision in chapters 11 and 12 clearly refers to the end of human history. It concludes in chapter 12 with the resurrection and judgment of the dead (Daniel 12:2.) The vision describes what will happen to believers, regardless of race, at the end. The attack on the holy covenant (Daniel 11:28,30) and the breaking of the power of the holy people (Daniel 12:7) refers to the attack of the contemptible person (Daniel 11:21) on the church. The holy covenant and holy people are the "your people" of Daniel 12. They do not refer to national Israel. Other texts do assert the revival of Israel at the end of history, but the revival is a revival to serve Jesus, not to the dead practices of temple worship. Faithful Jews will face the Man of Lawlessness and his persecution together with faithful Gentiles at the end. This vision promises a time of difficulty for the church that is so distressing that Daniel mourned for three weeks. Many today preach a gospel of ease and comfort. Those who will serve the Lord at the end of time must be prepared to face a time of distress such as has not happened since the beginning of nations.

The vision begins in chapter 11 with a prophecy about Persia and Greece. It is followed in Daniel 11:5-20 with a succession of attacks and counter attacks by kings from the North and South. Beginning in Daniel 11:21, a description of the Man of Lawlessness and his actions is presented through the end of the chapter. He is the Man of Lawlessness because of the following:

1. He exalts himself above every god and says unheard of things against the God of gods (Daniel 11:36.) This behavior can be compared with II Thessalonians 2:4 and Daniel 7:25, 8:11.

2. He desecrates the temple fortress, abolishes the daily sacrifice and sets up the abomination that causes desolation. The abomination that causes desolation is called the rebellion that causes desolation in Daniel 8:13 and is attributed to the Man of Lawlessness in that text. Likewise, the ending of the daily sacrifice and the surrender of the temple fortress are attributed to him in Daniel 8:11-13 (see also Daniel 9:27.)

3. He is a master of intrigue, causes deceit to prosper and will destroy many who feel secure (Daniel 11:21-24, 27, see also Daniel 8:23-25, II Thes. 2:10f.)

4. He will pitch his tents between the seas at the beautiful holy mountain (Daniel 11:45) just as is prophesied regarding Armageddon in Revelation 16:16, 20:9. There is no site called Armageddon, meaning Mount Megiddo, anywhere near Jerusalem. The location seems to be related to the Valley of Megiddo in the Holy Land. Various writers have proposed that Mount Megiddo could represent a fortress or city in the nearby vicinity. The Man of Lawlessness, at the end, camps in the Holy Land on the Holy Mountain and then is destroyed.

When the king (the Man of Lawlessness) is in place, there is a time of distress such as has not happened from the beginning of nations until then. This passage, quoted in the eschatological text in Matthew 24:21, refers to the events immediately prior to the return of Christ and the final judgment. The resurrection of the dead and the final judgment are described in verses two and three of Daniel 12.

Daniel asks when these things will occur and is told that it will be for a time, times, and half a time, when the power of the holy people has been finally broken, all these things will be completed. This breaking of the power of the holy people is a reference to the death of the church found in Daniel 8:24 and Revelation 11:7.

From the time the daily sacrifice is abolished and the rebellion or abomination that causes desolation is set up there will be 1,290 days. While it would be natural for the daily sacrifice to be abolished at the fall of Jerusalem and the destruction of the temple, it appears that some other event is in mind which occurs during the reign of the Man of Lawlessness. In Daniel 8:11-14, a small horn sets itself up to be as great as the Prince of the Host (Jesus), takes away the daily sacrifice from him and brings low the place of his sanctuary. From Gabriel's interpretation, it appears that all of this happens during the time of the stern-faced king who is destroyed but not by human power (i,e,. by God - Dan. 8:25.) The same imagery is found in Daniel 9 in which he (the ruler who will come) puts an end to sacrifice and offering and sets up the abomination that causes desolation on a wing of the temple. If it is agreed that both texts are referring to the Man of Lawlessness who is destroyed by the coming of the Lord Jesus, then the daily sacrifice is not the sacrifice in the temple in Jerusalem but is another way of speaking of true worship by the people of God.

The Man of Lawlessness has not yet been revealed. Rather than proposing the rebuilding of a temple which can have no legitimate function after Christ's sacrifice, Daniel must be describing true worship, which in his day would have involved sacrifice in the temple.

Some have proposed a transition from a reinstituted historic Old Testament Judaism in a rebuilt temple to an acceptance of Christ's sacrifice. This is impossible for two reasons:

1. A reinstitution of animal sacrifice would stand as a repudiation of Christ's sacrifice. It is not accidental that God allowed Rome to destroy the temple after Christ's death.

2. God has so confused the tribal structure of Israel that there is no Levitical priesthood to offer the sacrifices in accordance with the Law and from which to choose a high priest. One of the criticisms of Jeroboam was that he appointed priests who were not Levites (I Kings 12:31.) It was prophesied that Josiah would sacrifice these false priests who are called priests of the high places on Jeroboam's altar (I Kings 13:2.)

Since the temple has been destroyed, true worship involves the proper use of the sacraments and God's word purely preached. The Man of Lawlessness will act to eliminate this.

The abomination that causes desolation has been difficult to define because of disagreement about what it is and when it is set up. Some help in interpreting the abomination comes from the gospels where it is mentioned concerning the destruction of Jerusalem.

> *Matthew 24:15f* So when you see standing in the holy place the abomination that causes desolation, spoken of through the prophet Daniel—let the reader understand - then let those who are in Judea flee to the mountains.

> *Mark 13:14* When you see the abomination that causes desolation standing where it does not belong—let the reader understand— then let those who are in Judea flee to the mountains.

> *Luke 21:20* When you see Jerusalem being surrounded by armies you will know that its desolation is near. Then let those who are in Judea flee to the mountains, let those in the city get out, and let those in the country not enter the city. For this is the time of punishment in fulfillment of all that has been written.

These passages were assumed by the church to be referring to the Roman armies that set siege to Jerusalem and destroyed it in 70 AD. As a result, Christians fled to Pella and were not in Jerusalem when it finally fell to the Roman armies. It is true that the Luke 21 passage is speaking of the 70 AD destruction as is clear from the context. However, the gathering of armies around Jerusalem of Luke 21 is not the abomination that causes desolation described in the parallel passages in Matthew and Mark and the abomination that causes desolation was not set up during the Roman conquest in 70 AD. There are several elements in the Matthew and Mark gospel accounts that are inconsistent with the 70 AD destruction of Jerusalem.

1. Matthew and Mark warn of little time to escape. Matthew 24:17 says that those on the roof should not stop on their way out of the house to gather belongings. The Roman armies that gathered to destroy Jerusalem withdrew in 68 AD after the death of Nero. This allowed people in Jerusalem who were familiar with Jesus' prophecy to pack and escape with all their belongings. They had plenty of time to gather everything in their house, rent a cart, and move with their belongings to Pella.

2. Matthew and Mark call the period when all are to flee from Jerusalem a time of great distress unequaled from the beginning of the world. The 70 AD destruction of Jerusalem was no more severe than other destructions of cities. It certainly was not a time of distress unequaled from the beginning of the world. The time of great distress is quoted from Daniel 12:1. The time of distress in verse one is followed in Daniel 12:2 by the resurrection of the dead and the final judgment. In Daniel 12:4, Daniel is told to seal the words "until the time of the end." All of this points to the fulfillment of this prophesy at the end of human history. Matthew and Mark also say that no one would have survived if God had not cut short the days (Matthew 24:21f.) It is difficult to see how no one would have survived if God had not cut short the destruction of Jerusalem in 70 AD.

3. The context does not allow Matthew 24:15-25 to be understood as applying to the 70 AD destruction of Jerusalem. Verses one through nine describe religious opposition and the gospel being proclaimed. When the gospel has been preached in all the world "the end will come." It is inconsistent with the context to suggest that the 70 AD destruction of Jerusalem is referred to in verses fifteen to twenty-five after "the end will come." This problem is accentuated by the discussion of the return of Christ that occurs in verses twenty-six to fifty-one. The context supports a destruction of Jerusalem at the end of history that immediately precedes the return of Christ (see Ezekiel 38:14-23, Zech. 14:1-5, Rev. 20:7-9.) This is unlike Luke 21 where the context indicates that he is discussing the period after the death of Christ up to the destruction of Jerusalem in 70 AD. Luke says, "Before all this..." and refers to believers being handed over to synagogues which would only have occurred in the earliest history of the church.

4. Daniel 9 does not allow the Matthew and Mark passages to be interpreted as referring to the 70 AD destruction. The people of the ruler who will come destroy the city and the sanctuary after the Messiah is cut off (Dan. 9:26.) This is the 70 AD destruction. After the 70 AD destruction, the ruler who will come (the Man of Lawlessness) sets up the abomination that causes desolation (Dan. 9:27.) The abomination that causes desolation is set up at the end of history and so cannot be connected to the 70 AD destruction. Luke makes no mention of the abomination that

causes desolation and his description of events leading up to the 70 AD destruction is not connected to Daniel's prophecy.

It must therefore be concluded that the abomination that causes desolation is an unknown object or event that has not yet occurred. It waits for the Man of Lawlessness who will, after he sets up the abomination that causes desolation, gather the nations against Jerusalem and be destroyed by the coming of the Lord (see Joel 3:2, 9-16, Zeph. 3:8, Zech. 14:3-16, Rev. 16:14-16, 19:19-21, 20:7-9.)

The 1,290 days and the 1,335 days at the end of Daniel do not exactly match any symbolic period. They amount to slightly more than three and a half years and there is no obvious way to understand them as a combination of the 1,260 days of Revelation plus thirty days or seventy-five days. Because these times do not have any clear relationship to symbolism, it is most reasonable to understand these times literally. The 1,290 days is the period from the death of the two witnesses of Revelation 11 until their resurrection. If the 1,290 and 1,335 days are to be taken literally, the witnesses will be resurrected for forty-five days before the return of Christ.

Joel 2:28-3:27

The first half of Joel is directed toward Israel which has been laid waste. Joel's message is that Israel needs to repent before the day of the Lord.

The second half of the book, beginning in Joel 2:28, begins with the words, "And afterward." This is followed by the passage that Peter said was fulfilled at Pentecost when the Spirit came on the disciples. The second chapter concludes with extreme language that symbolizes the great and dreadful day of the Lord. While the description could be literal, the primary emphasis is that the great and dreadful day of the Lord is a day of judgement.

Chapter 3 of Joel in several places mentions the gathering of the nations to be judged (Joel 3:2, 9-16.) This is the same gathering of the nations by the Man of Lawlessness described in chapters 16, 19 and 20 of Revelation. Joel's language "harvesting and trampling grapes," used of God's judgment of the nations, is repeated in a similar context in Revelation 14:14-20, 19:15.

Zechariah 14

Zechariah describes in this chapter the gathering of nations by the Man of Lawlessness to fight against Jerusalem. In Matthew and Mark, there is a warning to avoid the city when the abomination that causes desolation is standing in the holy place. This abomination is unknown but will be set up by the Man of Lawlessness at the end of human history. The prophecy that he will set up the abomination has not yet been fulfilled. The reason for avoiding Jerusalem at the end of history is found at the beginning of Zechariah 14, "the city will be captured, the houses ransacked, and the women raped." Additionally, half the city will go into exile but the rest of the people will be left.

After this, the Lord will fight against those nations. The Mount of Olives will be split by a great earthquake (Zech. 14:4, see also Rev. 6:12, 11:13, 16:18f.) Then the Lord will come and all his holy ones with him. This is remarkably consistent with the description of the return of Christ with his angels in Matthew 24:30f.

Zechariah gives a graphic description of the destruction of the nations who are struck by the Lord.

> *Zechariah 14:12* This is the plague with which the Lord will strike all the nations that fought against Jerusalem: Their flesh will rot while they are still standing on their feet, their eyes will rot in their sockets, and their tongues will rot in their mouths.

This chapter is clearly describing the end of human history because the Lord is king over the whole earth (Zech. 14:9) and living water flows out from Jerusalem (Zech. 14:8, Rev. 22:1f.)

Passages in the Gospels

The Synoptic gospels all contain teaching by Jesus regarding the end of the age. There is a tendency to view parallel passages from these gospels as describing the same events in the same order. So, when Jesus teaches regarding the end of the age in Matthew 24, it is assumed that the passage in Luke 21 is the same teaching session with material presented in the same order. This is not a safe assumption to make. There are elements in Matthew that do not appear in Luke (e.g., the abomination that causes desolation spoken of by Daniel.) There are also elements in Luke that do not appear in Matthew (e.g., Jerusalem surrounded by armies and the desolation of Jerusalem.) It is reasonable to harmonize the two passages. Care should be taken to harmonize only those portions of the passages that parallel one another. The abomination that causes desolation in Daniel cannot be equated with the desolation of Jerusalem. The reason for this is that the abomination that causes desolation in Daniel is set up by the Man of Lawlessness at the end of history. The desolation of Jerusalem in Luke results in Israel being taken prisoner to all the nations and Jerusalem being trampled by the Gentiles.

A number of very wise biblical scholars have interpreted Revelation as referring almost exclusively to the destruction of Jerusalem in 70 AD. Their case has some merit because large parts of Revelation pertain to God's judgment of unfaithful Jerusalem. However, their evidence from the gospels focuses on the material in Luke's gospel referring to the 70 AD destruction of Jerusalem. They fail to see that the references to Daniel and the abomination that causes desolation in Matthew and Mark point to the Man of Lawlessness and the end of human history. They also fail to notice that while Luke 21 begins like Matthew and Mark, in verse 12 Luke changes direction. Jesus describes what will happen before all this (the end of the age) happens. Jesus describes what happens before the end of the age in Luke 21:12-24.

Matthew 24

The chapter begins with the disciples pointing out the temple and its buildings. Jesus' response is to prophecy the destruction of the temple in verse 2. Then as Jesus is sitting on the Mount of Olives, his disciples come to him privately and ask the question Jesus will be answering throughout the chapter. The question is in two parts but is about the same thing. Tell us, they say, when will "this" happen … It is clear, from the context of the previous two verses that the "this" must be the destruction of the temple. Jesus tells the disciples in Matthew 24 when the temple will be destroyed in the way that he has described. It is important that the interpreter not miss the point that the destruction of the temple must be like that described in Matthew 24:2.

The obvious connection between the 70 AD destruction of the temple and this prophecy by Jesus has been made by most commentators.

The problem is that in Matthew Jesus is not talking about the 70 AD destruction. There are several reasons this must be true, based on Jesus' description of the event in the text.

1. Jesus' description of the destruction is not literally fulfilled in the 70 AD destruction. Jesus said that not one stone would be left on another, but parts of the substructure of the temple are still visible on the east and west sides. The Wailing Wall is a part of the western substructure of the temple. If this were the only argument, Jesus' words could be an exaggeration reflecting terrible destruction. Exaggerated language appears elsewhere in Scripture in connection with destructions. This objection has value only if Jesus intends for the prophecy to be literally fulfilled.

2. The flow of the text argues against the 70 AD destruction and supports a destruction at the end of history. The question by the disciples appears to connect the temple destruction with the coming of the Lord and the end of the age. Matthew 24:4-14, clearly describes conditions leading up to the end of history. Matthew 24:26-51 describes the return of Christ and the final judgment. It is inconsistent with the context for the passage to go from "and then the end will come" in verse 14, to a discussion of events forty years in the future in verses 15 through 25, followed in the remainder of the passage by the return of Christ.

3. The reference to the abomination that causes desolation in verse 15 absolutely disqualifies the 70 AD destruction. In Daniel 9:24ff, the coming of the Messiah follows the decree to rebuild the city. The city is rebuilt and sometime after it has been built, the Messiah is cut off. After he is cut off, the city and sanctuary are destroyed by the people of the ruler who will come (the Man of Lawlessness.) The destruction described in Daniel 9:26 is the 70 AD destruction of Jerusalem. The 70 AD destruction occurs after Jesus died and involves destruction of the city and sanctuary.

In Daniel 9:27, the ruler who will come sets up the abomination that causes desolation. This occurs after the destruction of Jerusalem in 70 AD described in Daniel 9:26. The abomination that causes desolation is not defined in Scripture but is some symbol that is set up or event that occurs in the vicinity of the temple in Jerusalem. According to

Daniel 9:26f, the abomination that causes desolation occurs after the 70 AD destruction.

The abomination that causes desolation set up by the Man of Lawlessness must occur at the end of history because he comes at the end of history and is destroyed by the coming of the Lord (II Thes. 2:8.) The ruler who will come must be the Man of Lawlessness because he takes away the daily sacrifice (Daniel 8:11f, 9:27, 11:31), and is destroyed but not by human power (Daniel 8:25, II Thes. 2:8.)

4. The language describing events surrounding the setting up of the abomination that causes desolation does not fit the 70 AD destruction. The coming of the Roman armies was not so sudden that someone on the roof could not stop in the house to take anything out of the house (Matthew 24:17.) The Roman army withdrew and there was time to plan a trip to Pella (the mountains) before the Roman army returned. Additionally, the 70 AD destruction is not a time of distress unequaled from the beginning of the world until now (Matthew 24:21.) It is obviously not true that the time around the 70 AD destruction required that the days be cut short or no one would have survived (Matthew 24:22.)

Some have asserted that the temple in Jerusalem must be rebuilt, for everything that is prophesied to be accomplished. Jesus' words about the destruction of the temple can be literally fulfilled without the rebuilding of the temple. It is nowhere stated that the temple will be rebuilt and function as a worship center when it is destroyed so that "not one stone . . . will be left on another." Jesus does not assert that it will be destroyed by armies. The extent of the destruction is more likely to be the result of the final earthquake that is prophesied.

In Zechariah 14:4, the Lord splits the Mount of Olives with an earthquake that creates a valley. This earthquake is also mentioned in Isaiah 24:18-20, Ezekiel 38:19 and appears in several places in Revelation. Such an earthquake could easily cause every stone to be thrown down. Zechariah's earthquake immediately precedes the coming of the Lord with all his holy ones just as occurs in Matthew 24:29-31.

The second part of the question in Matthew 24:3 continues, . . . and what will be the sign of your coming and the end of the age? The second part of the question asks what they should look for as signs of the return of Christ and the end of the world. The signs of the end of the age include; false Christs, wars, famines, earthquakes (these are the beginning), persecution, some falling away, false prophets, and the love of most growing cold. While these signs are evil signs of the end of the age, there is a positive sign that appears as the conclusive sign of the end of the age, the preaching of the gospel in the whole world. Jesus concludes the section in Matthew 24:4-14 regarding the end of the age by saying:

> *Matthew 24:14* And this gospel of the kingdom will be
> preached in the whole world as a testimony to all nations,
> and then the end will come.

It is when the church has finished spreading the gospel to the whole world that her testimony is finished. This text is part of the background necessary for the reader to understand and interpret Revelation 11.

Verses 15-22 have been understood by the church to be identical to Luke 21:20-24 and to refer to the destruction of Jerusalem and the temple by Rome in 70 AD. The church benefited from the prophecy in Luke because many Christians survived the fall of Jerusalem to Rome by fleeing to Pella (the mountains.) As was mentioned earlier in this section, this passage in Matthew cannot be referring to the destruction in 70 AD because that destruction is prophesied as a separate event. In Daniel, the fall of Jerusalem in 70 AD occurs first (Daniel 9:26) and the abomination that causes desolation is set up later (Daniel 9:27.)

> *Daniel 9:26f* After the sixty-two 'sevens,' the Anointed One will be
> cut off and will have nothing. The people of the ruler who will
> come will destroy the city and the sanctuary. The end will come
> like a flood: War will continue until the end, and desolations have
> been decreed. He will confirm a covenant with many for one
> 'seven'. In the middle of the 'seven' he will put an end to sacrifice
> and offering. And on a wing of the temple he will set up an abomination that causes desolation, until the end that is decreed is
> poured out on him.

In verses 23-31 Jesus describes the signs of his coming. There will be false Christs and false prophets who will perform great signs and miracles. The false Christs and false prophets performing signs and miracles (Matthew 24:24) fits closely with the description of the time of the Man of Lawlessness.

II Thessalonians 2:9 The coming of the lawless one will be in accordance with the work of Satan displayed in all kinds of counterfeit miracles, signs and wonders ...

Revelation 16:13f Then I saw three evil spirits that looked like frogs; they came out of the mouth of the dragon, out of the mouth of the beast and out of the mouth of the false prophet. They are spirits of demons performing miraculous signs, and they go out to the kings of the whole world, to gather them for battle on the great day of God Almighty.

The false Christs and false prophets will suggest that Jesus has returned in secret. The church is warned not to believe it. The primary emphasis of the text is to prevent the church from following false Christs. However, the proof of the return of the true Christ is that his return is so visible. This discredits both false Christs and those who hold to a secret return of Christ.

Matthew 24:23 At that time if anyone says to you, 'Look, here is the Christ!' or, 'There he is!' do not believe it.

Matthew 24:26 So if anyone tells you, 'There he is, out in the desert,' do not go out; or, 'Here he is, in the inner rooms,' do not believe it.

The reason that the false Christs and false prophets are to be disbelieved is that the return of Christ will be so public, noisy, and visible that it cannot be missed.

Matthew 24:27,30,31 For as lightning that comes from the east is visible even in the west, so will be the coming of the Son of Man ... At that time the sign of the Son of Man will appear in the sky, and all the nations of the earth will mourn. They will see the Son of Man coming on the clouds of the sky, with power and great glory. And he will send his angels with a loud trumpet call, and they will gather his elect from one end of the heavens to the other.

It should be noted that this reasoning is invalidated if there is a secret return of Christ that is not publicly observed. If there were to be a secret return, then those who say here is the Christ or there he is (or he came and left you behind) could be telling the truth. In contrast with this, Jesus states that believers cannot be deceived by those who say that Christ has come because the return is visible, noisy, and unmistakable.

In verse 29, Jesus quotes from Isaiah 13, and 34. As discussed above, this extreme language is not used literally in the Old Testament and may not be intended to be taken literally in this passage. Just as it represents judgment in the Old Testament, here in the New Testament it represents the judgment that will occur at the return of Christ, whether the signs are literally fulfilled or not.

In verses 32-35, Jesus tells the disciples to look for the signs and when they see all these things, they will know that the time of the end is near. Then verse 34 says this generation will not pass away until all these things have happened. To avoid the difficulty of this passage (that the return of Christ did not happen while that generation lived) some have proposed translating generation as race. The result is that this race (i.e., Israel or humanity) will not pass away until all these things have happened. The question that must be asked then is whether any of the disciples thought Israel or the human race would pass away before the return of Christ. The statement so translated is meaningless. Of course neither Israel nor humanity will pass away until the return of Christ. No one ever thought Israel or humanity would pass away until the return of Christ. In this text, Jesus is not suggesting that the second coming will occur before this generation passes away. After all, he could not be talking about the time of his return if in verse 36 he says that he does not know the day and hour of his return. He is stating that the signs of the end of the world will all begin before this generation passes away. All of these signs have been observed in the world from the time of the apostles until now.

Verses 36-51 speak of the need to be prepared for the return of Christ. Everyone needs to be prepared because no one knows when Christ will return and there will be no warning. The consequences of unpreparedness are disastrous.

Some have interpreted verses 40 and 41 as teaching a secret rapture. The context of the passage will not allow such an interpretation. Verses 37, and 38 speak of Noah and the people who lived in his time. The flood was coming, Noah was making an ark, and all carried on with their normal activities as though they had a future. Noah entered the ark and was saved. The rest of the people were not prepared and were destroyed. Verses 40 and 41 warn that a similar judgment awaits the world. People will be performing their normal activities. Where two are together, one will be taken by the angels of verse 31 and the other will be left to face judgment. The time of Christ's return is not known, so believers are to always be ready.

Luke 21

This is a parallel passage to Matthew 24, but it contains a number of differences not to be overlooked. The nature of the destruction described in Luke 21:20-24 is different than that described in the parallel passages in Matthew and Mark.

1. There is no direct mention of the abomination that causes desolation from Daniel. Israel will be desolated or destroyed but it could be a different destruction than the one referred to in Matthew and Mark because of the lack of connection with Daniel.

2. The urgency to leave Jerusalem is not the same. People are told to leave Jerusalem and the language is similar in some ways to that in Matthew and Mark. However, Luke does not say that the situation is so urgent that someone on the roof will not have time to stop on the way through to pick up articles in the house.

3. Luke does not describe it as a time of such distress that the days had to be cut short or no one would have survived.

4. Luke's record of Jesus' words focuses on "this people" who are taken as prisoners to all the nations. The mention of Jerusalem being trampled "until the times of the Gentiles are fulfilled" ties his prophecy to the 70 AD destruction.

Because Luke is talking about the 70 AD destruction of Jerusalem, some interpreters have assumed that the parallel passages must also be talking about the same destruction. They are not. Luke includes some elements from Jesus' teaching not included in the parallel passages.

Whereas Matthew and Mark speak of the persecution of the disciples and follow that with a description of the end of the world, Luke approaches the same topic in a different order. Luke 21:12-24 is a parenthetical description of events in the near future. In Luke 21:12, after talking about fearful events and signs in the heavens, Luke quotes Jesus as saying, "Before all this,..." By going back to what occurs before the signs in the heavens, Luke is able to speak of the destruction of Jerusalem and the persecution of the church that began before 70 AD. The reference to being delivered to synagogues (Luke 21:12) applies only to the earliest history of the church. Believers were delivered to synagogues and prisons only up to the time that Jerusalem was destroyed. After that, they continued to be sent to prisons but they were not normally delivered to synagogues. The Jews had less religious freedom because of the rebellion against Rome. The Romans no longer needed Jewish charges in order to persecute Christians. The Christians' refusal to participate in Roman emperor worship violated Roman law. There was also less concern about being delivered to synagogues later in history because the church became more Gentile. The synagogues did not have jurisdiction over Gentile Christians.

The setting up of the abomination that causes desolation and the surrounding of Jerusalem by armies are two different events. Only if the abomination that causes desolation and the surrounding of Jerusalem with armies are equated can the parallel passages be speaking of the same event. Luke writes that the people in Jerusalem and Judea should flee when they see Jerusalem being surrounded by armies. This is only possible if the armies surrounding Jerusalem withdraw, so that those in the city can flee. This is what occurred when Rome came against Jerusalem in 66 AD and withdrew for a time after the death of Nero in 68 AD.

It is not uncommon for differences to exist between parallel passages in the gospels. That is because Jesus taught for years and would have repeated some of his lessons in different locations. Additionally, he healed so many people that some of the parallel passages describing his miracles look similar, but take place in different settings. An example of this can be seen in the healing that takes place prior to the Triumphal Entry in all three synoptic gospels. In Matthew 20:29-34, Jesus is leaving Jericho and heals two blind men sitting by the roadside. In Mark 10:46-52, when Jesus is leaving Jericho, a single blind man named

Bartimaeus is healed. It is not difficult to harmonize Matthew and Mark. Mark may have known the name of one of the blind men and so mentioned him by name. When Mark says there was a blind man, he does not exclude the possibility that there may have been others as well. In Luke 18:35-43, in a parallel passage, Jesus heals a blind man as he approaches Jericho. There is no way to reconcile the passages describing Jesus leaving Jericho with the passage where he approaches Jericho, so Luke is describing a different occasion. The passages are parallel but do not describe the same event.

Jesus prophecies that Israel will be taken as prisoners to all the nations and Jerusalem will be trampled on by the Gentiles until the times of the Gentiles are fulfilled. This time of the Gentiles is also mentioned elsewhere.

> *Romans 11:25* I do not want you to be ignorant of this mystery, brothers, so that you may not be conceited: Israel has experienced a hardening in part until the full number of the Gentiles has come in.

> *Revelation 11:2* But exclude the outer court; do not measure it, because it has been given to the Gentiles. They will trample on the holy city for forty-two months.

When the time of the Gentiles ends, the time of Israelite renewal begins. As will be seen later, this time of Israelite renewal occurs toward the end of history. The end of the "time of the Gentiles" occurring towards the end of history, as described in verse 24, makes a natural transition back to the signs in the heavens (Luke 21:25ff) as signs of the end.

In verses 34-36, there is a warning not to be weighed down by the anxieties of life, to prevent that day (the day of judgment) from closing unexpectedly like a trap. For it (that day) will come upon all those who live on the face of the whole earth. This is another clear statement that believers will face the return of the Lord and the subsequent judgment. For that day to come on all those who live on the face of the earth, it must come on believers and non-believers alike. While those who prefer a silent rapture suggest that they will not be on the face of the earth, the passage appears to be easier to interpret as all inclusive than to propose a removal of believers not discussed anywhere in this text. It would be expected that the Lord would announce judgment coming upon all those who "are left" if that were the case. The group of all those who live on the earth includes believers. The escape in verse 36 is an escape from the destruction facing those who are unprepared.

Passages From the Epistles

The epistles that include teaching regarding the return of Christ and the final judgment are written to encourage believers. Paul writes to the Thessalonians to encourage them in their faith. He does not want them to be ignorant regarding Christ's return or to be unsettled by letters claiming to come from him. In I Thessalonians, Paul encourages those concerned about fellow believers who have died. In II Thessalonians, Paul reminds the Thessalonians that certain signs must precede the return of Christ.

Peter writes to some who could be discouraged because Christ's return has been delayed longer than they expected. He advises believers that the certainty of Christ's return should result in holy and godly lives.

I Thessalonians 4:13-5:11

This text answers the question, what happens to those who die before the coming of the Lord? There is a play on the word asleep. In 4:14 Paul writes of those who have fallen asleep in Christ. Clearly he is speaking of those who have died. In verse 15 he speaks of those who have fallen asleep and in verse 16 he uses the term "the dead in Christ." All of these verses describe those who have died physically. Then in 5:6 he says, "let us not be like others, who are asleep" in reference to those who are spiritually dead. Later, in verse 10, he goes back to speaking of physical death by saying we will live with Christ, whether we are awake or asleep.

In comparing those who live until the return of Christ and those who have died before his return, Paul tells the Thessalonians that the dead will rise first and then those who are alive will join them in the clouds (I Thes. 4:15-17.) This is a noisy return of Christ and must be the end of the world because "we will be with the Lord forever.

Once again it should be pointed out that this is the return of Christ which Paul, speaking under the influence of the Holy Spirit, expects to participate in if he lives until the return of Christ. In I Thessalonians 4:15

Paul says "we who are still alive", and thereby includes himself among those who could participate in this noisy return of Christ. This return is both for Paul and for the Thessalonians because they are to encourage each other with these words (I Thes. 4:18, 5:11.) It would seem appropriate for them to encourage each other with these words only if there was a real hope of their seeing this return during their lifetime or during Paul's lifetime. If, as some have proposed, the next return of Christ was to be a removal of believers with the world continuing on, Paul and the Thessalonians would have had no hope of seeing the return of Christ described in this text except after they were raptured or after they died. This is clearly not Paul's expectation. This text describes the coming of the Lord which Paul hoped he would be alive to see.

II Thessalonians 2:1-12

In this text, Paul addresses concerns expressed by the church that the Lord might have come without their knowledge. Apparently, there were prophecies or rumors or other communications that had alarmed the Thessalonians. Paul reassures them, outlining certain events that must precede the coming of Christ.

If there was to be a secret rapture, Paul would not be addressing whether the day of the Lord had already come because the day of the Lord is the day of judgment. The coming of the Lord and our being gathered to him (verse 1) would have no relationship to the day of the Lord if there were a silent rapture (verse 2) because the silent rapture that has been proposed is not directly connected to the day of the Lord (the day of final judgment.) In verses 3 and 4, Paul describes the events that will precede the coming of the Lord, and in verse 5 reminds them that he had already told them these things.

Before the day of the Lord will come, the rebellion must occur and the Man of Lawlessness, who will call himself a god, must be revealed. He will support that statement with false miracles, signs, and wonders. The power of lawlessness is at work at the time that Paul is writing this letter. However, the Man of Lawlessness will not be revealed until that one who holds back the power of lawlessness is removed. The imprisonment of Satan in the Abyss is holding back the Man of Lawlessness. When he is released, the Man of Lawlessness will be revealed. The timing of this revelation is in God's hands; therefore he will be revealed at the proper time.

When he is revealed, the lawless one will be destroyed by the splendor of the Lord's coming.

The point Paul is making in this text is that the Thessalonians need not worry about the coming of the Lord until this event occurs. Any return of Christ must be after the Man of Lawlessness is revealed. Since he is destroyed by the coming of the Lord, it appears that only one return of Christ, which includes the final judgment, is in Paul's mind. This is supported by his description of the coming of Christ in I Thessalonians 4:13ff.

II Peter 3:1-18

Peter begins his discussion of the return of Christ by confronting those who deny that Christ will return. These scoffers claim that everything is as it always has been. Peter's response is that those who scoff choose to forget that God destroyed the world in the past through a flood. Peter compares the destruction of the world during the time of Noah with its destruction in the day of judgment. In Noah's time the world was destroyed by water. In the future, the world will be destroyed by fire in the day of judgment.

The day of the Lord, the day of final judgment, will come like a thief, unexpectedly. When the day of judgment occurs, the world will be destroyed by fire. This text clarifies that the world will not go on in its fallen state forever. This world must be destroyed and its place will be taken by the new heaven and new earth (II Peter 3:13), the new Jerusalem of Revelation 21 and 22.

Peter makes it clear that the destruction of the world calls forth a response from believers. They are not afraid of the destruction. The look forward to it (II Peter 3:12) and desire to speed its coming. Their response is to put forth an effort to be holy, blameless, and spotless before the Lord.

SECTION TWO

An Overview of Revelation

In examining the book of Revelation the reader is confronted with a mysterious book that has been interpreted in many ways to support a variety of eschatological views. The introductory material in Section One of this book may have clarified some of the issues regarding how Revelation should be interpreted. Yet, having read Section One, the average student of the Bible will not find Revelation easy to understand. Section Two is an interpretive summary of Revelation that shows how the principles in Section One and the definitions in Section Three should be used. What follows is not intended to be a commentary. Rather, its purpose is to give an explanation of how the author would interpret Revelation in light of the principles of interpretation outlined in Section One and the definition of symbols provided in Section Three.

It is natural to come to Revelation with some preconceived notions of how some or all of the book is to be interpreted. No one can or should dispose of knowledge already gained through study of the Scriptures. The reader should be cautious however, that what is already known can be supported by the biblical text in context. Some popular teaching regarding Revelation uses proof texts in a way that is inconsistent with their context. Such interpretations sometimes treat this vision as though it were a newspaper report. Many images in Revelation are interpreted within the text non-literally and other images within the text are similar or identical to images from other parts of Scripture that are interpreted non-literally. The many symbols and non-chronological ordering of events makes it impossible to treat the text like a news story. The symbols have meaning, and their meaning is to be taken literally. That does not mean the symbols themselves should be understood literally.

Revelation is the Word of God as much as any other New Testament book. Its message is hidden from the casual reader through its symbolism but it is accessible to those who really know the Old and New Testament Scriptures. Revelation was written by John for the edification of the church. Its benefit is similar to that of the other books of the New Testament.

Those who have the most interest in this subject probably already have an eschatological position. The goal of this section is not to be faithful to a particular eschatological view but to be faithful to the meaning of the text. It will be clear to those familiar with the classical eschatological positions that the interpretation of Revelation in this chapter does not completely fall within any of the historic eschatological views.

Revelation 1:1 - 3:22
Introductory Messages to the Seven Churches

In the introductory paragraph in chapter 1, John begins by defining the purpose of the book. It is the revelation of Jesus Christ, which God gave him to show his servants what must **soon** take place. John warns that the events described in the book will occur **soon**. He repeats this warning in verse 3, where the words must be taken to heart because the time is near. In showing his servants what must soon take place, Jesus is not suggesting that all of the events prophesied will occur equally **soon**. The fulfillment of some events occurs within the century after John finishes writing. Other events, including the many prophesies about the return of Christ, await fulfillment. John's Revelation consists of a series of related visions that conclude with the return of Christ or the final judgment. Sometimes the visions present future events in chronological order. At other times, the visions are topical and have no chronological elements. The events described in chronological visions must occur in their proper sequence. Both the return of Christ and the final judgment occur at the end of every chronological sequence. The biblical texts consistently speak of the second coming as imminent because of the uncertainty of its timing and because their purpose is to encourage believers to be prepared when Christ returns.

The book is addressed to seven churches. This is similar to Paul's letters, many of which are also addressed to churches. While Revelation contains images, prophesy, and exhortation rather than the instruction, counseling, and advice Paul provides, the purpose is the same. Revelation's goal is to encourage and edify the seven churches and all believers. The benefits to the reader are similar to those derived from reading Paul's writings. Paul tried to be encouraging while confronting unhealthy situations within the churches. John's vision addresses current conditions in the churches (in chapters two and three) and then presents information about the future through imagery. Paul's writings are of benefit to the modern church in spite of being addressed to first century churches. Likewise, John's vision is of benefit to the modern reader although addressed to seven first century churches (Rev. 1:4,11, 22:16.)

Following the prologue, there is a section praising God. Regardless of one's interpretation of various images within the book, all should agree that one of the most important and valued elements within Revelation are the many songs that praise God throughout the vision.

John greets the seven churches in Revelation 1:4f and then proceeds to a blessing or what might be called an introductory benediction. A similar blessing appears at the beginning of all of Paul's letters and at the beginning of Peter's epistles. The blessing comes from three persons. The first person is "him who is, and who was, and who is to come". If there was any question, the identity of this person appears in verse 8. He is the Lord God, the Almighty. The third person is Jesus Christ, the faithful witness, the firstborn from the dead, and the ruler of the kings of the earth.

The second person does not at first glance seem to be a person at all. It is a group called the **seven spirits of God** that are before the throne of God Almighty. Revelation is the only book that mentions seven spirits in connection with God. Elsewhere in Scripture, seven spirits that gather are always evil and they gather to possess a person completely (Matthew 12:43-45, Luke 8:2, 11:24-26.) The number **seven** represents completeness in Scripture, so the seven spirits should be translated the sevenfold Spirit of God, the Holy Spirit. This translation appears in the New International Version (NIV) as a footnote. The greeting from the three persons of the Godhead is a Trinitarian formula.

Three major themes within Revelation are first mentioned in verse 9. John introduces himself as a brother of those to whom he writes. He then calls himself a companion in the suffering, kingdom, and patient endurance that are ours in Jesus. The seven churches and the church throughout history will necessarily face suffering in this fallen world. The theme of sharing in suffering is found throughout Scripture (Rom. 5:3f, II Tim. 3:10-13, James 1:2-4) and is a repeated theme in

Revelation (Rev. 2:3,10, 3:10, 12:11,17, 13:7,15f.) The church must recognize the inevitability of suffering so that no one will be disheartened by the affliction that the faithful will face. While there will be suffering related to persecution, most suffering will be due to the Fall. That is why it is so important to mention in Revelation 22:3 that there will no longer be any curse in the new Jerusalem. The faithful will suffer because they are fallen people, living among fallen people in a corrupt and fallen world. Even the church, which should be a safe haven, will consist of fallen people who will inevitably sin against one another. The church should be a place where the faithful love to be, not because it is perfect, but because there is reconciliation, forgiveness, and love available for those who are suffering.

The promise of the kingdom is sandwiched between suffering and patient endurance to emphasize that it is not to be attained in isolation from suffering, and endurance. This is not a kingdom that will be some day. John is a companion in the kingdom in his own day. The kingdom of God is reigning both now and into eternity. The people of God are to reign on the earth (Rev. 5:9f, 11:5f, 20:4.) The final destiny of the people of God is the new Jerusalem. It comes down out of heaven from God and the faithful dwell in it with God.

Perseverance, and patient endurance are necessary for the church that endures persecution. The theme is repeated throughout Revelation that the faithful must remain faithful in the midst of persecution (Rev. 2:19, 3:10, 13:10, 14:12.)

Beginning in verse 12, the first major character in John's vision is presented. This person is described in terms that are similar to those used to describe the man in Daniel 10:4-6. The man in Daniel 10 is not identified except that he works with the archangel Michael and he announces what will be. The man in Revelation is the **First and Last**, the Living one who was dead and is alive forever and who holds the **keys** to death and Hades. From this it is clear that he is Jesus.

Jesus stands in the midst of seven golden **lampstands** and he holds **seven stars** in his right hand. These images are interpreted by Jesus in verse 20. The **seven** golden **lampstands** are the seven churches to whom this letter was written and the **seven stars** are the **angels** or messengers of the churches. When these symbols appear later in Revelation, they will be interpreted in the same way. It is this consistency within the symbols that makes the interpretation of the book possible.

The individual messages to the churches are addressed not to the churches but to the **angels** of the churches. If this were to be interpreted to mean that **angels** were assigned to those churches, the benefit of addressing the message to them is not clear. It is obvious that the message is meant for the people within the churches or the leadership of the churches. A better approach is to translate the word "angelo" messenger which is its primary meaning in Greek. The only way to distinguish between the two meanings of "angelo" is the context. In this case, the context could allow either meaning, so the translator must determine which meaning better fits the context. The clear intent is to provide instruction to the members of each church. An appropriate point of contact would be the pastor whose role it is to act as the messenger of God. It would be reasonable to send this letter through the pastor to ensure that the topics covered in the warnings would be addressed in the sermons preached.

The messages to the churches have several elements in common. They all are addressed to the messenger of the church. They all are introduced as the words of Jesus and he is usually described using the images that appear in chapter one. The description of Jesus at the beginning of the message relates to some action he will take or some circumstance the church will face. Each message concludes with the statement, "He who has an ear, let him hear what the Spirit says to the churches." Various images are used to illustrate the promise of eternal life for those who overcome.

Ephesus

The Ephesian church is commended by Jesus as a church that has endured and persevered through hardships. They have tested those travelling preachers who have come to them cla. ning to be apostles and have discovered those who were not apostles. In this way, they maintained their purity at a time when the church had a more difficult time remaining doctrinally pure because there was no universally accepted canon of Scripture.

Jesus is described in verse one as holding the **seven stars** in his right hand and walking among the **lampstands**. In verse 5, he threatens to remove the church's **lampstand** if it does not repent and do what it did at first.

While the church is pure, its members have lost their first love. They have lost the depth of love for God that they had at first which resulted in works of love. This problem is of sufficient seriousness that failure to repent will result in the destruction of their church.

They hate the practices of the **Nicolaitans**, a gnostic sect, whose practices are described in Revelation 2:14f. The Nicolaitans were antinomians who believed that since matter (and specifically the human body) was evil, and only the spirit was pure, ungodly physical actions made no difference. This resulted in sexual immorality, participation in meals dedicated to pagan gods and other accommodations to evil practices within the society.

If they overcome, they will eat from the tree of life that grows in the New Jerusalem in chapter 22.

Smyrna

Smyrna was closely tied to Rome and was a center for emperor worship. There was a large Jewish community in the city that was strongly antagonistic toward Christianity. The church was financially poor but was commended by Jesus because they were spiritually rich.

Jesus is the **First and Last** who died and came to life again. This image reminds the members of the church that Jesus faced harsh persecution just as they will. Using Jesus as the model, the text alludes to the promise that those who die in the Lord will come to life again.

The church has experienced afflictions and is about to experience even harsher sufferings. They are warned that some will be imprisoned. Furthermore, the warning to be faithful even to the point of death suggests that some will die in the persecution. The persecution will be for only ten days. This is not a literal ten days any more than any of the other time references in Revelation are literal. Ten days is a symbol representing a short time.

If they overcome, they will not be hurt by the **second death** that is later defined as the lake of fire.

Pergamum

Pergamum was the primary seat for emperor worship in Asia as the capital city of the Roman province of Asia. In addition to having a temple dedicated to Augustus, Pergamum had a large altar dedicated to Zeus, and a temple of Athena on its acropolis. Pergamum was also the center of worship for the serpent god of healing, Asclepios.

Jesus is described as having a sharp double-edged sword. That sword is a threat to those who hold to the teachings of the **Nicolaitans** because Jesus will fight against them using the sword of his mouth (Rev. 2:16.)

The church is commended for remaining faithful even after one of their number, Antipas, was put to death. The details regarding his death are not provided. Because of the magnitude of idolatry in the city, it is called the place where Satan has his throne and where Satan lives.

The church has a failing in that some of its members hold to the teaching of Balaam and the teaching of the **Nicolaitans**. From the structure of the Greek in this text it is clear that these are two descriptions of the same heresy. In verse 14, the teachings attributed to Balaam define the teaching of the **Nicolaitans**. The church must repent or the Lord will come and fight against that portion of the church involved in these evil practices.

If they overcome, they will be given some of the hidden manna. Hebrews 9:4 describes the gold jar of manna stored in the ark of the covenant. Later, in Hebrews 9:23f, the man-made sanctuary is called a copy of the heavenly one. The hidden manna is probably a reference to the true manna in heaven which is Jesus, the bread of life, and the true bread from heaven (John 6:25-35) who is available only for the redeemed.

The overcomers also will be given a **white stone** with a name written on it. While the precise meaning of the **white stone** is not known, it may refer to the **white stone** that was used to represent acquittal by a jury. It may also refer to a white stone that could be used as an admission ticket to a festival (such as the wedding feast of the Lamb.) No matter which meaning is preferred, the **white stone** is an emblem of redemption.

Thyatira

Thyatira had many trade guilds. Membership in the trade guilds was required for those who wanted to participate in trade. These trade guilds would have held social gatherings where the members shared a meal. Such meals would have been dedicated to a pagan deity and would have concluded with morally improper behavior. One question that Christians in this church would have wrestled with was how to participate in commerce without compromising their values.

Jesus is described as the Son of God whose **eyes are like blazing fire** and whose **feet are like burnished bronze**. The blazing eyes represent his searching the hearts, and minds of the members of the churches. His feet, looking like burnished bronze, represent authority and the ability to dash the nations to pieces like pottery (Rev. 2:26f.)

The church is commended for their deeds, love, faith, service, and perseverance. They are growing spiritually because they are doing more than they did at first.

Their problem was tolerance of a woman who claimed to be a prophetess. She encouraged accommodation with the evil behavior of the society. She taught that it was acceptable for Christians to participate in sexual immorality and eat food offered to idols. This was permissible because the body and all matter was believed to be impure, and idols were nothing. This would have been tempting to those who wanted to fit into the trade guilds. She has been warned and will be punished with illness. Her followers (those who follow her but have reservations about accepting her teaching) will suffer, and her children (those who have completely accepted her views without reservation) will die.

It is because the members of the church who have nothing to do with the prophetess' teaching are growing that no further requirement is laid on them. They should continue to do what they are doing and continue to grow.

If they overcome, they will have authority over the nations like the authority of the one who rules with the **iron scepter** (Jesus.) The overcomer will be given the **morning star**, who is identified in Revelation 22:16 as Jesus.

Sardis

Sardis was an industrial center that benefited from being the cross-roads of several major Roman roads. The city had a reputation for indulgence and relaxed moral standards.

Jesus holds the **seven spirits of God** and the **seven stars**. The **seven spirits** represent the Holy Spirit who gives life to believers (regeneration) and to the church (fellowship and worship.) The **stars** represent the **seven** messengers of the churches (the pastors) who must do their work to supply what this church needs. Without an infusion of life from the Spirit and the effective ministry of the pastor to wake them up (Rev. 3:2), Jesus will come as a thief in the night to those who are unprepared and spiritually dead.

The church has a reputation for being alive but Jesus tells them they are dead. They have the superficial elements of religion without the commitment and the condition of heart necessary for true religion. Although not completely dead, they are not far from it. Jesus tells them there is something still alive that needs to be strengthened before it dies. Their near-death condition is not from failing to hear the truth; rather they have left behind what they received, and heard.

The church has a remnant who have remained pure. They are promised that they will be dressed in **white**. Being dressed in **white** is defined in Revelation 7:14 as belonging to those who have come out of **the great tribulation**. Some will argue that Revelation 7:14 applies only to those who appear in Revelation 7:9. If the images in Revelation have the same meaning wherever they appear, the **white** robes given to the martyrs in Revelation 6:11 anticipate their inclusion among those in **white** robes who are defined in Revelation 7:14. The inclusion of the martyrs from chapter 6 with those coming out of **the great tribulation** leads to the conclusion that **the great tribulation** must begin prior to the death of the first Christian martyr. In that case, all of the faithful in Sardis would be included among those who came out of **the great tribulation**.

Those who overcome will be dressed in **white**, will have their name included in the **book of life**, and be acknowledged by Jesus.

Philadelphia

Philadelphia was located on a main geological fault line and as a result, experienced frequent earthquakes. While the city's name means brotherly love, it did not receive its name through the character of its citizens but from King Attalus Philadelphus who reigned from 159 to 138 BC. A false rumor that his brother Eumenes II had been assassinated caused Attalus to accept the crown. When his brother returned safely from Greece, Attalus abdicated in favor of his brother. It is also reported that Rome encouraged Attalus to overthrow his brother and he refused. For these acts of faithfulness, Attalus was given the title Philadelphus, "lover of his brother."

Jesus is described as holy and true, and holding the **key** of David. He is holy and true in contrast to those from the synagogue of Satan who claim to be Jews but are not. Their claims are false (being based on physical and racial lineage rather than spiritual lineage) so they are liars. The assertion that the Jews in Philadelphia are not really Jews comes from Paul's definition of what it means to be a true Jew.

> *Romans 2:28f* A man is not a Jew if he is only one outwardly nor is circumcision merely outward and physical. No, a man is a Jew if he is one inwardly; and circumcision is circumcision of the heart, by the Spirit, not by the written code. Such a man's praise is not from men, but from God.

The Jews in Philadelphia were physically Jews but their hearts were not right with God, so Jesus calls their synagogue a synagogue of Satan. Jesus holds the **key** of David, an image that comes from Isaiah.

> *Isaiah 22:22* I will place on his shoulder the key to the house of David; what he opens no one can shut, and what he shuts no one can open.

In Isaiah, God promises to remove Shebna who is in charge of Hezekiah's palace (In Isaiah 36:3 he is called the Secretary) and replace him with Eliakim (who in Isaiah 36:3 is called the palace administrator.) In the message to Philadelphia, Jesus holds the **key** of David. As the holder of the **key**, Jesus has authority over all Israel. Jesus will force those who claim to be Jews, but who are not because they lack the inward circumcision of the heart, to acknowledge his love for this Gentile church.

This is a weak yet faithful church. They have been enduring patiently and so will be kept from the persecution that is coming. They will be marked with three names. They will bear God's to show they belong to him (Rev. 14:1, 22:4.) They will bear the name of the new Jerusalem to show they are citizens of it. They also will bear the new name of Jesus, the name that no one knows but he himself (Rev. 19:12) as evidence that they belong to Jesus as well.

Laodicea

Laodicea was a wealthy city, a prestigious hub of banking and industry. It was sufficiently wealthy that after a severe earthquake in 60-61 AD, it was able to rebuild without the financial assistance from Rome that other cities required. A major medical school was located in Laodicea which was known for a component called "Phrygian powder" that was used in eye-salve.

Jesus is described as the faithful and true witness and the ruler of creation. Jesus is a true witness in contrast to the Laodiceans who are blind and need salve to put on their eyes. As the ruler of creation, he will give the overcomer the right to sit with him on his throne.

This church suffers from self-satisfaction. The people are so comfortable in their finances that they have been blinded to their spiritual condition which is wretched, pitiful, poor, blind, and naked.

Jesus assures them that his love will be expressed in rebuke and discipline in the hope that they will repent. He stands at the door of the professed believers in Laodicea and knocks. He is not knocking to evangelize them but to call them back as believers to a more intimate relationship.

Revelation 4:1-8:1
The Scroll and Seven Seals

In Revelation 4:1, John moves beyond the present ("I will show you what must take place after this".) But throughout Revelation 4, the future is in the presence of God and the only futuristic elements are the **twenty-four elders** who lay their crowns before the throne.

Revelation 4 is the old song of praise to God for his work as Creator (Rev. 4:11) while in Revelation 5, the new song of the redemption of the people of God is sung (Rev. 5:9,10,12.) Chapter 4 describes the scene in heaven where God is being praised by angels and **twenty-four elders/rulers.**

Revelation 4 begins with a voice speaking like a **trumpet.** The person with the trumpet-like voice was identified in Revelation 1 as one like a son of man who describes himself in Revelation 1:18 in terms that can only refer to Jesus. John is to come up to be shown what must take place after this. Following so closely after the admonitions to the seven churches regarding the current situation, the "after this" at the end of verse 1 must point to events that begin in the near future. The events described begin in the near future but include events occurring at the end of human history. It would be expected that events beginning in the distant future would be described using language pointing to the end of time (e.g., I will show you what must take place at the end.)

There is a throne surrounded by twenty-four thrones on which are seated **twenty-four elders.** They are dressed in **white** (representing holiness) and are wearing **crowns** of **gold** (indicating their status as rulers.) From the throne comes lightning, rumbling, and thunder. This is **extreme language** reflecting God's judgment (see the discussion of extreme language in section 1.) The lightning and thunder are less extreme than that described elsewhere in Revelation. The reason for this is that no specific judgment is being pronounced. The purpose here is to introduce the concept of judgment which is a major theme throughout the book. It is also designed to clarify for the reader that all judgment, including that which will occur later in Revelation, comes from him who sits on the throne.

There are **seven lamps** blazing before the throne. These **lamps** represent the **seven spirits** (or sevenfold Spirit) of God (Rev. 4:5.) The connection between **lamps** and **lampstands** should not be overlooked. The **lamps** (spirits) are the reason that there are **lampstands** (churches - Rev. 1:20.) The failure to repent and return to the first love will result in removal of the **lampstand** (and by implication the removal of the **lamp**/spirit - Rev. 2:5.)

The translation sevenfold Spirit (New International Version footnote) is preferred because there is nowhere in Scripture a description of **seven spirits of God**. Additionally, in Revelation 1:4f it appears that a

Trinitarian formula is being used in which the sevenfold spirit is equated with the Holy Spirit.

> *Rev. 1:4f* Grace and peace to you from him who is, and who was, and who is to come, and from the sevenfold spirit before his throne, and from Jesus Christ, who is the faithful witness, the first-born from the dead, and the ruler of the kings of the earth.

The one who is, and who was, and who is to come, is identified in Revelation 1:8 as the Lord God, the Almighty. The third person from whom the blessing is invoked is clearly identified as Jesus. That leaves the seven spirits or sevenfold spirit to be identified. If a Trinitarian formula is being used, the seven spirits must be a reference to the Holy Spirit and should be translated the sevenfold spirit.

The number **seven** represents completeness in Scripture (**seven** days in a week, also **seven** seals, **seven** trumpets and **seven** last plagues in Revelation) and describes the majesty and completeness of the Spirit of God who dwells in the seven churches as their light (**lamp**.)

There are **four living creatures** (Rev. 4:6) which are similar but not identical to the four creatures in Ezekiel 1. The differences between them include the shape of their bodies and the number of wings they have. In Ezekiel, the creatures are all like men and have four faces each. In Revelation, the creatures are in the form of three animals and a man. The creatures in Revelation have six wings like the seraphim in Isaiah 6 whose words are partially quoted by these **four living creatures**. Their purpose is to sing constant praise to God and their praise plays a counterpoint to the praise of the elders. The elders bow and lay their **crowns** before God as a sign of their adoration of him. Their song is the old song with which the new song of chapter 5 is compared. The focus of their song is the worthiness of God to receive praise because he is the creator.

Revelation 5 is a continuation of the praise of creation toward the **Lamb**. In chapter 5, God the Father is holding a **scroll** in his right hand that has been sealed with **seven seals**. The number **seven** indicates the completeness of its sealing which is such that no one can open or even look into it. The opening of the **scroll** and the **seals** is so important to John that when no one can open it he weeps and weeps. This reaction would be inappropriate if he did not know either the content of the **scroll** or that the opening of the **scroll** would be beneficial.

Since several of the **seals** are representative of various forms of death it may be surprising that John wants the **scroll** opened. However, the overriding theme of the **seals** is the conquest of the Lord over the earth and over the fall of creation. The creator who is praised for creating is also to be praised for redeeming his creation from its corruption.

A **lamb**, which looks as if it has been slain, takes the **scroll** from the Father. The **four living creatures** and the **twenty-four elders** sing a new song. It is new because it is the song of redemption of creation by the **lamb**, who acted as the sacrifice for sinful mankind. The **lamb** clearly represents Jesus who was slain and who bought men for God with his blood (Rev. 5:9.) His qualification to open the **seals** is his death. Through his death the people of God become priests (I Peter 2:5) who reign on earth. Revelation 5:9 clearly states that the redeemed will reign on earth. This text should be remembered when reading the analysis of Revelation 20 later in this section.

Ten thousand times ten thousand angels sing (to the **lamb** and to the Father on the throne) a song of praise. This is followed by a song sung by "every creature in heaven and on earth and under the earth and on the sea, and all that is in them." This song is sung to the Father and to Jesus together in a way that would be totally inappropriate if Jesus were not an equal with the Father. It would be blasphemous to sing a song of praise in which a creature was praised equally with God. It would be unthinkable that both would be given similar praise forever and ever. This is another evidence for the deity of Christ, supplementing the evidence of the divine titles which are ascribed to Jesus throughout the book.

In Revelation 6, the **lamb** begins to open the **seven seals**. These **seals** represent dangers to mankind. They act as a warning to all humanity that life is temporary, that the greatest dangers are outside the control of most people, and that the issue of one's relationship with the Lord must be confronted.

Seal 1—Danger of the Conquering Lord When the first **seal** is opened, from out of the **scroll** comes a rider on a **white horse**. The rider is wearing a **crown** which shows that he is a ruler who is reigning. He is not hoping to reign some day, but he is reigning on the earth through the church as is stated in I Corinthians 15:25.

> For he (Christ) must reign until he has put all his enemies under his feet.

He has a single **crown** because he is known as the God of Israel. As he goes out and conquers, he will not be known as the God of a single nation, but as the God of all the earth. This rider appears again in Revelation 19:10,11 where he is wearing many crowns, indicating that he has conquered many nations. His name, provided in Revelation 19, is the **Word of God** and he has the name **King of kings and Lord of lords** written on his robe and on his thigh. The first **seal** therefore represents the conquering Lord Jesus Christ. This **seal** is dangerous, as are most of the **seals**, for those who stand in opposition to this conquering king. They will be swept away by this conqueror and his armies.

Seal 2—Danger of War When the second **seal** is opened, a rider on a fiery **red horse** comes forth to take peace from the earth. In Zechariah 1:8ff, a man riding a **red horse** describes the whole world as at rest and in peace. An **angel** who is present reports that the Almighty is angry with the nations that feel secure and he describes how **Babylon** will be plundered by their slaves (Zech. 1:15, 2:9.) There is clearly a parallel in this passage in which God is displeased with peace on earth and he gives the rider power to take peace from the earth. It cannot be asserted that God likes war. The horse is **red** which is symbolic throughout the book of wickedness. War is not good, nor does God like war, it is rather a normal result of the corruption brought into the world by the Fall of man. War causes insecurity and pain, which God uses to draw men's attention to the fact that they cannot live in comfort without the Almighty.

Seal 3—Danger of Famine When the third **seal** is opened, a rider on a **black** horse comes forth holding a pair of scales. He represents famine as can be seen from the excessive prices for wheat and barley that are pronounced. This parallels the prices for wheat and barley described in II Kings 7:1 during a siege. Elisha prophecies that tomorrow, when the siege ends, seven quarts of flour will cost a shekel (this is in contrast with the cost of five shekels for half a pint of seed pods on the day he makes the prophesy.) The color **black** does not symbolize wickedness like the color **red**, but it is a color of doom and signifies the pain and death that starvation brings. Famine occurs as part of the corruption of the earth due to the Fall and the sinfulness of humanity. Through famine, God unleashes on man one of the inevitable effects of sin. The disharmony with nature caused by the Fall results in crops failing and a lack of sufficient food. Artificial famines have been created throughout history when a wartime siege has caused starvation of those in the city.

The danger of famine is designed to draw the reader's attention to the Lord who is in control of this impact of the Fall. He alone has the solution for this danger (i.e., to serve the risen and glorified Christ both now and in eternity.)

Seal 4—Danger of Sudden or Violent Death The fourth **seal** is opened and a rider on a pale horse comes forth. His name is Death and Hades (the residence of the dead) is close behind him. The types of death described contrast with the kinds of death most people imagine would be most favorable. This rider unleashes war (the sword), famine, plague, and mauling by wild animals on a fourth of the earth. To those who think they will live to an old age and who believe that they can consider the Lord later, this danger is greatest. This **seal** warns that death may be sudden and unexpected.

Seal 5—Danger of Martyrdom The fifth **seal** is directed to those who are believers. The warning is that more of the followers of Christ will be killed. The purpose of this warning of danger is to have believers count the cost (is their faith worth dying for?) and to ensure that no one is disheartened by Christian martyrdom. Later, in Revelation 13:10 and 14:12, additional warnings of persecution are followed by the statement "this calls for patient endurance and faithfulness on the part of the saints." Christians must expect persecution and endure it as a witness against the world. They can be encouraged because, in dying, they will live. Those who are attacked will be avenged and, in their ultimate destiny, those who are powerless will be the victors. They are given **white robes** indicating that they come out of the great tribulation (Rev. 7:14.) They are told that they must wait until their number is completed.

Seal 6—Danger of Final Judgment The opening of the sixth **seal** in Revelation 6:12 is accompanied by **extreme language** drawn from several Old Testament sources. By bringing together **extreme language** from different biblical texts, the vision emphasizes that the sixth **seal** is an unusually powerful judgment. It would be clear that this imagery represents judgment even if the Old and New Testament use of extreme language, which symbolizes the devastating nature of God's judgment, had not been explained. Within the text, all kinds of people want the earth to hide them from the face of him who sits on the throne and from the wrath of the **lamb**. The "great day of their wrath" reinforces that this is a day of judgment by using the same language found in the Old Testament describing judgment (see The Day of the Lord in Section One.) From the severity of the **extreme language** in this passage and the attempts to hide from the wrath of the **lamb**, it is clear that the image is depicting the final judgment. The **earthquake** described in the sixth **seal** and elsewhere parallels the assertion in Ezekiel 38 and in Zechariah 14 that there will be a great **earthquake** at the end.

Ezekiel 38:19 In my zeal and fiery wrath I declare that at that time there shall be a great earthquake in the land of Israel.

Zechariah 14:3-5 Then the Lord will go out and fight against those nations, as he fights in the day of battle. On that day his feet will stand on the Mount of Olives, east of Jerusalem, and the Mount of Olives will be split in two from east to west, forming a great valley, with half the mountain moving north and half moving south. You will flee by my mountain valley, for it will extend to Azel. You will flee as you fled the earthquake in the days of Uzziah the king of Judah. Then the Lord my God will come, and all the holy ones with him.

Great **earthquakes** continue to appear in Revelation in conjunction with passages describing the very end of human history (Rev. 8:5, 11:13,19, 16:18f.)

The seventh chapter of Revelation continues to describe the impact of the sixth **seal**. There are four **angels** having the power to harm the land and the sea. They are not to harm land or sea until the servants of God have been sealed. The number sealed is **144,000** from all the tribes of Israel, 12,000 from each tribe. It is difficult to hold to a literal interpretation of these numbers. The number 1000 is symbolic of completeness in Scripture and numbers are often rounded to the nearest 1000 when large numbers are reported in Scripture. The number twelve is symbolic of the people of God (twelve sons of Jacob, twelve tribes, twelve apostles.) If the numbers were to be taken literally, they would describe the number of Israelites sealed and would not apply to those who are not Israelites but are sealed. Since the sixth **seal** describes the final judgment, the **144,000** reflects the completeness of the spiritual restoration of the Jewish church on earth at the time of the return of Christ.

After those from the Jewish church are sealed, there appears a multitude that no one can count from every nation, tribe, people, and language wearing **white robes**. The **white robes** are not unique to the martyrs but must be worn by everyone in the congregation who stands before the throne. This is similar to Matthew 22:11-14 where the one who was not wearing the wedding clothes was cast out into the darkness. This immense congregation is holding **palm branches** in their hands.

Palm branches were a sign of national victory. A Roman general who had won many victories was called a man of many palms. Israel carried palm branches into the temple when they captured and cleansed it during the Maccabean revolt. Jesus was welcomed into Jerusalem with palms and the people sang songs expressing hope for national victory in calling him the Son of David and the king of Israel. Palms are used in this passage to symbolize the victory of the Lord over all of his opponents.

The multitude sings songs of praise for the one on the throne and for the **lamb**. This again emphasizes the worthiness of the **lamb** to receive praise alongside the Father on the throne.

Another clue that helps interpret this passage is the question asked, 'Who are these in **white robes** and where did they come from'? The answer is that these are they who have come out of (i.e., died during) **the great tribulation**. It is important to note that they did not come out before **the great tribulation**. They did not avoid the tribulation through a rapture. They lived and died during **the great tribulation**.

This question and answer causes some distress to theories about a tribulation period of seven years or less. Those wearing the **white robes** have come out of the great tribulation period. If the number of those who come out of **the great tribulation** period is a number that no one can count from every nation, tribe, people, and language (Rev. 7:9) it is difficult to see how this could be accomplished in seven years or less. Based on this text, any theory proposing a short tribulation period would require that there be a bloodbath where millions of Christians would be killed. Such a theory cannot be held because the group under the altar in Revelation 6:9, consisting of all those who have been slain because of the Word of God and their testimony (i.e., all martyrs), are also wearing

white robes. They are given **white robes** to represent that they too have come out of the great tribulation (Rev 7:14.) It is awkward to suggest that the **white robes** in Revelation 7:9 represent coming out of **the great tribulation**, but the **white robes** fifteen verses earlier do not bear the same symbolism.

If the time of **the great tribulation** includes those described in Revelation 6:9, **the great tribulation** must have begun before the first martyr died. **The great tribulation** lasts for an indefinite time but covers at least the lifetimes of all Christian martyrs. Not all the multitude who died during the great tribulation were martyred. Since the tribulation period covers most if not all of the time since the death of Christ, many would have died a natural death. If all the multitude who came out of **the great tribulation** were martyrs they would have appeared under the altar with the other martyrs. In Revelation 6:9ff, the martyrs appear to be a group limited in number.

Some have suggested that this text is not referring to the great tribulation period but to personal struggles. The King James Version translates this, "These are they which came out of great tribulation …," which could suggest that they are people who faced difficulties. Most modern translations (e.g., the New King James Version, the Revised Standard Version, the New American Standard Version and the New International Version) say, these are they which have come out of **the great tribulation**. The Greek text contains a repeated definite article (the great the tribulation) which supports the translations by the newer versions. Abbott writes that the repetition of the definite article "adds weight and emphasis to the article." [4] The repeated articles emphasize that the vision refers to a specific tribulation period.

The sixth **seal** concludes by describing the nurturing of the people of God by their God into eternity.

Seal 7—Danger of Exclusion From God's Rest In Revelation 8:1, the seventh **seal** is opened and there is silence. As in Genesis 2 where God rested on the seventh day after having finished his work of creating the world in six days, so he rests on the seventh **seal** after having finished his work of warning the world of death and judgment during the six **seals**. The promise of entering God's rest is discussed in Hebrews 3:7-4:11 as a warning against unbelief. Similarly, this **seal** warns the readers that they must do everything in their power to be robed in white in the sixth **seal** and thereby to enter God's rest.

Revelation 8:2-11:19
The Seven Trumpets of Judgment
The Death and Resurrection of the Church

Where one section ends with the victory of the Lord and the church over Satan and the Fall, the next tells the same story from a different point of view. In this section, **seven angels** with **seven trumpets** of destruction represent God's overcoming, but from a different perspective. The **seven trumpets** describe God's judgments on a fallen world. Some of the judgments are familiar in that they parallel plagues described in Exodus. It is clear that these **trumpets** are sounded for judgment from the **extreme language** that appears in Revelation 8:5. An angel with a golden censer offers both incense and the prayers of the saints before the **throne** (from Revelation 4:2.) He then fills the censer with fire and hurls it to earth, resulting in thunder, lightning, and an earthquake. The shaking of the earth is common in Old Testament **extreme language** (see Isaiah 2:17,19, 13:13, 24:18, Joel 2:10, 3:16.) God coming with thunder and lightning in judgment is also a common Old Testament theme (Isaiah 29:6, Jer. 25:30, Joel 2:11, 3:16, Hos. 6:5, Zech. 9:14.) Some of the contexts where the Lord comes with thunder and lightning contain more typical **extreme language** (darkened sun, moon, and stars falling from heaven.)

There are two groupings of **trumpets**. The first four are reflective of how the Fall has damaged creation and how fallen humanity's mismanagement of creation after the Fall has contributed to that damage. Whereas man was to care for creation, fallen man injures creation and himself. The second grouping, called three woes, reflects how the Fall has impacted and will continue to impact humanity. It concludes with God's restoration of the earth through the return of Christ. When Christ returns and the world is judged, part of that judgment is God's destruction of "those who destroy the earth" (Rev. 11:18.) The **seven trumpets** tell the story of fallen man's destruction of a fallen world.

First Trumpet—The Deterioration of Horticulture One-third of all plants are destroyed as is all of the green grass. The use of hail in the imagery is reminiscent of Exodus 9:13 where God destroyed the crops of the Egyptians through a plague of hail. This text should not be taken chronologically or literally. In Revelation 9:4 the locusts are told not to harm the grass of the earth that was all burned up in Revelation 8:7.

Second Trumpet—The Deterioration of the Seas

The image of the huge mountain that destroys the seas is drawn from Jeremiah 51:25 where God calls **Babylon** a destroying mountain that destroys the whole earth. At the end of the verse God promises to make the destroying mountain a burned out mountain. The image of **Babylon**, the destroying mountain that is destroyed, is used in Revelation to portray the destruction of the seas that occurs because of humanity's falleness.

When the burning mountain of the second **trumpet** is thrown into the seas, one-third of the seas are turned to blood. The damaging of the seas is similar to the turning of the waters in Egypt to blood in Exodus 7:14. The Fall's impact and man's mismanagement of the oceans will result in the death of one-third of the sea creatures and the destruction of one-third of the ships.

The sea creatures die because fallen man harvests them for food and other uses (whereas prior to the fall man ate the fruit of trees and did not use living things as expendable commodities.) They also die through the polluting of the oceans. The ships are destroyed through severe, destructive storms, and through naval wars, both of which occur because of the Fall.

Third Trumpet—The Deterioration of Fresh Water

A third of the fresh water is made unusable and people die because of it. The water is bitter not because it tastes bad, rather it is either poisoned or so salty as to be undrinkable. Bitter water was used for judgment in several places in the Old Testament.

In Numbers 5:11-31, if a man suspected his wife of unfaithfulness, she was required to drink "bitter water" made from holy water and dust from the tabernacle floor. If she was guilty, she would swell up and suffer pain. If she was innocent, she would suffer no ill effects.

Bitter water was also mentioned in connection with judgment in Jeremiah 9:15 and 23:15, where God stated that he would make his unfaithful people, and the lying prophets eat bitter food and drink poisoned water.

The **star** which is an **angel** (**stars** represent **angels** in Revelation) called **Wormwood** is unknown elsewhere in Scripture. He shares his name with a bitter and mildly poisonous plant. There are several varieties of wormwood in Palestine, none of which is deadly when mixed with water. The **angel Wormwood** symbolizes the poisoning of fresh water through various pollutants as part of the Fall's impact and man's mismanagement of God's creation.

Fourth Trumpet—Deterioration of the Air The darkening of one-third of the sun, moon, and stars is similar to the plague of darkness imposed on Egypt in Exodus 10:21.

There are a number of ways that the lights of heaven are blocked due to the Fall. Genesis 2:4-10 describes the Garden of Eden as being watered by streams and mist. Destructive storms, which are so common in a fallen world, did not exist prior to the Fall. These massive storms can block the lights in the heavens for days at a time. An additional way that those lights are diminished is through air pollution and exterior lights at night in modern society. These products of fallen man reduce the light of the sun, and moon, and hide many of the stars. David points out that the heavens declare the glory of God and the skies proclaim the work of his hands (Psalm 19:1.) It is not surprising that fallen humanity's actions would supplement the impact of the Fall, diminishing creation's expression of the glory of God. While it might seem extreme to suggest that exterior lighting is a sign of man's falleness, it is nonetheless true that many street lights and lights outside homes are kept lit at night primarily to deter crime. These lights make it difficult to see most stars in the vicinity of any major city.

There is a break after the fourth **trumpet** for the pronouncement of three woes on the inhabitants of the earth. This draws attention to the change from judgments impacting the earth to judgments pronounced against humanity.

Fifth Trumpet—The First Woe, Man's Mismanagement of His Own Needs and Desires A **star** falls from the sky to the earth. **Stars** in Revelation represent **angels**, and this **angel** is given the **key** to the Abyss. Jesus holds the **keys** of death and Hades (Rev. 1:18) and he is the **angel** who has the **key** to the Abyss in Revelation 20:1-3.

Jesus alone could seize Satan and bind him in Revelation 20. In Jude 9, the Archangel Michael could not do anything but say "the Lord rebuke you" to Satan. If Michael was forced to rely on the Lord to deal with

Satan, it is clear that only Jesus would be able to handle Satan in the way depicted in Revelation 20.

If Jesus has the **key** to the Abyss in Revelation 20, it is reasonable to expect that he was given the **key** in Revelation 9. It is difficult to propose that the **star** in Revelation 9 is a wicked character because there is a beast that resides in the Abyss (Rev. 11:7) whose release is under God's control. A wicked character would be likely to release the beast, not the locusts who harm those not having the seal of God on their foreheads (Rev. 9:4.) The **star** must represent Jesus who came to earth from heaven. Jesus opens the Abyss to release locusts who have as king over them the angel of the Abyss (i.e., Satan.) This demonstrates Jesus' control of all things, even forces opposed to him. When the Abyss opens, the smoke from it darkens the sun and sky. The smoke of the Abyss, by darkening the sky, represents the dark and foreboding doom of those not marked with the **seal** of God. On earth, those opposed to God do not see the flame of the lake of fire. But they live without hope and without God in the world. Their experience is as though they smell and taste the pit where Satan is imprisoned.

The locusts parallel one of the plagues in Exodus; however, they are not literally locusts because they harm people rather than crops. They do not harm believers but only those lacking the **seal** of God on their foreheads. While some have proposed that these locusts are Germanic tribes who attacked and sacked Rome, the limitations imposed on these locusts and their origin does not support this view. The Germanic tribes were no more Satanic than the Romans they attacked and they did not exclude Christians from their plunderings. The agony of the non-believers is like a scorpion sting and it lasts only five months. This five months is a short period in comparison with **forty-two months** that appears elsewhere in Revelation. Since the **forty-two months** represent the duration of the time of the Gentiles, the five months probably represents the length of a human life. This would suggest that the stinging lasts throughout the life of non-believers. The locusts do not kill, but those who are stung wish they could die.

To interpret this the reader must determine what pain, not experienced by believers in this fallen world, is experienced by those who do not believe and is of sufficient seriousness that they would want to die. It appears that the pain inflicted by the locusts represents the unrelieved impact of the Fall with its alienation from God and all its attendant hopelessness, sin, guilt, conflict, and isolation. Believers experience the beginning of the reversal of the Fall. They are no longer alienated from God. They are being changed by the Spirit, and their guilt has been taken away. Conflict and isolation are replaced with fellowship in the body of believers, the family of God. They have hope in the midst of their struggles.

The attributes of the locusts represent the unsatisfied desires of fallen humanity which remains in opposition to God. They wear something like **crowns** of **gold**, representing the desire to rule creation as Adam did. They are like **crowns**, but are not **crowns**. Man substitutes personal power, and egotism for the God given authority that he had before the Fall. The faces of the locusts resemble human faces but are not human faces. Their faces represent the diminishment of the image of God in man. Humanity has become imperfect physically, mentally, emotionally, and spiritually through the Fall. The teeth of the locusts are like lions' teeth, representing the danger and conflict of fallen humanity. Their desires cause them to attack one another, not only physically but also through manipulation and intimidation. James 4:1-6 warns that fights and quarrels come from desires that battle within those who think they can exist in friendship with the world. Believers are to submit, humble themselves, and draw near to God. The locusts have breastplates of iron representing fallen man's hardness of heart.

Sixth Trumpet—The Second Woe, Man's Mismanagement of Relationships with Others This woe sounds the death of a third of mankind by three plagues of fire, smoke, and sulphur. This death of so many is from God (it is at his command and those killed are killed by his angels.) Such a disaster could lead people to repentance just as the threat of a similar disaster caused widespread repentance in Ninevah in the time of Jonah. However, those who are left, who have witnessed the death of so many, do not repent (Rev. 9:20,21.) By not repenting, the survivors ensure that they will face further judgment.

Some contend that the two hundred million mounted troops suggest an attack launched from China and the horses suggest mechanized weapons. The death of a third of mankind would, according to this proposal, also suggest the use of nuclear weapons. But it should be noted that a third of mankind is killed by the plagues that come from the horses. For this to be fulfilled, the Chinese army and their weapons would have to be directly responsible for the death of a third of humanity, without considering any losses suffered by the Chinese. This scenario makes the Chinese army a tool in the hands of the four angels who have been kept ready. The text observes that those not killed by the plagues did not repent. This suggests that repentance is a natural response to the carnage described in this vision. It is difficult to see how a savage attack by a Chinese army would motivate those lacking in faith to repent.

It is more appropriate to see this as symbolism. Fire and sulfur were rained down on Sodom when God judged that city. In Ezekiel 38:22, God asserts that he will execute judgment on Gog with plague, bloodshed, and burning sulfur. Burning sulfur is reserved for the wicked who are cursed by God (Genesis 19:24, Deut. 29:23, Job 18:15, Psalm 11:6, Isaiah 34:9, and Luke 17:29.)

The text is not predicting a single battle that kills one-third of humanity. Rather, this image represents wars that have existed throughout history. War is the supreme mismanagement of interpersonal relationships and the mistreatment of others is a major impact of the Fall of man.

These **angels** of death are released to kill. They kill a third of mankind through armies of mounted troops. This suggests that the horrors of war are designed to call humanity to repentance (see Revelation 9:20f.) The death of a third of mankind to these plagues is spread over centuries. This text emphasizes that God's judgment, even when imposed through something as terrible as war, does not stir the wicked to repentance.

In Revelation 10, there appears an **angel** whose **face is like the sun**. This **angel** is Jesus (see Rev. 1:16) and he is holding a **scroll**. He states that in the days when the seventh **angel** is about to sound his **trumpet**, the **mystery of God** will be accomplished (Rev. 10:7.) Since the seventh **trumpet** is the final judgment of God, the **mystery of God** will be accomplished right before the end of human history. Throughout Scripture there is a common meaning for the term "**the mystery of God**," which is that Gentiles are to be included with Israel in God's redemption of his fallen world (see article on **Mystery of God** in Section 3.) This inclusion of the Gentiles in God's plan is briefly mentioned in Revelation 11:1-13. The falleness portrayed by the first six trumpets is experienced throughout the whole of human history. The "**mystery of God**" is a part of God's plan that he has already revealed.

Jesus gives John the **scroll** to eat and it tastes sweet but makes him sick. This is similar to Ezekiel 3:3 where Ezekiel ate a **scroll** on which were written words of lament, warning, and woe on both sides. When Ezekiel ate the **scroll**, it was as sweet as honey. By its close similarity with the Ezekiel passage it is clear that this **scroll** that John eats bears words of lament, and woe though the text does not mention it. Ezekiel tasted the sweetness without any sickness because the end of the judgment of God was going to be Israel's restoration. However, John's **scroll** makes him sick: while the people of God will be redeemed (which is the sweetness of the scroll), it also prophecies the death of the church through satanic attack which John describes in the passage that follows. John is not the only one made sick by this message. Daniel's face turned pale at the vision he saw in Daniel 7 and he lay ill for several days as a result of the vision he recorded in Daniel 8 (Daniel 7:28, 8:27.) The vision Daniel records in Daniel 10-12 is so distressing that he mourns and fasts for three weeks (Daniel 10:2f.) The visions Daniel saw record the same destruction of the church that John describes in Revelation 11.

Revelation 11:1-14 describes history from John's time until the end. The passage describes a time of the Gentiles followed by the death and resurrection of the church. The trampling of the holy city by the Gentiles for **forty-two months** was previously prophesied in Luke 21:24 which says that the Gentiles will trample Jerusalem until the times of the Gentiles are fulfilled. This time of the Gentiles is described in Romans 11:25-27 and is the time during which Israel is hardened in part. This time of hardening will not end until "the full number of the Gentiles has come in." This **forty-two month** period lasts from the death of Christ until the church finishes her testimony (see **forty-two months** in Section Three.) What happens at the end of the **forty-two month** 'time of the Gentiles' is described in Revelation 11:7ff.

There are **two witnesses** which are also called two **olive trees** and two **lampstands**. They have great power similar to that demonstrated by Moses in the plagues on Egypt (they can turn water into blood and strike the earth with plagues.) Their ability to perform these wonders suggests that they have divine approval and authority. Based on the definitions of terms in Revelation 1, the witnesses must be churches because **lampstands** represent churches (Rev. 1:20.) Additionally, the two **olive trees** represent the Jewish and Gentile branches of the church.

The image of the **olive trees** first appears in Zechariah 4. Zechariah sees a golden **lampstand** with seven lights on it and two **olive trees** on the right and left of the **lampstand**. The seven lights represent the Holy Spirit. Zechariah 4:6 explains the image by promising to Zerubbabel, "Not by might nor by power, but by my Spirit, says the Lord Almighty." He then identifies the seven lights (Zech. 4:10) as the seven eyes of the Lord that range throughout the world. The seven eyes of the Lord have been previously defined in Revelation 5:6 as the **seven spirits** or seven-fold Spirit (the Holy Spirit) of God sent out into all the earth. Zechariah also asks for an explanation of the **olive trees** on either side of the **lampstand** (Zech. 4:11f.) He is told (Zech. 4:14) that they are the two who are anointed to serve the Lord of all the earth. It would be difficult to define the two anointed from Zechariah if there were no other passages that used the image. However, the two **olive trees** are defined elsewhere in Scripture. The image of the two **olive trees** appears in Romans 11 where the Gentile church is a wild olive tree and the Jewish church is a natural olive tree. Paul's use of the two **olive trees** to represent the two branches of the church, particularly in a section where he discusses the ultimate restoration of Israel, provides a clear precedent for John's use of the same imagery.

While John could easily have been aware of Paul's letter to the Romans written only ten years earlier, his knowledge of Romans is only relevant if John was writing this letter out of his own knowledge and experience. Did John write down exactly what he saw in his vision, or did he take the information in the vision and, at certain points in the text, provide the reader with clues to the meaning using other biblical images? No matter how this is answered, the purpose in referring to the witnesses as **lampstands** and **olive trees** is to define the **two witnesses** for the reader. God may have directly identified the witnesses as the Jewish and Gentile churches in the vision through the images he inspired in Zechariah and Romans. Or John may have taken what he understood from the vision and added references to images from other biblical texts to clarify potentially obscure characters for the reader. The purpose of these images is to provide helpful clues to the believer who should recognize that similar images have been defined elsewhere in Revelation or in other portions of Scripture.

The two branches of the church prophecy for **1,260 days** (which is the same as **forty-two months**) and is the period that the **woman clothed**

with the sun (Rev. 12:1ff) is kept safe. They cannot be harmed by their enemies and anyone who wants to harm them is destroyed by fire from their mouths. This text does not suggest that all of the opponents of the church are burned up. It affirms God's protection of both branches of his church and their ability to continue their ministries after their opponents are dead and gone. This image may also reflect the final destiny of opponents to the church in the lake of fire where they are burned up forever. The church continues to conquer and overcome until it completes its testimony.

When the **two witnesses** finish their testimony, the **beast from the Abyss** will attack and kill them and leave them exposed for all to see in the **great city** (i,e,. Jerusalem.) Matthew 24:14 mentions the finishing of the testimony of the church. The gospel will be preached in the whole world and then the end will come. The **beast from the Abyss** is Satan. He appears again in Revelation 17 as a scarlet beast on which the great **prostitute** sits (Rev 17:8.) The **beast from the Abyss** (Satan) kills the church (see article on **Beast from the Abyss** in Section Three.)

If the reader agrees that the **beast from the Abyss** is Satan and that the **two lampstands/olive trees** are the Jewish and Gentile churches, the conclusion is inevitable that Satan will come up from the Abyss when he is released (Rev. 20:7) to attack and kill the church. Revelation 11 provides additional details regarding the actions of the beast from the Abyss, who will be released in Revelation 20. In Revelation 20 the text is concerned exclusively with Satan's release and the gathering of the nations. If both texts describe the same event from different perspectives, the **1000 years** that the people of God will reign with Christ in Revelation 20 must occur prior to the death of the church during the time of the Gentiles, also called **forty-two months** or **1,260 days**. It will be demonstrated later that the millennium is the period from the resurrection of Christ until the death of the church.

While the text attributes the death of the church to Satan, it is clear from Daniel and elsewhere in Scripture that he accomplishes his purpose through the **Man of Lawlessness** who is revealed when Satan is released from the Abyss. Satan works through a representative to whom he gives his power so that his purpose can be achieved. This death of the churches is not the death of all individual Christians within the church but is the death of the visible church. Its death occurs in the denial, by the most visible portions of the Christian church, of some element or elements necessary for them to be Christian as opposed to merely religious. This could involve the denial of the deity of Christ, the denial of the Trinity, or the denial of the necessity of Christ's sacrifice for all who are to be saved.

This death of the church is found elsewhere in Scripture. There is a small **horn** in Daniel 7 that represents the **Man of Lawlessness**. This small **horn** wages war against the saints and is defeating them until the Ancient of Days takes his power away and destroys him forever (Daniel 7:21f, 26.) This defeating of the saints is what is called the death of the **two witnesses** in Revelation and the destroying of the holy people in Daniel 8.

In Daniel 8:24, the **Man of Lawlessness** *destroys* the mighty men and *the holy people.* This section is interpreting Daniel 8:12 which reports that the host of the saints were handed over to him. The text is not referring to isolated persecution or the killing of individual Christians. Rather, the host of the saints, the visible church, is what is being destroyed. After he destroys the holy people, the **Man of Lawlessness** is himself destroyed by the coming of Christ (Daniel 8:25.)

In Daniel 12:1-7, the end of the world is described. Verses one through three describe a time of distress and the final judgment. Then in verse six, Daniel asks how long it will be before these things are fulfilled. He receives the answer that it will be for a time, times, and half a time, when the *power of the holy people has been finally broken* all these things will be completed. The two churches (the holy people of God) have been given power from God (Rev. 11:3), and it is represented by the images of fire coming from their mouths, the sky shut up so that it will not rain, and the earth being struck with plagues. The breaking of that power, in the death of the church, results finally in the return of Christ. Believers who are still alive are gathered by the angels and the final judgment occurs (Rev. 11:12,18.)

Daniel chapters 7, 8, and 12 provide Old Testament support for interpreting the images in Revelation 11 as teaching the death of the visible church. After the churches' death, Christ returns and judges the world.

When the churches die, there will be celebration and gift giving for a time called **three and a half days** by those who oppose the church. This **three and a half day** period is not literal but is indicative that this time of celebration will be short. Daniel 9:27 mentions this **three and a half day** period where the **Man of Lawlessness** puts an end to sacrifice and offering and sets up the **abomination that causes desolation** in the middle of one 'seven' (in the middle of the week or for **three and a half days**.) The setting up of the abomination that causes desolation is related to the death of the church. The abomination is set up in the middle of the week (or at the beginning of the second three and a half days of the week.) The abomination is set up in Jerusalem on a wing of the temple and it symbolizes the non-sectarian world religion that replaces the visible church.

There are two elements in Daniel's prophesy that provide helpful insights to the actions of the **Man of Lawlessness**. The first element is that he puts an end to sacrifice and offering (or the daily sacrifice - Daniel 8:11-13.) At the time Daniel was writing, true and faithful worship involved the daily sacrifice and offerings. The fulfillment of this passage does not require that worship in the temple be re-instituted. Such a practice would be a repudiation of the once and for all time sacrifice of Jesus Christ. Rather, Daniel refers to the true worship of God. In its current form, true worship involves the preaching of the word of God and the proper use of the sacraments. In some way, the **Man of Lawlessness** will put forward a distortion to true worship which will be widely accepted. This idea is supported by Daniel 8:12 which describes the activities of the Man of Lawlessness by saying,

> "Because of rebellion, the host of saints and the daily sacrifice were given over to it. It prospered in everything it did, and truth was thrown to the ground."

The host of saints and daily sacrifice being given over to it suggests his control of the church and its worship. The statement that truth is thrown to the ground suggests the replacement of truth (and true worship) with a lie. The ability of the **Man of Lawlessness** to do this comes out of his position as a Christian authority figure. I John 2:18f describes the pattern for antichrists. They go out from the church, but they do not really belong to the church. The **beast out of earth** is represented as exercising Christian authority by the symbols used of him. He has two **horns** like a **lamb** but a voice like a **dragon**. **Horns** represent authority or power and the **lamb** is the symbol for Jesus. While he is a Christian authority figure his voice is that of a **dragon** (Satan). In the interpretation of Daniel's vision, the **Man of Lawlessness** will destroy the holy people and cause deceit to prosper. This supports the proposal that the church dies under his control.

The second element is the setting up of the **abomination that causes desolation**. The Scriptures do not define what the **abomination that causes desolation** is. Matthew and Mark record Jesus' warning to escape from Jerusalem and flee to the mountains when they see the abomination that causes desolation standing in the holy place. While some have thought that this was fulfilled when Jerusalem was destroyed in 70 AD, the prophesy in Daniel 9 describes the 70 AD destruction of Jerusalem and the temple as taking place after the death of the Anointed One (Daniel 9:26.) Later, in Daniel 9:27, the setting up of the **abomination that causes desolation** is depicted as a different event, toward the end of human history. Jerusalem is attacked and destroyed, but after its destruction the Lord returns to destroy the **Man of Lawlessness** and his armies.

The literal length of the **three and a half days** may be provided in Daniel 12:11f since the lengths of time in this passage do not match any symbolic reference to time elsewhere in Scripture. If the time is to be taken literally, the church will be dead for 1,290 days or slightly over three and a half years (three years plus 195 days.) Under this theory, the 1,335 days of Daniel 12:12 represent the 1,290 days that the church is dead plus the revival of the church which lasts forty-five days.

The **witnesses** (churches) rise from the dead in Revelation 11:11 through a breath of life from God. This breath from God is a spiritual awakening under the direction of the Holy Spirit that reestablishes the visible church. The revival of the **two witnesses** occurs after the time of hardening of Israel has ended. The time of the Gentiles ends at the conclusion of the **forty-two months** when the **witnesses** die. Since Romans 11 says that the hardening will last until the full number of the Gentiles has come in, it is unlikely that the Gentile portion of the church will see as much revival as the Jewish church. The resurrection of the Jewish church will involve the restoration of a majority of all Jews. Paul states, in Romans 11:26, "and so all Israel will be saved" suggesting a large scale revival of the Jewish church. This restoration of the Jewish church at the end of history is prophesied in Hosea 3 as being similar to the restoration of Hosea's relationship with his wife.

Hosea 3:4f For the Israelites will live many days without king or prince, without sacrifice or sacred stones, without ephod or idol.

> Afterward the Israelites will return and seek the Lord their God and David their king. They will come trembling to the Lord and to his blessings in the last days.

Hosea's prophesy must refer to the end of history because of the reference to being without king and sacrifice for many days. While Assyria conquered Israel as Hosea prophesied, the temple was not destroyed and they continued to have a king. Nebuchadnezzar destroyed the temple, but it was rebuilt about seventy years later. Since Hosea's prophecy, the only extended period when Israel has been without king or prince, without sacrifice and ephod has been since the destruction of Jerusalem by the Romans in 70 AD. Israel has not yet come trembling to the Lord and his blessings, but she will in the last days.

The resurrection of the church causes terror for those who sent gifts to celebrate the church's death. This terror is well founded, because after the resurrection of the churches, Christ will return and believers will be gathered to heaven in a cloud. God calls for the churches to be with him with a loud voice and the churches ascend as their enemies look on. This is clearly the loud and visible return of Christ seen in Matthew and I Thessalonians.

The Seventh Trumpet—The Third Woe, Man's Mismanagement of the Relationship with God The sounding of the seventh **trumpet** gives the natural conclusion to that which has gone before. It is a woe for those who are out of relationship with God. Whether they are living or already have died, they must face the judgment of the God whom they have spurned. Christ has returned and taken the church to be with him, so all that remains is for the Lord to reign and the final judgment (Rev. 11:18.) This judgment results in the rewarding of the saints and the destruction of those who destroyed the earth in their falleness. This section (Rev. 11:19) ends with **extreme language** representing God's judgment of the wicked.

Revelation 12:1-14:20
The Dragon, The Woman, Beasts and The Lamb

A new vision begins in Revelation 12 with a sign in heaven, a **woman clothed with the sun**. This woman has a **crown** of twelve stars and gives birth to a son (Jesus) who will rule the nations with an **iron scepter**. The woman must be the church, through both Old Testament and New Testament periods. She precedes the birth of Christ since she is pregnant and gives birth to Jesus. In the Old Testament she has the twelve tribes (symbolized by her twelve stars.) In the New Testament she is taken care of after the son is snatched up by God to his throne, for a **time, times, and half a time** or **1,260 days** (compare Rev. 12:6,14.)

The woman goes to a place in the desert prepared for her by God. The image of the desert is designed to communicate the nature of the church's ministry which is of humble dependence under the guiding hand of the heavenly father.

> *Deuteronomy 8:2-5* Remember how the Lord your God led you all the way in the desert these forty years, to humble you and to test you in order to know what was in your heart, whether or not you would keep his commands. He humbled you, causing you to hunger and then feeding you with manna, which neither you nor your fathers had known, to teach you that man does not live on bread alone but on every word that comes from the mouth of the Lord. Your clothes did not wear out and your feet did not swell during these forty years. Know then in your heart that as a man disciplines his son, so the Lord your God disciplines you.

The time in the desert is a time of testing, teaching, and nurturing for the church.

The woman (the church) is protected for a finite period, only **1,260 days**. At that time she either no longer needs protection or she is simply no longer protected. The period that she is protected is identical with the **1,260 days** that the **two witnesses** prophecy in Revelation 11. The **1,260 days** begin when the Son is snatched up to God's throne. While there is no mention of what happens to her at the end of the **1,260 days**, it does appear that her fate must be identical with that of the **two witnesses** because both she and the witnesses represent the church.

The child is born and snatched up to God and his throne. It would not normally be expected that Jesus' birth, life, death, and ascension would be handled in such a compressed fashion. The reason for this is that the focus of this vision is on the woman and her offspring in conflict with Satan. The life and death of the **lamb** are dealt with in other biblical texts. The purpose of this text is to encourage the church, which will be facing persecution, to remain faithful. Support for this is found in Revelation 12:11 that commends those who overcame Satan by not shrinking from death.

The **dragon** is identified as Satan (Rev. 12:9) and he wants to kill the child of the **woman clothed with the sun**. He is **red** because that is the color of evil in Revelation. He is pictured as having lost a war in heaven and having been cast down with his angels to earth. Having failed to kill the child, the **dragon** attempts to kill the woman (the church), but she is taken care of in the desert, out of the dragon's reach, for **1,260 days**. As was seen in Revelation 11, at the end of that time her protection ends and the church dies. When the **dragon** sees that he cannot harm the woman, he goes off to war against her offspring, those who obey God's commandments.

Revelation 13 introduces a **beast who comes out of the sea**. This beast comes out of the sea just as the four beasts in Daniel 7 came up out of the sea (Daniel 7:3.) This is not the only similarity. The beast in Revelation has qualities of a leopard, bear, and lion, which are the first three beasts described in Daniel 7. These similarities suggest that the symbols in both texts have the same or a similar meaning. The leopard, bear, and lion in Daniel represent world empires and the meaning of these images in Revelation must be the same.

This beast has **ten horns**, **seven heads**, and ten **crowns**. The **ten horns** represent ten kings who have not yet received a kingdom (Rev. 17:12) but who will receive authority as kings along with the beast. The kings are ten evil rulers of world empires whose reigns stand in opposition to God and the church. They use their authority to persecute the church after the demise of the Roman Empire. The **seven heads** are **seven** hills and **seven** kings (Rev. 17:9,10.) The image of the seven hills is a clear reference to the city of Rome.

Of the **seven** kings, five have died, one is currently ruling and the other has not yet come. These **seven** kings are Roman Emperors who persecute the church. The five who have died are all of the emperors since Jerusalem was captured (Julius Caesar, Augustus, Tiberius, Caligula and Claudius.) The one who now is ruling is Nero. The one who is yet to come is Vespasian, who was ruling when the temple in Jerusalem was destroyed. There are several emperors who reigned for short periods (less than a year) between Nero and Vespasian. The year 69 AD is called the year of the four emperors because Nero died in 68 AD and there were three emperors who reigned before Vespasian took power in December of 69 AD. Vespasian must be the emperor referred to in Revelation because the text says when the seventh king comes he must remain a little while. The three emperors that preceded him never consolidated their power so that they could be said truly to rule.

The beast is not the **dragon** (Satan) but he derives his power from the **dragon** (Rev. 13:2) and men worship the beast and the **dragon**. The beast wars against the saints and overcomes them. This is different from the killing of the witnesses by the beast from the Abyss in Revelation 11. While Satan will be released and kill the institutional church, this beast persecutes individuals within the church and kills them. He is Satan's agent during the **forty-two months (1000 years)** that Satan is bound in the Abyss. He has authority over all nations and everyone who does not belong to the **lamb** will worship this beast.

From the imagery surrounding the beast, and the similarity of his form to the great beasts who came out of the sea in Daniel 7, it is clear that the **beast out of the sea** is the authority of persecuting world powers. He accomplishes his imposition of persecution and idolatry through political power. In Daniel, a lion, a bear, and a leopard represent world empires in Babylon, Media/Persia, and Greece. There is a fourth beast with ten horns, and one of the horns speaks boastfully. This horn wages war against the saints and defeats them until God pronounces judgment in favor of the saints, and the time comes when they possess the kingdom. This fourth beast is interpreted to Daniel as a fourth kingdom that will appear on earth. History shows that this fourth kingdom is Rome and the civilization that continued after Rome. The beast's ten horns are ten kings who will come from this kingdom. When this image is compared with Revelation 17, the ten kings must be persecuting leaders of world powers, arising out of the Roman empire, who act both to persecute the church and to attack Israel. Another king will arise (the **Man of Lawlessness**) who will speak against the Most High and the saints will be handed over to him for a **time, times, and half a time**.

After the **time, times, and half a time** he will be destroyed forever.

The **beast out of the sea** is the power that is called the secret power of lawlessness in II Thessalonians 2:7. This power of lawlessness is at work at the time Paul is writing II Thessalonians. The beast is national political power of nations and empires that act in hostility toward the gospel. At times there are great leaders who act in greater hostility toward the church and Israel for a short time. These ten kings are satanically inspired to war against the church and to attack Israel, but they are overcome by the lamb (Rev. 17:12ff.)

The power of lawlessness will ultimately culminate in the person of one called the **Man of Lawlessness** when "the rebellion" occurs (II Thes. 2:3, Daniel 8:12f.) The **Man of Lawlessness** will not appear until the end of time because he is destroyed by the splendor of the coming of Jesus Christ (II Thes. 2:8.) At the time John is writing, this power of lawlessness has authority in Rome and will have authority in the civilization that continues after Rome has gone. The worship of the **dragon** and the beast represents idolatry in all its forms. One major source of idolatry, which provides a strong temptation to Christians at the time John is writing, is emperor worship. Persecution can be avoided by a simple action (worshipping the emperor) that does not require any commitment. That is why John warns Christians that those who worship the beast (and specifically those who are tempted to participate in emperor worship) do not have their names in the **book of life**. As a result, he calls on believers to be faithful and to patiently endure. In verses 9f, John reminds his readers that there is no escaping what God has in store for them. The structure is similar to passages in Jeremiah where God warns that he is about to judge Judah and Egypt.

> *Jeremiah 15:1f* Then the Lord said to me: "Even if Moses and Samuel were to stand before me, my heart would not go out to this people. Send them away from my presence! Let them go! And if they ask you, 'Where shall we go?' tell them, 'This is what the Lord says: " 'Those destined for death, to death; those for the sword, to the sword; those for starvation, to starvation; those for captivity, to captivity.'

> *Jeremiah 43:10f* Then say to them, 'This is what the Lord Almighty, the God of Israel, says: I will send for my servant Nebuchadnezzar

king of Babylon, and I will set his throne over these stones I have buried here; he will spread his royal canopy above them. He will come and attack Egypt, bringing death to those destined for death, captivity to those destined for captivity, and the sword to those destined for the sword.

The warning followed by the call for patient endurance cautions believers against accommodation with the beast out of the sea because they cannot avoid their fate.

The **beast out of the earth** is another beast who has two **horns** like a **lamb** but speaks like a **dragon**. The **horns** like a **lamb** suggest that he has some sort of Christian authority. **Horns** are used throughout Scripture to represent power and authority (Jeremiah 42:17, Lamentations 2:17.) The comparison with a **lamb** is a comparison with Jesus who is represented as a **lamb** throughout Revelation. The beast speaks like a **dragon** indicating that while in externals he may exert Christian authority, his character is like the **dragon**, Satan. He proves the text that says, out of the fullness of the heart, the mouth speaks (Matthew 12:34.)

The **beast out of the earth** requires people to worship the first beast and kills those who do not. This beast is from the earth and is the final man in the line of those who will act lawlessly. He is the **Man of Lawlessness**, the ultimate embodiment of the spirit of lawlessness. He forces everyone to receive a mark. This mark is not physical, any more than the mark of God on believers' foreheads (Rev. 14:1, 22:4) is physical. The mark represents idolatry, the worship of something or someone other than God, which may take a form similar to the emperor worship existing during John's time. Since he is destroyed by the coming of the Lord (II Thes 2:8), he did not live during John's time. Therefore, his identity and the form of idolatry he will attempt to propagate is yet to be revealed.

He has a man's number, indicating that he is a man; and he has the power to force people to worship the first beast. The text says **666** is man's number or a man's number. Either can be the correct translation. It is difficult to see the significance if **666** is man's number. Is the vision informing the reader that the beast is human? How does "man's number" make that any more clear? Since the significance of the number **666** is understandable, but calls for wisdom and can be calculated by someone with insight, it must be a particular man's number. The **Man of**

Lawlessness' identity can be verified by using numerology to see if a particular candidate's name adds up to **666**. John provided no more information and the identity of the man was unknown during the time of the early church fathers. Irenaeus comments,

> "We will not, however, incur the risk of pronouncing positively as to the name of Antichrist; for if it were necessary that his name should be distinctly revealed in this present time, it would have been announced by him who beheld the apocalyptic vision." [5]

The **Man of Lawlessness** has not yet been revealed and so it is not surprising that his identity has not been made known. At the time he is revealed, those with wisdom and insight will be able to confirm his identity by calculating his number. Numerology should not be used for speculation. The purpose of **666** is to provide final confirmation when someone fulfills those things prophesied regarding the **Man of Lawlessness** (putting an end to sacrifice and worship, performing signs and wonders, and setting up the **abomination that causes desolation**.)

Revelation 14 begins with the singing of a new song of praise to the **lamb** from a group who are called firstfruits to God and the **lamb**. This group is described as **144,000** who had been redeemed from the earth. It appears that this is a different group than the **144,000** who came from the twelve tribes of Israel (Rev. 6:4-8.) They are distinct in that they did not defile themselves with women. There is no indication that this was true of the group in Revelation 6. The members of the group in Revelation 14 are not identified as Israelites. The characteristic that sets this group apart is that they are male virgins.

The number **144,000** is clearly symbolic. It consists of twelve groups of 12,000 in Revelation 7, but is not broken into smaller groups in Revelation 14. The symbolic nature of this number is suggested by its connection with the numbers twelve and **1000**. The number **144,000** consists of twelve squared times **1000**. Twelve is an important symbolic number in Scripture (12 tribes, 12 apostles.) The number 1000 (**1000 years**) is used symbolically in Revelation 20 to represent an indefinite but complete period. The combination of twelves and **1000** appears to represent the entirety of a group of indefinite number.

After this, three **angels** appear who proclaim three messages from God. The first **angel** announces that everyone is to fear God, give him glory, and worship him because he is about to judge. The second angel announces the fall of **Babylon** (Jerusalem.) The third **angel** warns against idolatry (particularly emperor worship at the time John is writing.) Anyone who worships the beast and his image will drink God's wrath and be tormented forever. This last warning is followed by the repeated statement "this calls for patient endurance on the part of the saints." Those who die in the Lord (having endured and overcome) will rest from their labor for their deeds will follow them.

The end of the chapter describes the harvesting of the earth. This is another image of the final judgment. This harvest describes, in graphic and symbolic terms, the judgment of those who are the enemies of God. They are thrown into the winepress of God's wrath and they are crushed. This image comes from Joel 3:12f where it is also used to depict the final judgment.

Revelation 15:1-16:21
The Seven Bowls of God's Wrath

In Revelation 15, a new sequence in the vision begins. This is the final sign, the seven last plagues, which are being prepared. These are the last plagues because "with them God's wrath is completed." If they are the last plagues that complete God's wrath, the plagues must be poured out toward the end of human history. It is clear that at least the last two plagues describe events occurring at the end of human history. The sixth plague is the gathering of the nations for battle on the great day of God Almighty. The seventh plague uses **extreme language** to represent the final judgment. Plagues one through five reflect the intensification of the judgments pronounced in **trumpets** one through five from Revelation 8-11. These seven plagues are judgments by God, poured out on the earth, from the time that the **Man of Lawlessness** is revealed until his destruction.

Revelation 15:2, describes the **beast out of the earth** and the image to whom he gave life as having already lost. The beast that appears must be the **beast out of the earth** because the ones standing beside the sea were victorious over the beast and his image (which might lead one to think it is the **beast out of the sea**) and the number of his name. Only the **beast out of the earth** has a number associated with his name. So the beast in Revelation 15:2 who also appears in Revelation 16:2,10 is the **beast out of**

the earth. The plagues are poured out on the beast out of the earth (Rev. 16:10), the **Man of Lawlessness**. The revealing of the **Man of Lawlessness** on earth occurs at the same time as Satan's release from the Abyss. That is why some actions attributed to Satan are performed by the **Man of Lawlessness**.

The **angels** who are to pour out the plagues are dressed in clean, shining linen to emphasize that while what they are about to do is not pleasant, those who do it are holy. The **bowls** are filled, not with arbitrary disasters, but with the wrath of God. The plagues that come from the pouring of the contents of the **bowls** on earth are expressions of God's wrath against the increasingly evil behavior of non-believers. As fallen humanity becomes increasingly wicked, God allows the world to live out its opposition to him. God has not established arbitrary rules to prevent people from enjoying life. The opposite is true. God's rules define how life can be lived with the greatest satisfaction and pleasure. When Adam sinned it not only affected him but also damaged all creation (Genesis 3:17-19, Romans 8:20f.) During the reign of the **Man of Lawlessness**, the breaking of God's law is at such an extreme level that all of creation feels the effect.

The seven final plagues in Revelation 16 parallel the seven **trumpets** of Revelation 8-11 and to a lesser extent, the plagues of Exodus. The seven **trumpets** proclaimed fallen humanity's destruction of a fallen world and the pain associated with falleness. The seven **bowls** express God's wrath at the increased corruption of the world and of humanity, and take the destruction described in the seven **trumpets** to an extreme level. By pouring out the **bowls**, God causes the damage resulting from sin to impact humanity and all creation. Those devoted to sin live out the consequences of their behavior during the time of the **Man of Lawlessness**.

The first three plagues involve events not requiring the obvious intervention of God. There is no comment about how the victims of the plagues refuse to repent because they may not have recognized God's wrath being poured on them. The fourth and fifth plagues are extraordinary and are recognized as God's handiwork. In spite of this, the opponents of God do not repent.

First Bowl of Wrath

The first **bowl** is poured out on the land. This is similar to the first **trumpet** that caused hail and fire to be cast down to the earth. Unlike the first **trumpet**, the impact of the first **bowl** is not on horticulture. It is assumed that the grass and trees have already been damaged to the point that they can no longer protect humanity from this plague. The **bowl** causes painful sores that fall only on those who participate in the activities of idolatry symbolized in Revelation as the **mark of the beast**.

There is a parallel between this passage and the plague that fell on Egypt in Exodus 9:9-11. The passages are similar. In both, God is judging a people who stand in opposition to his people. In both passages, those on whom the plague falls do not repent due to hardness of heart. There is another similarity in that God protects his people from the plague that injures his enemies.

Since most of the images in Revelation are symbolic, it would not be reasonable to suggest that this image, in the midst of a section filled with non-literal imagery, is one of the few that is to be taken literally. If it were literal, the sudden appearance of sores only on non-believers and not on believers would certainly draw attention to the judgment of God. Instead, this plague is thought to be merely an unhappy circumstance by those marked by the beast. The opponents of God do not recognize His hand in these plagues until the fourth **bowl** is poured out. It makes no difference because even when they recognize God's involvement they refuse to repent.

The first plague represents the diminishing of human health as a result of the damage done to the trees and vegetation on earth. The passage does not explain how God protects his people from this plague. In Egypt, some of the plagues did not occur in the area where Israel lived. Other plagues, like the angel of death, were avoided by obedience to specific commandments. In the time of the **Man of Lawlessness**, believers can expect that one element in God's protection will be the keeping of His commandments. No matter how it is accomplished, those marked by the beast are the only ones affected by this plague.

The Second Bowl of Wrath

The second **bowl** turns the sea to coagulated blood and every living thing in the sea dies. The second **trumpet** caused the sea to turn to blood and a third of the living creatures died. This plague is an intensification of the second **trumpet**.

The plague of turning the Nile to blood is similar to this plague (Exodus 7:17-21), but the Nile is inland fresh water and this plague is much larger in scope. All of the fish in the Nile died just as the fish die in this plague. The results of this plague are similar. Just as Pharaoh refused to relent and hardened his heart, there is no softening of the hearts of those who use the seas for food or commerce.

The turning of the oceans to blood suggests death, bloodshed, and ruthlessness. A comprehensive description of the results of this plague cannot be developed from such a brief passage. It can be stated that the intensification of the judgment proclaimed in the second **trumpet** suggests disaster for the fish of the oceans and for shipping.

In Scripture the failure to acknowledge God results in evil practices and in death of wildlife.

> *Hosea 4:1-3* Hear the word of the Lord, you Israelites, because the Lord has a charge to bring against you who live in the land: "There is no faithfulness, no love, no acknowledgment of God in the land. There is only cursing, lying and murder, stealing and adultery; they break all bounds and bloodshed follows bloodshed. Because of this the land mourns, and all who live in it waste away; the beasts of the field and the birds of the air and the fish of the sea are dying.

John prophecies that the reign of the **Man of Lawlessness** leads to bloodshed and the death of the fish of the sea. The Hosea passage makes the connection between the refusal to acknowledge God and death of man and beast. A nation's unfaithfulness toward God leads to murder, bloodshed, and the death of wildlife on a large scale.

The Third Bowl of Wrath

The third **bowl** is poured out on the fresh waters, rivers, and springs, and they are turned to blood. This is an intensification of the judgment proclaimed in the third **trumpet**. The third **trumpet** proclaimed the mismanagement of fresh water by fallen humanity such that a third of the fresh water was unusable. The third **bowl** makes all of the waters unusable.

There is a strong similarity between the turning of the Nile to blood (Exodus 7:17-21), and this third plague. All of the waters were fouled in Egypt so that the people had to dig in the ground to find fresh water that could be used to drink. The third plague is the same except on a larger scale. All running water on the surface of the earth is polluted. If the judgment pronounced by the third **trumpet** is intensified, the third **bowl** also will intensify the consequences of the third **trumpet**. Since in the third **trumpet** some die by drinking the fouled waters, it would be expected that even more would die from drinking water after the third **bowl** has been poured out.

The symbolism of turning the water to blood, is both a literal and figurative judgment in Revelation 16:5-7. The pollution of the waters represents God's judgment on humanity who must drink the corrupted water (i.e., they must drink blood.) God literally pronounces judgment on those who have corrupted the fresh water. At the same time he symbolically pronounces judgment on the persecutors of the church by having them drink "blood." God declares in Leviticus 17:10-14 that he will set his face against anyone who eats (or drinks) blood and they will be cut off from (his) people. So God stands in opposition and hostility toward these people who in their sin have ruined the fresh water and shed the blood of the saints and prophets.

The Fourth Bowl of Wrath

The fourth **bowl** is poured on the sun and the result is a searing heat that is recognized to be the work of God. The problems with nature permitted by God in the first three plagues were not recognized as the work of God. God's hand in this fourth plague is more obvious so the people curse God and refuse to repent. The refusal to repent reflects people's awareness of God's involvement in bringing this plague.

This searing heat is similar to that described in Isaiah 24.

> *Isaiah 24:4-9* The earth dries up and withers, the world languishes and withers, the exalted of the earth languish. *The earth is defiled by its people;* they have disobeyed the laws, violated the statutes and broken the everlasting covenant. Therefore a curse consumes the earth; its people must bear their guilt. Therefore earth's inhabitants are burned up, and very few are left. The new wine dries up and the vine withers; all the merrymakers groan. The gaiety of the tambourines is stilled, the noise of the revelers has stopped, the joyful harp is silent. No longer do they drink wine with a song; the beer is bitter to its drinkers.

The cause for the searing heat that burns or scorches the people is the same in both Isaiah and in Revelation. God has control over this plague (Rev. 16:9, Isaiah 24:1.) He devastates the earth in response to the sinfulness of humanity. The Isaiah text is in an eschatological passage that also includes the great **earthquake** (Isaiah 24:18-20), the reference to "that day" which is the final judgment (Isaiah 24:21f) and **extreme language** (Isaiah 24:23.) The eschatological content of Isaiah 24 encourages connecting the searing heat of Revelation 16 with that in Isaiah 24. The heat burns or scorches the earth's inhabitants so that all song and celebration stops. Those who stand against the Lord and the church respond to this clear judgment from God by cursing him (Rev. 16:9.)

At first glance it might be thought that there is no connection between the fourth **trumpet** and the fourth **bowl**. In the fourth **trumpet**, a third of the heavenly bodies are darkened while in the fourth **bowl**, the sun scorches people with intense heat. However, if it is true that the fourth **trumpet** represents the mismanagement of the air resulting in air and light pollution as has been proposed, the searing effects of the sun could result from the intensification of the effects of pollution.

The searing heat sounds similar to current theories regarding global warming and the reduction of the ozone layer. There is no reason to think that the **Man of Lawlessness** is ruling now. It is therefore not certain that any of the phenomena that concern scientists now will be used by God to impose judgment. It might be interesting to ponder how this could happen, but it must be recognized that such considerations will remain speculation until the prophesy is fulfilled.

The Fifth Bowl of Wrath

The fifth **bowl** is poured on the throne of the beast and his kingdom is plunged into darkness. The darkness is not merely dark but is a source of agony (Rev. 16:11.) The intensification of the judgment of the fifth **trumpet** would be expected to include both darkness and pain. When the Abyss was opened at the sounding of the fifth **trumpet** (Rev. 8:2), the sun and sky were darkened by the smoke from the Abyss. The smoke from the Abyss suggests the taste and smell of the judgment to come. The locusts from the Abyss tortured those not having the **seal of God on their foreheads**, causing agony (Rev. 9:5.) The fifth **bowl** is poured on the throne of the **beast out of the earth**, and his kingdom is plunged into the darkness of the smoke from the Abyss. The followers of the **Man of Lawlessness** gnaw their tongues in agony. This represents an intensification of the hopelessness, sin, guilt, conflict, and isolation belonging to fallen man alienated from God. Under the rule of the **Man of Lawlessness**, the increase in sin and the rejection of God will cause an increase in the pain experienced by the community of the ungodly. They will be forced to live out the consequences of their godless practices and their movement away from relationship with God.

The darkness of the fifth **bowl** is similar to the plague of darkness that fell on Egypt in Exodus 10:21-23. The plague of darkness was a darkness so deep that it could be felt. The result of this plague, which occurred immediately before the final plague on the firstborn, was that Pharaoh suggested that the Israelites could leave if they left their flocks behind. When Israel rejected that offer, Pharaoh's heart was hardened and he refused to let them go.

The Sixth Bowl of Wrath

The sixth **bowl** is poured on the river Euphrates and its water is dried up. If the previous images were being interpreted literally, there would be no water in the Euphrates, only blood. The Euphrates is dried up to make it easier for the kings from the east to transport their armies. God is making it easier for the kings of the whole world to gather for battle on the great day of God Almighty. God's purpose in allowing (and even assisting) these nations to gather at Armageddon is to bring them together to the place where they will be judged.

The sixth **trumpet** described four **angels** bound at the river Euphrates, who were released to kill a third of mankind. There were two hundred million mounted troops who rode horses that inflicted injury both from their heads and from their tails. The description of the warriors was followed by the story of the death and resurrection of the church. The **two witnesses** testified regarding Christ, were killed, and after three and a half days were resurrected and ascended to heaven in a cloud. The sixth **trumpet** contained images of the reign of the **Man of Lawlessness**.

In the sixth **bowl**, the **dragon**, the **beast out of the earth** and the false prophet gather the nations to **Armageddon** where they will be destroyed by Jesus (Rev. 19:19-21.) The spirits of demons perform miraculous signs (Rev. 16:14). This is similar to Matthew 24:24, where false Christs and false prophets appear and perform great signs and miracles to deceive. False signs and miracles are also included as marks of the end in II Thessalonians 2:9. Matthew 24:29ff relates that the return of Christ will happen immediately after the distress of those days. This is a more detailed description of the reign of the **Man of Lawlessness** than was provided in the sixth **trumpet**.

The **false prophet** appears in Revelation 16:13 for the first time without introduction or interpretation. Since the **beast out of the earth** always appears with the image he brought to life, it appears that the **false prophet** is the image of the **beast out of the sea** mentioned at the beginning of this section in Revelation 15:2.

Jesus says that he comes as a thief. This language is repeated both in Revelation and elsewhere. All should take to heart the warning that the return of Christ will come unexpectedly and the people of God must be prepared.

The kings are gathered against the Lord at **Armageddon**, the precise location of which is unknown. A Valley of Megiddo exists, but Har Megiddo (Mount Megiddo) does not. Mount Megiddo may be a fortress or stronghold near Megiddo. It is also possible that the Valley of Megiddo will become a mountain when the **earthquake** described in Zechariah 14:3-5 splits the Mount of Olives. This gathering of the nations by the **Man of Lawlessness** to the vicinity of Jerusalem appears in Daniel 11:45, Joel 3:2,9-16, Zephaniah 3:8, and Zechariah 14:3-5,12. It is called the great day of God Almighty which is a variation of the day of the Lord (i.e., the day of judgment.)

The Seventh Bowl of Wrath

The seventh **bowl** is poured out and the voice from the throne says, "It is done." In Revelation 16:18-21 there is **extreme language** representing destruction and judgment. The seventh **bowl** is the final judgment of God. This corresponds to the seventh **trumpet** which asserts that the kingdom of the world has become the kingdom of our Lord and of his Christ and that the time for judging the dead has come. The description of the seventh **trumpet** concludes with **extreme language** and an **earthquake** representing the enacting of final judgment.

The **earthquake** associated with the seventh **bowl** is unlike any since man has been on earth (Rev. 16:18.) This is similar to the **earthquake** from Zechariah 14:3-5 that splits the Mount of Olives. After that great **earthquake**, the Lord will come and all his holy ones with him (Zech. 14:5.)

The language of verse 20 is similar to that in Revelation 6:14 which is the sixth **seal** representing the final judgment. Additionally, verses 18 and 19 are similar to Revelation 11:13, at the conclusion of the sixth **trumpet**, which depicts a severe **earthquake** that occurs after the people of God have gone up to heaven in a cloud.

Revelation 17:1-19:10
The Great Prostitute, the Scarlet Beast
and the Fall of Babylon

Revelation 17 begins a new section in which a **prostitute** is introduced whose punishment is to be shown to John. She bears the title, **Babylon** the Great on her forehead and all of chapter 18 and part of chapter 19 are devoted to a celebration of her destruction. The **prostitute** is in sharp contrast to the **woman clothed with the sun** from Revelation 12. The **woman clothed with the sun** represented the church throughout the ages. Likewise, the **prostitute** represents a people. The **prostitute** is drunk with the blood of the saints (Rev. 17:6) and so must be a persecuting power. At the time John is writing, Roman persecution has been limited, while a great persecution in Jerusalem has scattered Christians out into Judea and Samaria and eventually into the whole world (Acts 8:1-4.) She is called the **great city** which combined with the fact that she sits on a beast having **seven** heads respresenting **seven** hills (Rev. 17:9) has led some to believe that she is Rome. However, she is not Rome. In Revelation 11:8 the **great city** is defined as the place where the Lord was crucified. So when the woman who is repeatedly called **Babylon** the great is also defined as the **great city** in Revelation 17:18, it becomes clear that both the **great city** and **Babylon** are Jerusalem.

It should be noted that the woman is sitting on the **scarlet beast** not on its heads. This beast has **seven heads** which are seven hills. The woman, sitting on a beast having seven heads representing seven hills, is seen by some as a city sitting on seven hills, (i.e., Rome.) However, she is not sitting on the heads meaning that she is not sitting on the seven hills.

There are a number of features that require that the woman be Jerusalem in addition to her being identified as the great city, which was previously defined as Jerusalem. First, she is a prostitute. God repeatedly calls unfaithful Israel a prostitute in the Old Testament. God warns Israel not to prostitute themselves through idolatry and disobedience in Numbers 15:39. He predicts that Israel will prostitute herself to foreign gods in Deuteronomy 31:16. Israel prostituted themselves in idolatry at the high places in II Chronicles 21:11,13. Israel is compared to a prostitute, acting unfaithfully with the gods of other nations in Jeremiah chapters 2 and 3, Ezekiel 16 and 23 and in Hosea 4:12,15 and 9:1. God would not be inclined to call Rome a prostitute for being unfaithful in the same way that he would tend to call unfaithful Israel a prostitute.

The clothing the woman wears is another clue to her identity. She is wearing purple, scarlet, gold, precious stones, and pearls. A comparison of her dress with the ephod of Aaron in Exodus 39:8-14 reveals a remarkable similarity. The ephod is made of gold, blue, purple and scarlet yarn, and of finely twisted linen. On it are mounted gold and precious stones. The tabernacle in Exodus 26:1 also is made of the same colors and materials. There are some differences, but these are for a purpose.

The prostitute does not wear linen. In Revelation 19:8, fine linen stands for the righteous acts of the saints. Since the prostitute behaves wickedly, she has no right to wear linen.

The prostitute does not have any blue in her clothes. In Numbers 4, the most holy things from the tabernacle including the ark of the covenant were covered with blue cloths. In Numbers 15:38-40 the significance of the color blue appears to be that of consecration and holiness:

Speak to the Israelites and say to them: 'Throughout the generations to come you are to make tassels on the corners of your garments, with a blue cord on each tassel. You will have these tassels to look at and so you will remember all the commands of the Lord, that you may obey them and not prostitute yourselves by going after the lusts of your own hearts and eyes. Then you will remember to obey all my commands and will be consecrated to your God.

The **prostitute** is wearing pearls which do not appear on the ephod or the tabernacle. This is a sign of the wealth that the prostitute has received for her unfaithfulness.

Another reason that it would be difficult to hold that the great city is Rome is that the blood of the prophets is found in "**Babylon**". While it could be asserted that the blood of saints would be found in Rome, there is no biblical or historical evidence that any Old Testament prophets died in Rome. It could be proposed that New Testament prophets died in Rome and they are the prophets mentioned in the text. However, Israel was known for killing the prophets (Matthew 23:37.) Revelation 18:24 says that in this city was found the blood of all who have been killed on the earth. Rome as a recent persecutor does not fit this description.

All of the arguments above could be persuasive by themselves, but the most compelling argument is that the **prostitute** dressed in scarlet is found in Jeremiah 4 and is identified as unfaithful Jerusalem. In Jeremiah 3, Jeremiah prophecies against faithless Israel and unfaithful Judah. Israel is compared to an adulterous wife and a prostitute.

Jeremiah 3:1-3 "If a man divorces his wife and she leaves him and marries another man, should he return to her again? Would not the land be completely defiled? But you have lived as a prostitute with many lovers - would you now return to me?" declares the Lord. "Look up to the barren heights and see. Is there any place where you have not been ravished? By the roadside you sat waiting for lovers, sat like a nomad in the desert. You have defiled the land with your prostitution and wickedness. Therefore the showers have been withheld, and no spring rains have fallen. Yet you have the brazen look of a prostitute; you refuse to blush with shame.

Israel and Judah are like two sisters who are married to God. Both act unfaithfully and their idolatry is like adultery against God.

Jeremiah 3:8,9 I gave faithless Israel her certificate of divorce and sent her away because of all her adulteries. Yet I saw that her unfaithful sister Judah had no fear; she also went out and committed adultery. Because Israel's immorality mattered so little to her, she defiled the land and committed adultery with stone and wood.

Jeremiah 3:20 "But like a woman unfaithful to her husband, so you have been unfaithful to me, O house of Israel," declares the Lord.

God promises Israel that if she returns and puts away the idols that he will bless her. Judah faces condemnation and destruction because she makes a pretense of returning to God but remains unfaithful. The warning to Judah begins in Jeremiah 4:3. A powerful army will come against her from the north. The Lord proclaims judgment against Jerusalem in this prophecy in Jeremiah 4:11,14, and 16. The symbol of Jerusalem as a prostitute in a scarlet dress appears at the end of Jeremiah 4.

Jeremiah 4:30-5:1 What are you doing, O devastated one? Why dress yourself in scarlet and put on jewels of gold? Why shade your eyes with paint? You adorn yourself in vain. Your lovers despise you; they seek your life. I hear a cry as of a woman in labor, a groan as of one bearing her first child - the cry of the Daughter of Zion gasping for breath, stretching out her hands and saying, "Alas! I am fainting; my life is given over to murderers." "Go up and down the streets of Jerusalem, look around and consider, search through her squares. If you can find but one person who deals honestly and seeks the truth, I will forgive this city.

The use of a prostitute dressed in scarlet in Jeremiah as a symbol of Jerusalem gives final verification that the **prostitute** in Revelation 17 is Jerusalem.

The **prostitute** is sitting on the beast having seven heads representing seven hills because she has exchanged faithfulness to God for accommodation with Rome and the wealth that cooperation with Rome will bring.

The **prostitute** sits on many waters which are peoples, multitudes, nations, and languages. This refers to her commercial endeavors throughout the world. Support for this is found in Revelation 18 where many people express sorrow at losing "**Babylon**" as a trading partner.

The **scarlet beast** is similar to the **beast out of the sea** in chapter 13 which also had **ten horns** and **seven heads**. He is evil both because of his similarity to the **beast out of the sea** and by his **scarlet** color. This beast once was, now is not, and will come up out of the Abyss. This description requires that the beast be Satan. He once was, before he was bound and cast into the Abyss by Jesus (Rev. 20:1-3.) He now is not, indicating that he is not present on earth at the time John writes because he remains in the Abyss until he is released. He will come up out of the Abyss (Rev. 11:7) when he is released by Jesus for a short time (Rev. 20:3) and go to his destruction (Rev. 17:11, 20:9,10.)

The beast has **seven heads** which are seven hills (representing Rome) and seven kings. The seven kings, because they come from the same symbol (**seven heads**), must be from the city indicated by the seven hills (Rome.) The seven kings are Roman kings or emperors who persecute first Old Testament Israel and later the New Testament church. (For the identity of the seven kings, see the discussion of Revelation 13.) The beast is called an eighth king in verse 11, patterned after the seven kings. While Satan cannot directly act as an eighth king, his representative, the **Man of Lawlessness**, can do the things that are attributed to Satan. The **Man of Lawlessness** derives his power and authority from Satan, so his actions can be ascribed to Satan. If he is like the seven Roman emperors, he must have authority similar to a Roman emperor and must be a world ruler.

The **ten horns** represent ten kings who have not yet taken power who will reign and make war against the **lamb**. These are kings who reign after the Roman empire has been destroyed. They make war against the **lamb** (and his church) but are overcome. These kings not only persecute the church, they also persecute the **prostitute** (Jerusalem), bringing her to ruin, leaving her naked, eating her flesh, and burning her with fire. The attacks directed against the **prostitute** are more descriptive of how Jerusalem and the Jewish people have been treated than a description of Rome. These kings are significant world leaders or empires who act both as persecutors of the church and persecutors of Israel (anti-semites.)

By their anti-semitism, which is sometimes attached to Christian celebrations or justified by using inaccurate Christian theology, these leaders have acted to drive a wedge between Judaism and Christianity. Historic examples of this include Russian programs that were sometimes initiated during the Easter season and efforts by Hitler and others to gain popular support for destroying the Jews by characterizing them as Christ killers. These leaders and empires have stood in opposition to Christianity and have persecuted true Christians. Their actions have contributed to the temporary hardening of Israel (Rom 11:25f.) At the end of history there will be no division between faithful Israel and Gentile Christians. All will honor Jesus together as the Messiah who saves us from our sins.

In Revelation 18, the church celebrates the fall of unfaithful Jerusalem (vs. 20) because of her crimes and because in her was found the blood of the prophets and the saints (vs. 24.) This is not anti-semitic because it is written by a faithful Israelite against that portion of Israel that has repudiated the Messiah of God. The text addresses this destruction as a future event. For the destruction of Jerusalem to be a future event, Revelation must have been written before 70 AD. The destruction of the city will be sudden, occurring in one day (Rev. 18:8) and in one hour (Rev. 18:10,17,19.) The burning of the city (Rev. 18:9,18) and the suddenness of its destruction matches Jerusalem's destruction but not Rome's.

Revelation 19 begins with praise to the Lord for avenging the blood of his servants on Jerusalem. This is followed by a song of praise to God and celebration at the wedding supper of the **lamb**. As in the wedding supper in Matthew 22, wedding clothes are provided. The wedding clothes at the wedding supper of the **lamb** are **fine linen** which represents the righteous acts of the saints. This **fine linen** was given to the bride rather than belonging to the bride. This reinforces the teaching of Philippians 2:13 that the righteousness of the saints is from God who works in them to will and to act according to his good purpose.

Revelation 19:11-20:15
The Seven Bowls of God's Wrath (Continued)
Satan Bound, Released and Destroyed
The Judgment of All Mankind

The next image depicts a rider on a **white horse** who is clearly identified as Jesus Christ. He is **King of kings and Lord of lords**, and his name is the **Word of God**. He rode out as a conqueror in Revelation 6:2 wearing one **crown**. The **crown** he was wearing was symbolic of his reign over creation but it was also symbolic of his reign over Israel. Prior to the spread of the gospel, he was known as the God of Israel, the God of Abraham, Isaac, and Jacob. In this passage he has many **crowns** and an army following him riding **white horses** and dressed in **fine linen**. The soldiers' weapons are not described. The army does not need weapons because it is not their power but the power of the one on the **white horse** that will overcome the enemies. The rider on the **white horse** has made all believers a kingdom and priests. He has determined that believers will reign on earth (Rev. 5:9f), spreading his reign over even more of the earth. The conqueror has conquered and he therefore reigns over faithful followers from many nations. He wears many **crowns** because he has made himself known to many nations and has a people who come from many nations.

Jesus rules the nations with an iron scepter. This image comes from Psalm 2 where it is used messianically. With the iron scepter he will dash the nations to pieces like pottery. Jesus will tread the winepress of the furious wrath of God. The image comparing God's wrath to treading a winepress has several Old Testament precedents. In Isaiah 63:2f, in the day of vengeance and in the year of the Lord's redemption, God tramples the nations in his anger and pours their blood on the ground. In Lam. 1:15, God tramples Judah in his winepress. In Joel 3:14, God tramples the nations who have gathered in the Valley of Jehoshaphat. In the context, Joel's description of the judgment of the nations precedes the description of the holy Jerusalem. The pattern is identical to that found in Revelation where the nations gather for destruction in Revelation 19 and 20 after which the new Jerusalem descends.

An **angel** cries out to the birds in the vicinity to gather to eat the bodies of the enemies of the Lord. This is similar to the destruction of Gog and his armies in Ezekiel 39:4, 17f. God calls to the birds and wild animals to feast on the flesh of mighty men who he is about to slay. A parallel passage is found in Ezekiel 29:5 where God prophecies that the Egyptian army will be food for the beasts and the birds.

The kings of the earth gather to war against the rider and his army. This is a continuation of Revelation 16:12-16 where the **dragon**, beast, and **false prophet** gathered the kings of the earth for battle at **Armageddon**. This is the same event described in Revelation 20:7-9 where the nations gather for battle after Satan's release. In this passage, the nations have been gathered for battle, to be led by the **false prophet** and beast against the forces of the rider on the **white horse**. The section ends with the final judgment in which the **false prophet** and beast are thrown alive into the lake of burning sulphur. The army that they had gathered is destroyed by the Lord.

The latter half of Revelation 19 is not a prelude to the events about to be discussed in Revelation 20. Rather, chapter 20 is a new section providing a different perspective and additional information of the same event by considering Satan's role in the world. Revelation 20 parallels chapter 19 because the army that is destroyed in Revelation 19:21 is again devoured by fire in Revelation 20:9. Another reason that they must be the same event is that in Revelation 16:13f, the **dragon** (Satan), the **beast out of the earth** (the **Man of Lawlessness**) and the **false prophet** (the image of the **beast out of the sea**) together gather the kings of the whole world for battle on the great day of God Almighty (the final judgment.)

Revelation 20 begins with an **angel** coming out of heaven who has the key to the Abyss. This **angel** must be Jesus because only Jesus could treat Satan as he is treated in verses 2 and 3. Even Michael the archangel could say only "the Lord rebuke you" to Satan (Jude 9.) Satan, who is also called a **dragon**, ancient serpent, and the devil in this text, is thrown into the Abyss for **1000 years**. This **1000 year period** is not a literal **1000 years** but it does represent a time in human history.

To determine what this **1000 year** period represents one must be able to answer the following questions:

1. What is the **first resurrection**? John identifies the **1000 years** with the **first resurrection** (Rev. 20:4f) and if the **first resurrection** can be defined in a clear way, the **millennium** also can be defined because the two are the same.

2. Who reigns for this **1000 year** period with Christ?

3. What is the **second death** that does not have power over those who reign with Christ for **1000 years**?

The first two questions are closely related and must be addressed together. Those who reign with Christ are a group of people sitting on thrones who have authority to judge (Rev. 20:4.) Included with those who are judging are those who were beheaded for Jesus. They did not worship the beast or receive his mark (Rev. 20:5.) This requires that they lived during the time that the beast lived and that he was marking people. If they had not lived during the time of the beast and his mark, saying that they had not worshipped him or received his mark would be foolish. It would be like saying that a man had chosen never to give birth to children. These believers came to life and reigned with Christ. To do this they must have been dead before this **1000 year** period. This coming to life is called the **first resurrection**. The critical issue in this text is whether the first resurrection is a physical resurrection or a spiritual resurrection.

If this refers to a physical resurrection, a small group who lived during the time of the beast, who died (some through beheading), and who are already seated on thrones to judge, come back to life. Since they refused to worship the beast and did not receive his mark, why is there any reason to mention the second death has no power over them? They were already dead, they were already seated on thrones, and of course they are blessed and holy. Also, where is Christ when Satan is released and deceives the nations? If Christ is reigning physically on earth, Satan would not dare attack the Lord and his people who are reigning. The **first resurrection** cannot be a physical resurrection. (See article on **first resurrection** in Section 3.) It is most reasonable to assert that the people of God, who are born dead in their transgressions and sins (Ephesians 2:1) are first resurrected to new life with Christ. The language used in this passage supports this interpretation. John did not see the bodies of those who had been beheaded but their souls (Rev. 20:4.) If the **first resurrection** was a bodily resurrection, it would be expected that John would see the people themselves (their bodies) rather than their souls. Instead, John sees their souls because they are resurrected spiritually, made alive in Christ through regeneration. New life with Christ, spiritual rebirth, is the **first**

resurrection (see article on the **first resurrection** in Section Three.)

In the song of praise in Revelation 5:9f, included in the song to the **Lamb** is the statement that those purchased by his blood are a kingdom of priests and they will reign on the earth. It is the reign of those participating in the **first resurrection** to which both Revelation 5:10 and Revelation 20:4 refer. Since the first resurrection is regeneration or spiritual rebirth, those who come to life and reign with Christ are all those who are true believers from the time of the death of Christ until the release of Satan.

If it is true that believers are reigning with Christ from his death until the release of Satan, it must be demonstrated from Scripture that Christ and the church are reigning now. There are several passages that support this.

> *Romans 5:17* For if, by the trespass of the one man, death reigned through that one man, how much more will those who receive God's abundant provision of grace and of the gift of righteousness *reign in life* through the one man, Jesus Christ.

> *I Corinthians 15:24f* Then the end will come, when he hands over the kingdom to God the Father after he has destroyed all dominion, authority and power. For he must reign *until* he has put all his enemies under his feet.

> *Revelation 1:5* ...and from Jesus Christ, who is the faithful witness, the firstborn from the dead, and the ruler of the kings of the earth.

> *Revelation 5:9f* And they sang a new song: You are worthy to take the scroll and to open its seals, because you were slain, and with your blood you purchased men for God from every tribe and language and people and nation. You have made them to be a kingdom and priests to serve our God, and they will reign on the earth.

While it might have been expected that those who receive God's grace and the gift of righteousness would reign after life, Romans 5 promises that they will reign in life. It could be expected that I Corinthians would speak of Christ reigning *after* he puts his enemies under his feet but he reigns *until* they are under his feet. This requires that he be reigning while those enemies are not yet subjugated. In Revelation 5, Jesus is praised for purchasing all who are saved with his blood from every nation. This same group, made up of all believers, will reign on earth. If all believers reign on earth, it is an easy step to see the **millennium** as a description of that earthly reign by all who have come to life through the work of the Spirit in their hearts.

The **beast out of the sea** and the **mark of the beast** exist throughout the Christian era. The **mark of the beast** is the alternative to having the name of the **lamb** and his Father's name on one's forehead (Rev 14:1.) The **mark of the beast** is idolatry. Idolatry exists throughout the time of the **beast out of the sea** (Rev. 13:4.)

The group which does not come to life until the **1000 years** are over are those who remain dead in their sins, unbelievers. They come to life after the **1000 years** to face the final judgment and the **second death** (the lake of fire.) Since the **first resurrection** is regeneration, Christ is currently reigning on earth and Satan is bound while the church is alive.

This text fits closely with Revelation 11, although it provides a different perspective. In both passages Satan comes up out of the Abyss and attacks the church. In both, the reigning of Christ on earth through the unconquerable church ends at the point that Satan is released. The conclusion is the same in both passages: Satan deceives the nations, but is destroyed by the return of Christ. The **second death** has no power over those who reign with Christ for **1000 years** because they are, by definition, the redeemed. The purpose of this passage, besides providing additional information about the end of time and the return of Christ, is to encourage those who face persecution. Those facing death need to know that the **second death** will have no power over them, so it is worthwhile to die rather than deny Christ.

The **millennium** is not an innovation by John, unknown elsewhere in Scripture. It is Jesus Christ, reigning through the church in a manner consistent with the teaching of other parts of Scripture. It does not begin after the tribulation period; it is at the same time as the **great tribulation**. The church faces opposition and tribulation but at the same time overcomes through the power of the Lord and defeats all of her oppressors until her testimony is completed (as in Rev. 11:4-12.) Even when the church is killed by Satan, the situation is not without hope. The church must die before she can be resurrected. When she is resurrected the time is short and she will stand as a witness until the return of Christ. Jesus Christ will return to destroy Satan and his allies and to establish his kingdom in the new Jerusalem.

When Satan is released, he intensifies and unifies the opposition against the church using his human representative, the **Man of Lawlessness**, as the personification of his power. Since Revelation 11 describes the resurrection of the church, and Romans 11 prophecies the end of the hardening of Israel after the time of the Gentiles, it is not surprising that Satan gathers his armies to attack Jerusalem. Most of Israel comes to faith in Christ after the death of the church (Romans 11:26,27.)

Joel 2:18-3:21 describes the Lord's redemption of Israel at the end of history. The text describes the same gathering of the armies of the kings of the world at **Armageddon** culminating with their destruction by the Lord found in Revelation 19 and 20. **Extreme language** (Joel 2:30f) depicts "wonders in the heavens and on the earth ... before the coming of the great and dreadful day of the Lord." This is followed by a number of verses pertaining to the judgment of the nations portrayed in Revelation 16:12-16, 19:17-21 and 20:7-9.

> *Joel 3:2* I will gather all nations and bring them down to the Valley of Jehoshaphat. There I will enter into judgment against them concerning my inheritance, my people Israel, for they scattered my people among the nations and divided up my land.

> *Joel 3:10-16* Beat your plowshares into swords and your pruning hooks into spears. Let the weakling say, "I am strong!" Come quickly, all you nations from every side, and assemble there. Bring down your warriors, O Lord! "Let the nations be roused; let them advance into the Valley of Jehoshaphat, for there I will sit to judge all the nations on every side. Swing the sickle for the harvest is ripe. Come, trample the grapes for the winepress is full and the vats overflow - so great is their wickedness!" Multitudes, multitudes in the valley of decision! For the day of the Lord is near in the valley of decision. The sun and moon will be darkened, and the stars no longer shine. The Lord will roar from Zion and thunder from Jerusalem; the earth and the sky will tremble. But the Lord will be a refuge for his people, a stronghold for the people of Israel.

Similarities are numerous between this passage and the texts in Revelation describing the gathering of the nations for judgment. Joel prophecies that all of the nations of the world are gathered for judgment. The analogy of the winepress above is repeated in Revelation 14:14-20 and describes the harvesting of the earth, the final judgment. The winepress of God's wrath is also mentioned in Revelation 19:15 prior to the destruction of the nations gathered by the beast and the **false prophet**. The use of **extreme language** in Joel 2:30f and 3:15f is consistent with similar language regarding the final judgment in Revelation 6:12ff, 16:18ff.

While it might be asserted that the location (the Valley of Jehoshaphat) appears to be inconsistent with the topography suggested by the name Armageddon (Mount Megiddo), there are several possible explanations. The phrase valley of Jehoshaphat means 'the Lord Judges' and could be a symbolic identification. With the size of the army gathered, it is conceivable that the army could camp between the Valley of Jehoshaphat (perhaps the Kidron Valley) and the hill, fortress, or city of Megiddo. Or, the location could be both a mountain and a valley if the splitting of the Mount of Olives to create a mountain and valley (Zech. 14:4f) were to be literally fulfilled. The description of Jerusalem in Joel 3:17-21 is similar to the peaceful and prosperous new Jerusalem.

This same gathering, judging, and destroying of nations is promised in Zephaniah 3:8. Zephaniah then concludes his prophesy by describing the restoration of a purified Israel to a position of honor among the nations.

In Zechariah 14:3-21, God fights against the nations and conquers them. The reference to living water (Zech. 14:8) is similar to the water of life in the new Jerusalem (Rev. 22:1,17.) The coming of the Lord God with all his holy ones (Zech. 14:5) is identical with the various New Testament descriptions of the return of Christ (Matthew 24:30f, I Thes. 4:17, Rev. 19:14.)

All these Old Testament passages describe the same gathering and destruction of the nations as is found in Revelation 19 and 20. Just as the destruction of the nations is followed by the final judgment, and peace and prosperity in the new Jerusalem in Revelation 21 and 22, these Old Testament passages maintain that after the judgment there will be an unending period of peace and prosperity as the Lord reigns.

When the nations have gathered, and just as it appears Satan will win, the church hears "Come up here" (Rev. 11:12.) Those who are left face the day of the Lord described in II Peter 3:10:

"...The heavens will disappear with a roar; the elements will be destroyed by fire, and the earth and everything in it will be laid bare."

Or as Revelation 20:9 describes, "But fire came down from heaven and devoured them." This destruction of the armies by fire is graphically described in Zechariah 14:12-15 as a rotting of flesh, eyes, and mouth.

The dead are judged using two sets of **books**. There are **books** (plural) opened and another book (singular) is opened which is the **book of life**. If anyone's name is not found in the book of life he is cast into the lake of fire. If a name is found in the **book of life**, that person is a child of God and will live. The other books are lists of what each person has done, and all are judged according to what they have done (Jer. 17:10, Matt. 16:27, Romans 2:6, II Cor. 5:10, Rev. 22:12.) The difference between the righteous and the wicked in this judgment is dramatic and distinct (like the difference between night and day.) Only the good things the righteous have done are recorded in the **books** and the wicked have recorded only the wicked things they have done (See Ezekiel 18:21,22,24, 33:13-16.) God promises through Ezekiel that none of the sins committed by believers will be remembered against them. This is similar to Paul's teaching in Ephesians 6:8. Writing to believers, he says the Lord will reward everyone for whatever good he does. For the wicked, none of their righteous acts will be remembered, so they will be punished and there will be nothing to reward.

Revelation 21:1-22:21
The New Jerusalem

In Revelation 21, the fallen heaven and earth have passed away. This passing away of the heavens and earth is prophesied in Isaiah 51:6 where the temporary nature of the heavens and earth is compared with the permanence of God's salvation. The heavens will vanish like smoke, the earth will wear out like a garment, but God's salvation will last forever. The heavens and earth are burned up in fire as described in II Peter 3:10, quoted above. The fallen earthly Jerusalem has been replaced by the perfect new Jerusalem that comes down from God. As before the Fall, God will dwell with men (Rev. 21:3); they will be his people and he will be their God. In this unfallen world there will be no more death, mourning, crying, or pain. God on the throne says it is done, indicating that this is not a fond hope or wish, but it is already accomplished. It is the future of the people of God. For those who are opposed to God, and whose behavior exemplifies that opposition, their future is just as certainly the lake of fire, the **second death**. For most of the rest of this chapter John describes the beauty of the new Jerusalem.

At the end of the chapter, differences are pointed out between this new world and the former fallen world. There is no temple because God dwells with his people. There is no sun or moon because the glory of God provides sufficient light. Isaiah provides a similar description of the new Jerusalem.

> *Isaiah 60:19f* The sun will no more be your light by day, nor will the brightness of the moon shine on you, for the Lord will be your everlasting light, and your God will be your glory. Your sun will never set again, and your moon will wane no more; the Lord will be your everlasting light, and your days of sorrow will end.

There is no night in the new Jerusalem because the glory of the Lord is never diminished in any way. At the end of Revelation 21, the warning from the previous chapter is repeated. Only those whose names are in the **lamb's book of life** will come into that city.

Life in the new Jerusalem is no longer harsh and unyielding as it was in the fallen world. Instead, all of creation is a source of health, strength, and life. The water of life and the tree of life are in that city. John emphasizes the change from falleness to unfalleness by commenting that "no longer will there be any curse" (Rev. 22:3.) The people of God will reign forever and ever.

In contrast to Daniel who was told to seal up the words he heard (Daniel 12:4), John is not to seal them because Jesus is coming soon (Rev. 22:7,10,12,20.) There is little difference between Jesus' statement in this text that he is coming soon and the statement in the beginning of the book that Jesus will show the seven churches what must soon take place. In Revelation 1:1,3, John's vision is to show the seven churches and all who read this book what will happen from the time of this vision until the return of Christ. Those who read and hear it are to take the words to heart because the time is near. In Revelation 22, John warns that Jesus' return is near so that no one will think that they can be careless, as though they could respond to the message later. John continues to emphasize that this book is addressed to the seven churches (Rev. 22:16.) It is not a vision for only that portion of the church still alive when Jesus returns, it is for the seven churches first of all. It is to be read by those who come after in the same way that Paul's letters are read. As Scripture it has value for the whole church no matter where in history the reader is. For those coming after the seven churches, the warnings and promises of Revelation are always timely. The warning of continual opposition, even from governments opposed to the gospel, helps to reader to not lose heart. The warning of a tribulation period that lasts to the end protects believers from complacency or confusion. Believers should expect troubles, opposition, and persecution. The promises of God energize the believer and encourage him to stand in the face of opposition, because the benefits of faithfulness far exceed the cost.

The book closes with the offer of the gospel. The water of life, representing the grace of God, is available to those who come and take it. This is followed by a warning not to add to or remove anything from this book. Clearly, changing any portion of this book would cause it to lose its coherence. The Old and New Testament foundations are only meaningful when the symbols from the other parts of Scripture are replicated as they are in Revelation. Additionally, the definitions that are provided are necessary for the reader to make any sense of the book. The need for coherency would be reason enough to warn against changing anything in the book. However, the primary reason for such a strongly worded prohibition against changing the content of the book is that to change it is to change that which God has determined to communicate through John's vision. To alter it is to alter what God revealed and had John write for the strengthening and encouragement of the church. Anyone who would change the text would have to believe he knew better than God what the future will be and what the book should say.

SECTION THREE

Terminology and Imagery

666 - [Rev. 13:18] The number **666** is a clue to the identity of the **Man of Lawlessness** (II Thes. 2.) In Daniel he is called a little horn that spoke boastfully (Daniel 7), a stern-faced king and master of intrigue (Daniel 8), and the king who exalts himself (Daniel 11.) In Revelation he is the **beast out of the earth** (Revelation 13 - see the article on beast out of the earth for clarification.)

The number of the beast out of the earth appears to be a use of what is known as gematria. Gematria is the assigning of values to letters of the alphabet. It was commonly used in the ancient world. A variety of systems of numbering were used to permit shorthand representations of numbers using letters. Out of this grew a practice, that existed prior to the Christian era, of using numbers to represent names. A numeric total was reached by assigning a value to each letter and adding the values for the letters in a person's name. The values for the letters were assigned as follows:

Alpha =	1	Iota =	10	Rho =	100
Beta =	2	Kappa =	20	Sigma =	200
Gamma =	3	Lambda =	30	Tau =	300
Delta =	4	Mu =	40	Upsilon =	400
Epsilon =	5	Nu =	50	Phi =	500
Stigma =	6	Xi =	60	Chi =	600
Zeta =	7	Omicron =	70	Psi =	700
Eta =	8	Pi =	80	Omega =	800
Theta =	9				

Stigma was an obsolete Greek letter that has an "ST" sound as in stop. It was not used as a letter in the alphabet but was used to represent 6 in gematria during the New Testament period.

The meaning of the number can be discerned by someone with wisdom who should be able to figure out or calculate the number. Irenaeus, an early church father, said:

> "We are not bold enough to speak confidently of the name of the Antichrist. For if it were necessary that his name should be declared clearly at the present time, it would have been announced by him who saw the revelation." [6]

If the identity of the Man of Lawlessness (also called the **Antichrist**) had been deciphered by the early church, it could be expected that his identity would have been passed down with the other traditions of the church. Irenaeus seems to suggest that when the name is to be known, it will be understood by the wise within the church, based on the 666 numerology. John does not provide the number to allow the church to identify the Man of Lawlessness prior to his coming to power. He gives the church the number to allow the wise in the church to confirm the identity of the Man of Lawlessness when he has begun to do what is attributed to him in Scripture.

Some suggest that the number 666 represents man's number, a reduction by one of each digit from what would be God's number 777, a number of completeness. The problem with this view is that it is not clear how the applying of man's number to the beast out of the earth requires wisdom or insight or communicates anything of substance about the beast. If the only point to be made was that he is a man, the point could be made (and is in Daniel) without resorting to numerology.

It has also been suggested by some that Nero or another persecutor is the beast out of the earth. Using gematria on Nero Caesar does not result in 666 unless one performs some contortions by changing the Greek name to Hebrew (an extraordinary thing for Asian churches to think to do) and even so the name must be modified. If, as is being proposed, the beast out of the earth is the Man of Lawlessness, he is destroyed by the coming of the Lord (II Thes. 2:8.) This requires that he be a figure from the future and disqualifies all of the historic figures who have been proposed.

1000 Years - [Rev. 20:1-7] This text, the only passage in Scripture referring to the **millennium**, is one of the greatest sources of controversy in Revelation. The correct interpretation of this text will define how this millennium is the **first resurrection** and what is meant by the **second death**. It also will clarify how, for those involved in this first resurrection, the second death has no power. Some have proposed a literal understanding of this passage and the 1000 year timeframe. These interpretations describe a millennium that is not seen anywhere else in Scripture. John does not define the term "first resurrection." This suggests that the reader should already know what it is. Since the first resurrection is identical to the millennium it is unlikely that the millennium could be something new in Scripture.

John defines the term "second death" in Revelation 20:14, and 21:8 as the fiery lake of burning sulphur. In Revelation 20:6, those involved in the first resurrection do not participate in the second death.

> *Revelation 20:6* Blessed and holy are those who have part in the first resurrection. The second death has no power over them, but they will be priests of God and of Christ and will reign with him for a thousand years.

It is clear that those who do not face the lake of fire (the second death) are the people of God, but what portion of the people of God participate in the millennium?

A literal interpretation of this passage would require that the first resurrection consist only of those who had been beheaded, and those John saw seated on thrones to judge. This group of people must have had the opportunity to reject worshipping a beast and receiving the mark of the beast. (It would not be praiseworthy that they had not worshipped the beast and refused the mark of the beast unless the pressure to receive a mark and to worship the beast existed.)

Some propose that the resurrection described in Revelation 20 is a first, physical resurrection coinciding with the temporary detention of Satan. In such an interpretation, all believers are raptured prior to the millennium. At the millennium, Christ reigns on earth for 1000 years (there is some debate about whether this period is literal) with a small group of his followers who have been resurrected. At the conclusion of Christ's reign, Satan is released and destroyed, and the final judgment occurs.

A major problem with this interpretation is that no hint of such a "first resurrection", involving only some believers who have been confronted by the mark of the beast and rejected it, is found anywhere else in Scripture. Other passages that are proposed as supporting texts make no mention of the beast and do not give any clear teaching regarding a resurrection of a small subset of all believers. In most cases, it appears that the texts offered are referring to the eternal state in heaven. Efforts by supporters of this position to produce a historical timeline, inevitably rely on speculation, because there are no other biblical texts that describe a sequence of events similar to that believed to exist in this passage.

Others propose that the believers who come to life to reign with Christ do so in eternity. It is argued that the first resurrection is not a rest ration of physical life but rather describes believers coming to life in the presence of God. However, there is no biblical support for equating "coming into the presence of God" with a resurrection. To be resurrected requires that one first be dead. While the bodies of believers die, their souls, which enter the presence of the Lord, are not dead. In Scripture, the death of a soul is normally equated with its eternal destruction in hell.

> *Matthew 10:28* Do not be afraid of those who kill the body but cannot kill the soul. Rather, be afraid of the One who can destroy both body and soul in hell.

Those who hold this position do not normally assert that the bodies of believers are resurrected but rather that their souls are resurrected. If their souls were not dead, they cannot be resurrected.

A better alternative is to understand the first resurrection as a reference to the spiritual resurrection that takes place when the spiritually dead awaken to new life in Christ. There is biblical support for this sort of language and it would certainly be true that those who participate in this resurrection would have nothing to fear from the lake of fire. (See article on **first resurrection** for a more in depth discussion.)

When Satan is bound by the **angel** having the **key** to the Abyss (i.e., Christ), he is unable to interact directly with mankind as a deceiver and opponent (as in Job.) His binding occurs during the church age.

While he is no longer loose in the world, his presence continues to be felt through his representatives and through the evil that will always exist in a fallen world.

Those John saw on thrones and the martyrs, came to life, not after their physical death, but during their lives, when they were made alive spiritually by the Spirit of God. This is the reason John saw their souls rather than their bodies (Rev. 20:4.) Instead of the **mark of the beast** (see article below) they received the **name of God on their foreheads** (see article below.) The mark of the beast is idolatry that exists during the time of the beast out of the sea as well as during the time of the beast out of the earth. The mark is particularly mentioned during the reign of the beast out of the earth because he will establish some particular idolatry in place of Christian worship. The reign of resurrected believers is not for a literal 1000 years but is during the church age. Each of them does not live for the entire figurative 1000 years (the church age), but it is during this time that they come to life in Christ and the church grows and prospers. They will be priests of God as described in Isaiah 61:6, I Peter 2:5,9, and Revelation 5:10.

The reigning of the church with Christ is seen in the growth of the church with its positive impact throughout history. Several passages speak of Christ and the church reigning on earth during the church age.

> *Romans 5:17* For if, by the trespass of the one man, death reigned through that one man, how much more will those who receive God's abundant provision of grace and of the gift of righteousness *reign in life* through the one man, Jesus Christ.

> *I Corinthians 15:24ff* Then the end will come, when he hands over the kingdom to God the Father after he has destroyed all dominion, authority and power. For he must reign *until* he has put all his enemies under his feet. The last enemy to be destroyed is death.

If he must reign until all of his enemies are under his feet and if the list of enemies to be overcome includes death, then he must be reigning now. His reign will end after the judgment when he hands the kingdom over to God the Father.

> *Revelation 5:9f* And they sang a new song: You are worthy
> to take the scroll and to open its seals, because you were slain,
> and with your blood you purchased men for God from every
> tribe and language and people and nation. You have made them
> to be a kingdom and priests to serve our God, and *they will reign
> on the earth.*

The impact of this reigning is more than spiritual in that the Christian mindset has had a profound influence on science and history. This is part of what theology calls common grace.

The dead who did not come to life until the 1000 years ended are those who do not come to spiritual life, i,e,. those who never come to faith in the Lord. They come to life after the 1000 years to face the final judgment and the **second death**.

The release of Satan in Revelation 20 is described earlier in the book when in Revelation 11:1-12 the two **olive trees** and **lampstands**, which represent the Jewish and Gentile portions of the church, finish their testimony. When the church has completed her testimony by preaching the gospel through the whole world, the **beast from the Abyss** (Satan) kills the witnesses. He accomplishes this through his representative, the **Man of Lawlessness**, and they lay dead in the city where their Lord was crucified (Jerusalem.) But after a short time, life from God enters them, they stand on their feet and ascend to heaven in a cloud. In Revelation 20, Satan is released at the end of the 1000 years and attacks God's people, surrounding the camp of God's people, the city that he loves (Jerusalem.) Satan is destroyed by fire and cast into the lake of fire.

The 1000 years is a figurative representation of the church age. It is identical to the **1,260 days** and the **forty-two months** that are used to describe this period elsewhere in Revelation. The 1000 year symbol expresses a completeness of time and depicts the indefiniteness of the period that the church will wait. This indefiniteness is reinforced by passages like Psalm 90:4 and II Peter 3:8 which describe 1000 years as like a day in the eyes of the Lord. In the II Peter passage, Peter moves from warning of the day of judgment which some will say is delayed, into a comparison of 1000 years to a day in God's sight. His point is that time is not the same for God as it is for his readers. John's 1000 years is equally indefinite, seeming short to the Lord but seeming much longer for those waiting for his return. Some could become discouraged if they thought

John meant to suggest that the wait would be only a few years when the Lord did not come back for centuries. By using 1,260 days, forty-two months and 1000 years to describe the same events, John helps the **seven churches** and the readers afterwards to avoid taking literally the times used in the book.

1260 Days - [Rev. 11:3, 12:6] See article on **forty-two months** for a discussion of the background of the use of three and a half years in Daniel and Revelation. This period is forty-two lunar (thirty day) months or three and a half years of thirty day months (360 day years.)

In Revelation 11:3, the two **witnesses**, who are also **olive trees** and **lampstands** and symbolize the church, prophecy for 1,260 days. The church is then overpowered and killed (Rev. 11:7.) Later, a breath of life from God causes them to stand on their feet (Rev. 11:11) and they go up to heaven in a cloud (Rev. 11:12.) Since the church has testified from its inception and can be expected to testify until the end, the 1,260 days reflect the church age.

In Revelation 12 there is a confrontation between a **dragon** who is Satan (Rev. 12:9) and a **woman clothed with the sun** who bears a son who rules with an **iron scepter**. From Revelation 19:11-16 it is clear that this child is Jesus Christ. The woman is then taken care of by God in the desert for 1,260 days. There is a direct connection between 1,260 days (Rev. 12:6) and **time, times, and half a time** (Rev. 12:14). In Revelation 12:14, the woman clothed with the sun goes to a place prepared for her in the desert for a time, times, and half a time. The woman clothed with the sun bears Christ and has other offspring who obey God's commandments and hold to the testimony of Jesus (Rev. 12:17.) She must be the church. Her offspring are not protected as she is and Satan makes war against them during this 1,260 day period (Rev. 12:17.) Satan's attack on the offspring of the woman is called the great tribulation in Revelation 7:14. The great tribulation lasts throughout the Christian era. Satan makes war against the offspring of the woman throughout the 1,260 days that she is kept safe. It would appear that this is the very nature of the great tribulation (Satan warring against the saints.)

The woman clothed in the sun is protected only for 1,260 days. Her destiny after that time is not discussed. Lacking any other information, it could be proposed that she would be attacked after the 1,260 days or the danger could pass. Revelation 11:1-12 describes what happens at the end of the 1,260 days. The church dies and is resurrected. Then Jesus Christ returns and executes judgment. So for 1,260 days (the church age) the church is kept safe, until her testimony is finished. Her children are attacked by Satan reflecting the difference between the visible church which is protected and sustained, and individuals within the church who will face persecution and death. The text promises that the church will be protected and victorious until her testimony is complete. The problems faced by groups and individuals within the church will require patient endurance and faithfulness if they are to overcome as part of the victorious church (Rev. 12:11, 13:9,10, 14:12.)

144,000 - [Rev. 7:4, 14:1,3] The number 144,000 is clearly symbolic. The symbolic nature of this number is suggested by its connection with the numbers twelve and 1000. The number 144,000 consists of twelve squared times 1000. Twelve is an important symbolic number in Scripture (twelve sons of Jacob, twelve tribes, twelve apostles.) It is a number representing the chosen people of God. The number 1000 (**1000 years**) is used symbolically in Revelation 20 to represent an indefinite but complete period. The combination of twelves and 1000 appears to be a representation of all those in a group of indefinite number who are set apart to God.

There are 12,000 people sealed with God's seal from each of the tribes of Israel in Revelation 7. These faithful people have the same seal of God as all those who dwell in the new Jerusalem (Rev. 22:4.) The purpose of this passage is not to give a precise number of people from Israel who will be faithful. Rather, it is designed to express, in the context of the sixth seal (final judgment), the complete spiritual restoration of the Jewish church at the time of the return of Christ. This is important because the hardening of Israel (Rom 11:25f) might lead some to think that God is no longer interested in Israel. However, Israel is still important and when the time of the Gentiles is fulfilled (Luke 21:24) there will be a revival of Israel.

The 144,000 in Revelation 14 who also have God's name written on their foreheads are a different group. Their nationality is unknown and apparently irrelevant. The criteria for belonging to this group is that one must be a male who has not defiled himself with women, or to say it another way, the members of this group are male virgins. They are a group set apart who are first fruits to God.

It should be noted that both references to 144,000 in Revelation conflict with the theology of the Jehovah Witnesses. The first group were Jews set apart by tribe and the second group were male virgins. There is no special group of 144,000 in Revelation that, understood literally, would include Gentiles who were not virgins or that would include any Gentile women.

Abaddon/Apollyon - [Rev. 9:11] This name for Satan means destruction and destroyer. Abaddon appears in several places in the Old Testament (Job 26:6, 28:22, 31:12, Psalm 88:11, Proverbs 15:11, 27:20) and is used to refer to the place of the dead. The destruction unleashed on the earth through the Fall of man is death and bondage to decay (Romans 8:20f.) This destruction has resulted in the agony of unredeemed mankind who suffer in their inability to find satisfaction without God.

Abomination That Causes Desolation - This term is not found in Revelation, but its use in Daniel and in the gospels makes it important for those who want to understand eschatology.

The abomination that causes desolation is set up by the **Man of Lawlessness** (Daniel 8:13, 9:27, 11:31.) It is mentioned in the gospels as standing in the holy place or standing where it does not belong (Matthew 24:15, Mark 13:14.) The passages in Matthew and Mark advise the reader to flee to the mountains from Judea when the abomination that causes desolation appears.

The warning to escape is important because at the end of history Jerusalem is going to fall to the armies that will be gathered by the Man of Lawlessness.

> *Zechariah 14:2* I will gather all the nations to Jerusalem to fight against it; the city will be captured, the houses ransacked, and the women raped. Half of the city will go into exile, but the rest of the people will not be taken from the city.

This text clearly refers to the end of human history because the coming of the Lord with all his holy ones is described in Zechariah 14:5.

In spite of the obvious references in Matthew and Mark to the abomination that causes desolation and its connection with the return of

Christ, this prophesy was thought by many to have been fulfilled when the Roman armies surrounded Jerusalem and destroyed it in 70 AD. This is because the parallel passage in Luke 21 does refer to the 70 AD destruction. Unlike Matthew and Mark, Luke focuses on the Lord's teaching regarding the years shortly after his crucifixion. In Luke 21:10f, the Lord begins to describe the signs of the end. In verse 12, he says, "But before all this, ..." and goes into a description of persecution occurring shortly after his death. The reference to being delivered to synagogues is significant because the synagogues were a normal source of persecution only prior to Jerusalem's fall. After that, the church was normally persecuted for failing to participate in emperor worship.

Matthew and Luke can be talking about the same event only if the setting up of the abomination that causes desolation by the Man of Lawlessness can be equated with the gathering of armies around Jerusalem in Luke 21. It does not appear that that connection can be made. Jesus' warning in Luke describes an escape after the city has been surrounded by armies. Normally that is the point at which it is too late to escape. In 68 AD the Roman armies did withdraw for a short time after the death of Nero allowing those familiar with Jesus' prophesy to escape. In Matthew and Mark, the abomination that causes desolation comes from Daniel's prophesy and is some symbol or event set up on one wing of the temple in Jerusalem. It is difficult to connect something set up on one wing of the temple with armies surrounding Jerusalem.

Some have felt that the parallel passages must be describing the same event. The abomination that causes desolation from Daniel would in this view be set up in 70 AD. However, it is clear from Daniel 9:26f that this is not true.

Daniel 9:26f After the sixty-two 'sevens', the Anointed One will be cut off and will have nothing. The people of the ruler who will come will destroy the city and the sanctuary. The end will come like a flood: War will continue until the end, and desolations have been decreed. He will confirm a covenant with many for one 'seven'. In the middle of the 'seven' he will put an end to sacrifice and offering. And on a wing of the temple he will set up an abomination that causes desolation, until the end that is decreed is poured out on him.

This passage indicates that there will be a destruction of the city and sanctuary after the Anointed One (Messiah/Christ) is cut off (Daniel 9:26.) That is the destruction of Jerusalem in 70 AD. Later, the Man of Lawlessness, the ruler who will come, sets up the abomination that causes desolation until the end decreed is poured out on him (i.e., his destruction at the return of Christ - Daniel 9:27.)

The abomination that causes desolation has not yet come because the Man of Lawlessness has not yet come. When he comes, he will set up the abomination that causes desolation and gather the nations to surround Jerusalem. It is at the end of history that the Man of Lawlessness will be revealed. At that time the abomination that causes desolation will be set up and Matthew's prophesy "then let those who are in Judea flee to the mountains" will be of great importance. When the abomination that causes desolation is set up, Zechariah 14:2ff will be fulfilled both in the capture of Jerusalem and in the return of Christ.

Alpha and Omega - [Rev. 1:8, 21:6, 22:13] This title is used both of the Lord God Almighty (Rev. 1:8, 21:6) and of Jesus (Rev. 22:13) in the book. That the first two passages describe God Almighty cannot be denied, but there are some who would question whether the third passage describes Jesus. There are several reasons why the passage in Revelation 22 must be seen to use this title to refer to Jesus:

1. The person speaking in the text is coming soon, which would describe Jesus rather than God the Father.

2. The speaker identifies himself as Jesus in verse 16.

3. One of the other titles used in verse 13 (the **First and the Last**) is used of Jesus in Revelation 1:17 and 2:8. In both Revelation 1:17 and 2:8, the person describes himself as one who died and came to life again, a description that can only fit Jesus.

The use of a title is reserved for the one to whom it applies. A title used of God is inappropriate for others to share. No one shares titles like The Almighty, The Lord, the Beginning and the End. However, Jesus is able to share the title, "The First and The Last" with God Almighty. This provides strong evidence for his deity, because he is called by the same title used of God Almighty.

Angels - The terms angel and angels appear eighty-four times in Revelation. In ancient Greek, the word angel can refer to a heavenly messenger, but the meaning of the word derives from angelia - a message, tidings or news - and refers to one who bears a message, a messenger. There is a tendency to translate the Greek word angelos, when it is found in the New Testament, as angel, and normally that is the correct translation. However, there are times when the messenger being described in Scripture is not an heavenly but an earthly messenger. This is particularly true in Revelation 1-3 where several messages are written to the angels of the churches.

Some have asserted that the angels of the seven churches are heavenly messengers who have responsibility for the spiritual oversight of these churches. It is difficult to reconcile this view with the statements, addressed to the angels, which tell the angels such things as;

> *Rev. 2:4* Yet I hold this against you: You have forsaken your first love.

> *Rev. 2:14* Nevertheless, I have a few things against you: You have people there who hold to the teaching of Balaam ...

> *Rev. 3:1f* I know your deeds; you have a reputation of being alive, but you are dead.

These comments are not being directed to heavenly messengers who mystically are going to rejuvenate sick churches, but to the churches themselves which are in need of change. The comments about being dead and forsaking the first love could properly be addressed to the pastors of churches, who would then call the congregation to repentance. Such comments, directed to angels would be as though the churches were reading a letter, addressed to someone else, that was discussing them. The members of the churches are expected to change or be encouraged by reading the message addressed to their church. The idea suggested by some that the churches are reading someone else's mail (namely their angel's) and benefiting from it is not helpful. If the letter were addressed to a heavenly angel, it would suggest that the angel is responsible for the deficiencies and that the angel must take action to change the situation. Nowhere in Scripture can a similar idea be found—that angels are responsible for deficiencies in churches or in the people in churches. Christians are held responsible for their failures and for the failures in their churches throughout Scripture.

In other parts of Revelation the messenger is an angel from God and in a few places the character being described as an angel is Jesus. In Revelation, the term **star** is used to represent an angel. A star was given the key to the shaft of the Abyss and, based on other texts (e.g., Rev. 20:1), the person with the key to the Abyss is Jesus. In some places it is not clear if the angel is God or not. In other places, angels refuse worship, showing that they are angels and not God.

This use of the term angel to describe God is consistent with Old Testament usage where the term "angel of the Lord" sometimes describes appearances of God in a visible form. In Judges 6:22f Gideon expresses fear that he will die because he has seen the angel of the Lord (i.e., God.) The same fear is expressed by Manoah in Judges 13:21f at seeing the angel of the Lord. In Genesis 16:7-13, Hagar calls the angel of the Lord "the God who sees me." In Exodus 3:2-6, the angel of the Lord appeared in the flames of fire of the burning bush to Moses and God called to him from within the bush. In some Old Testament passages the term angel of the Lord is used of an appearance by God, a theophany.

Antichrist - This term does not appear in the book of Revelation. It is used only in I & II John (I John 2:18,22, 4:3, II John 1:7) and is not normally used in the way that the term has been popularized. When the term "the Antichrist" is used in I John 2:22 and II John 1:7, it does not appear that a single individual is in mind.

> *I John 2:22* Who is the liar? It is the man who denies that Jesus is the Christ. Such a man is the antichrist—he denies the Father and the Son.

> *II John 1:7* Many deceivers, who do not acknowledge Jesus Christ as coming in the flesh, have gone out into the world. Any such person is the deceiver and the antichrist.

There is one place where an individual who is coming is called the antichrist.

I John 2:18f Dear children, this is the last hour; and as you have heard that the antichrist is coming, even now many antichrists have come. This is how we know that it is the last hour. They went out from us, but they did not really belong to us. For if they had belonged to us, they would have remained with us; but their going showed that none of them belonged with us.

This text indicates that the antichrist, assuming he follows the pattern of the many antichrists, will come out of the church.

The "Man of Lawlessness" from II Timothy 2:1-12, is the final antichrist mentioned in I John 2:18. He displays counterfeit miracles, signs, and wonders. He sets himself up in opposition to everything called God and is destroyed by the breath of Jesus' mouth and by the splendor of his coming. The Man of Lawlessness is preceded by the secret power of lawlessness that is already at work at the time Paul is writing II Thessalonians (II Thes. 2:7.) Likewise, John speaks of the spirit of the antichrist which is even now already in the world (I John 4:3.) John connects the antichrist and the spirit of the antichrist to a denial of Jesus Christ coming in the flesh (I John 2:22, 4:3, II John 2:7.)

John also asserts that many "antichrists" went out from the church but never belonged to it (I John 2:18.) There is a similar suggestion in Revelation that the antichrist or Man of Lawlessness comes out of the church. The **beast out of the earth** has two horns like a lamb. Horns represent authority and power and the similarity to a **lamb** suggests Christian authority since the lamb is a symbol for Christ. These texts appear to support the idea that just as many antichrists came out of the church, the final antichrist will be a person having authority within the church. They also suggest that the corruption of the church and worship by the antichrist, prophesied in Daniel, will occur through a denial of Jesus Christ.

The activities of the Man of Lawlessness are described in the visions in Daniel 7, 8, 9 and 11. He is also called the beast out of the earth in Revelation 13.

In Daniel 7, the Man of Lawlessness is called a little horn (Daniel 7:8,20f) having eyes like a man and speaking boastfully. He wages war against the saints (oppresses the saints - Daniel 7:25) and is defeating them until the Ancient of Days takes his power away and destroys him completely.

In Daniel 8, he sets himself up to be as great as the Prince of the host (Daniel 8:11), takes away the daily sacrifice and as he prospers, truth is thrown to the ground. Later (Daniel 8:23ff), he is called a stern-faced king, a master of intrigue, strong but not by his own power. This is similar to the description of the beast out of the sea who has the power, throne, and authority of the dragon (Satan - Rev. 13:2.) It is this same authority that the beast out of the earth exercises on behalf of the beast out of the sea (Rev. 13:12.) While the beast out of the sea is presented as a conglomerate of several world powers (he resembles the animals from Daniel 7 that represented world powers), the beast out of the earth is a man who has a man's number. He destroys the mighty men and the holy people (Daniel 8:24) and causes deceit to prosper. Finally, he is destroyed but not by human power (Daniel 8:25.) He is destroyed by the coming of the Lord Jesus Christ (II Thes. 2:8.)

In Daniel 9, the Man of Lawlessness confirms a covenant with many for one 'seven' (Daniel 9:27.) The one 'seven' is the period beginning when he is first revealed and continuing until he is destroyed. His reign does not last exactly seven years but is approximately seven years. His covenant is in opposition to God's covenant with his people, though its precise nature is not defined. In the middle of the 'seven' he puts an end to sacrifice and offering. The interruption of sacrifice and offering in Daniel 9 describes the three and a half days that the church is dead in Revelation 11. The death of the visible church will occur through the denial of some basic and foundational truth related to the person and work of Jesus Christ and will include the corruption of true worship. The Man of Lawlessness will set up the abomination that causes desolation on one wing of the temple and will gather armies from the nations to attack Jerusalem.

In Daniel 11, the Man of Lawlessness is described as a contemptible person who has not been given the honor of royalty (Daniel 11:21.) He seizes a kingdom through intrigue, acts deceitfully, and rises to power with only a few people. His heart is set against the holy covenant (i.e., against the church) and he will vent his fury against the holy covenant (Daniel 11:28-30.) His armed forces desecrate the temple fortress, abolish the daily sacrifice, and set up the abomination that causes desolation. He exalts himself above every god and speaks against the God of gods (Daniel 11:36.) He invades the Beautiful Land (Israel) and he pitches his royal tents between the seas at the beautiful holy mountain (this is the gathering of nations at **Armageddon**.) Then, he comes to his end.

In Revelation 13, the beast out of the earth is the Man of Lawlessness. The **beast out of the sea** resembles the world powers of Babylon, Media/Persia, Greece, and Rome from Daniel 7 and is the secret power of lawlessness (II Thes. 2:7.) The beast out of the earth is a man, having a man's number, who exercises authority of the world powers (i.e., he is an emperor.) He performs great and miraculous signs as is prophesied in II Thessalonians 2:9. It is this beast who with Satan and the false prophet gathers the nations to Armageddon (Rev. 16:13-16.) It is also this beast that is destroyed in Revelation 19:19-21.

Armageddon - [Rev. 16:16] The Hebrew equivalent for this would be Har Megiddo or Mount Megiddo. While there is a plain of Megiddo there is no mountain called Megiddo. It appears that this may be a reference to a fortress or city built on or near the plain of Megiddo that will be the focal point for the gathering of forces by the Man of Lawlessness immediately before the return of Christ. The plain of Megiddo was the scene of several important battles in Israel's history as is recorded in Scripture (Joshua 12, Judges 5, II Kings 9 and II Chronicles 35.)

The gathering of nations to a location in the Holy Land by the **Man of Lawlessness** is foretold in both the Old and New Testaments (Ezekiel 39:2-4, Daniel 11:45, Joel 3:2,9-16, Zeph. 3:8, Zech. 14:2, Luke 21:20, Rev. 16:14-16, 19:19, 20:8f.) The location is variously described as Jerusalem, the mountains of Israel, and the Valley of Jehoshaphat in the Old Testament. It is called Jerusalem and Armageddon in the New Testament. Another possible scenario is that when the **earthquake** from Zechariah 14:3-5 occurs, the plain of Megiddo will be displaced and become a mountain.

Babylon - [Rev. 14:8, 16:19, 17:5, 18:1,2,10,21] Babylon the Great is a symbol in Revelation for Jerusalem. The great **prostitute** bears the title Babylon the Great (Rev. 17:5) and is the **great city** that rules over the kings of the earth (Rev. 17:18.) At first glance it is natural to think that this refers to Rome. However, the great city has already been defined (Rev. 11:8) as the place where their Lord was crucified, so it must be Jerusalem. Additionally, in Babylon was found the blood of the prophets and of the saints (Rev. 18:24.) While Rome might contain the blood of the saints, it could not be described as containing the blood of the Old Testament prophets. However, Jerusalem is known as the city that kills the prophets (Matthew 23:37.)

The prostitute wears the title Babylon the Great on her forehead. Assuming that Babylon is one of her titles, Jerusalem must be Babylon because the prostitute represents Jerusalem. The truth of this is seen from Jeremiah 4 where the symbol of a prostitute dressed in scarlet first appears. In Jeremiah 3 both Israel and Judah are compared with adulterous wives who live as prostitutes.

> *Jeremiah 3:1-3* "If a man divorces his wife and she leaves him and marries another man, should he return to her again? Would not the land be completely defiled? But you have lived as a prostitute with many lovers—would you now return to me?" declares the Lord. "Look up to the barren heights and see. Is there any place where you have not been ravished? By the roadside you sat waiting for lovers, sat like a nomad in the desert. You have defiled the land with your prostitution and wickedness. Therefore the showers have been withheld, and no spring rains have fallen. Yet you have the brazen look of a prostitute; you refuse to blush with shame.

Israel and Judah are like two sisters who are married to God. Both act unfaithfully and their idolatry is like adultery against God.

> *Jeremiah 3:8,9* I gave faithless Israel her certificate of divorce and sent her away because of all her adulteries. Yet I saw that her unfaithful sister Judah had no fear; she also went out and committed adultery. Because Israel's immorality mattered so little to her, she defiled the land and committed adultery with stone and wood.

> *Jeremiah 3:20* "But like a woman unfaithful to her husband, so you have been unfaithful to me, O house of Israel," declares the Lord.

God promises Israel that if she returns and puts away the idols that he will bless her. Judah faces condemnation and destruction because she makes a pretense of returning to God but remains unfaithful. The warning to Judah begins in Jeremiah 4:3. The Lord proclaims judgment against Jerusalem in this prophesy in Jeremiah 4:11,14, and 16. The symbol of Jerusalem as a prostitute in a scarlet dress appears at the end of Jeremiah 4.

> *Jeremiah 4:30-5:1* What are you doing, O devastated one? Why dress yourself in scarlet and put on jewels of gold? Why shade your eyes with paint? You adorn yourself in vain. Your lovers despise you; they seek your life. I hear a cry as of a woman in labor, a groan as of one bearing her first child - the cry of the Daughter of Zion gasping for breath, stretching out her hands and saying, "Alas! I am fainting; my life is given over to murderers." "Go up and down the streets of Jerusalem, look around and consider, search through her squares. If you can find but one person who deals honestly and seeks the truth, I will forgive this city.

If the principle of interpretation called "internal consistency" from section one is accepted, the prostitute and Babylon must be Jerusalem.

Giving Jerusalem the title of Babylon expresses the complete loss of true religion in Jerusalem at the time that John is writing. It is an insult to the "people of God" to have their city, which is supposed to be the city of God, described using the name of a Gentile, idolatrous city. In Babylon was found the blood of all who have been killed on the earth (Rev. 18:24.) Rome as a recent persecutor would not fit this description.

Beast from the Abyss - [Rev. 11:7, 17:8] When the two **olive trees** or **lampstands** (Jewish and Gentile churches) have finished their testimony, the beast from the Abyss will attack, overpower, and kill them (Rev. 11:7.) This character, who in Revelation 11 kills both branches of the church must be Satan. He looks like Satan in Revelation 17 where he is a **scarlet beast** (like the red **dragon** that represents Satan in Revelation 12) having **seven heads** and **ten horns**. The fact that he once was, now is not and yet will come (Rev. 17:8,11) is consistent with the description of Satan who in Revelation 20 is loose, then is thrown into the Abyss for **1000 years** and after that will be set free for a short time. The description of this beast as coming out of the Abyss is consistent with the anticipation that Satan will come from the Abyss after he is released. Satan is the only character in Revelation who is cast into the Abyss, remains there for some predetermined time and then comes forth from the Abyss. If the 1000 years refers to the same timeframe as the **1,260 days** and the **forty-two months** as it appears that it must (see articles below), then the beast from the Abyss can be no one else but Satan.

While the beast from the Abyss is Satan, he accomplishes his work when he is released through the **Man of Lawlessness**. The Man of Lawlessness is empowered by Satan (Rev. 13:2,12) and is described as acting with Satan to gather the nations (Rev. 16:14-16.) Satan will be active and involved, but he will use his representative to do the things attributed to him (e.g., deceiving the nations.)

Beast out of the Earth - [Rev. 13:11-18, 15:2, 16:10,13, 19:19,20] This beast has two horns like a **lamb** but speaks like a **dragon**. The imagery conveys a picture of something or someone whose power (horns symbolize power) appears to be godly and good (like the lamb - Christ), but it reveals its true nature when it speaks like a dragon (it is from Satan.) The two horns like a lamb suggest that the beast out of the earth, who represents the **antichrist** or the **Man of Lawlessness**, exercises Christian authority. It should be expected that the antichrist/Man of Lawlessness would be a renegade Christian because I John 2:19 describes many antichrists coming out of the church as a pattern for the final antichrist.

> *I John 2:18f* Dear children, this is the last hour; and as you have heard the antichrist is coming, even now many antichrists have come. This is how we know it is the last hour. They went out from us, but they did not really belong to us. For if they had belonged to us, they would have remained with us; but their going showed that none of them belonged to us.

The beast from the earth is the same person who is identified in II Thessalonians 2 as the Man of Lawlessness. He is called a little horn in Daniel 7, a stern-faced king in Daniel 8, a ruler who will come in Daniel 9 and he is a king who exalts himself in Daniel 11. He is tied to the **beast out of the sea** because he exercises the authority of the beast out of the sea on his behalf. In the same way, the Man of Lawlessness is tied to the secret power of lawlessness (II Thes. 2:7.) The little horn is tied to the fourth beast that prepares its way (Daniel 7:7), and the king who exalts himself grows in power out of the kingdom of the north. There are several striking similarities between the Man of Lawlessness, the beast out of the earth and the boastful horn or ruler described in Daniel.

The Man of Lawlessness exalts himself claiming to be God (II Thes. 2:4.) His coming will be displayed with counterfeit miracles, signs and wonders to deceive those who are perishing (II Thes. 2:9f.) He is destroyed by the coming of the Lord (II Thes. 2:8.)

The Man of Lawlessness is described in four passages in Daniel as a boastful ruler. In chapter 7, the little horn speaks boastfully (Daniel 7:8) and speaks against the Most High (Daniel 7:25.) He oppresses the saints and tries to change the set times and the laws (Daniel 7:25.) The saints are handed over to him for a time, times, and half a time (Daniel 7:25.) The fourth beast (and thereby the boastful horn) is slain when the court is seated and the **books** are opened (i.e., at the judgment.) After he is slain, he is cast into the blazing fire (Daniel 7:11.)

In chapter 8, the stern-faced king (also called a small horn - Daniel 8:9f) sets himself up to be as great as the Prince of the host (Daniel 8:11.) He will destroy the mighty men and the holy people (Daniel 8:24.) He will cause deceit to prosper and will be destroyed, but not by human power (so it must be by divine power, as in the return of Christ - Daniel 8:25.)

In chapter 9, he puts an end to sacrifice and offering (i.e., he impacts true worship) and he sets up an abomination that causes desolation until the end that is decreed is poured out on him.

In chapter 11, the king who exalts himself says unheard of things against the God of gods (Daniel 11:36.) He will be successful until the time of wrath is completed and he will come to his end with no one to help him (Daniel 11:36,45.) That he is the same character as those in chapters 7 and 8 is clear because his actions are similar. He desecrates the temple fortress, abolishes the daily sacrifice and sets up the abomination that causes desolation (Daniel 11:31, 8:11,13.)

Likewise, the beast out of the earth forces the whole world to worship the first beast. Since the beast out of the earth exercises authority on behalf of the beast out of the sea the world worships him (Rev. 13:12.) He performs great and miraculous signs to deceive the inhabitants on earth (Rev. 13:13f.)

The beast out of the earth is the beast mentioned beginning in Revelation 15:2 and continuing through Revelation 19:20. He gathers armies to oppose God's people, is destroyed by the coming of the Lord, and is cast into the lake of fire. It is clear that the beast out of the earth is being mentioned in Revelation 15:2 where it speaks of those who were victorious over the beast and his image and the number of his name. Only the beast out of the earth has a number associated with his name. Later in chapter 16, the same language is used (the beast and his image) that was used of the beast in Revelation 15:2. This consistency shows that it is the same beast. When darkness is poured on the throne of the beast (Rev. 16:10) it must be the same beast referred to in Revelation 15:2. If the text was describing a different beast than the one last mentioned, there would have to be some indication of the change within the text.

The beast out of the earth causes the beast out of the sea to be worshipped at first, but later he replaces the beast out of the sea with an image. The beast out of the sea (the secret power of lawlessness) is replaced by the beast out of the earth and an image that looks like the beast out of the sea. This occurs because the beast out of the earth, as the Man of Lawlessness, is the completion and personification of that power. The Man of Lawlessness replaces the secret power of lawlessness with an imitation power because he retains all true power. Since the beast out of the sea represents political and governmental power used in opposing the Lord and the gospel, the image as an imitation of the beast out of the sea is an imitation of real power. True power resides with the beast out of the earth once he appears. However, there are others, who appear to wield power but do so under the direction of the Man of Lawlessness. These imitation rulers are likely those referred to in Daniel 9:27 with whom he confirmed a covenant. The Man of Lawlessness appears when the **forty-two months** of the beast out of the sea are completed.

The image that the beast out of the earth orders erected is given breath (i.e., life) so that it can speak and it is able to kill those who refuse to worship it. As an imitation of the beast out of the sea, the image continues to appear with the beast out of the earth, it is worshipped, and eventually it is given the title of **false prophet**.

The mark on the hand or forehead is no more physical than God's mark of his people on their forehead is physical. It represents idolatry and the choice to stand in hostility against God.

The number of this beast is provided for those who will live when the Man of Lawlessness is revealed. The 666 will allow those who know the Scriptures to identify him so they are not misled by his signs and wonders.

Beast out of the Sea - [Rev. 13:1-10] This beast is made up of pieces of the lion, bear, and leopard creatures in Daniel 7, but is in fact the terrible fourth beast that appears after them. He comes up out of the sea just as the four beasts did in Daniel. The beast out of the sea and the fourth beast in Daniel both have **ten horns** which represent ten kings. At the time John is writing, the ten kings have not yet received a kingdom (Rev. 17:12.) They, for one hour (a short time), receive authority as kings along with the beast and agree to give the beast their power to rule (Rev. 17:12f, 17.) The similarity between the two beasts is not accidental. The purpose of the vision in Revelation 13 is to provide additional information regarding the fourth beast in Daniel 7. John's readers need to know about the ten kings and the one who comes after them.

The beast out of the sea exercises authority for **forty-two months**, which is the church age, the same time that the Gentiles trample the holy city (Rev. 11:2.) The beast out of the sea is not a single person or nation. It is national political power, during the Roman empire and in the civilization that grows out of the Roman empire, that actively stands in opposition to truth and the gospel. It continues from the time of the Roman empire until Satan is released from the Abyss. Further, it is what is called by Paul the secret power of lawlessness (II Thes. 2:7.) This political power, by which men jockey for position and authority, is worshipped (Rev. 13:4.) Those who gain power blaspheme against God (Rev. 13:6.) Many who aspire to authority without respect for God become persecutors, making war against the saints and conquering them. This is not the same as Satan's killing of the church in Revelation 11 where the visible church dies (Rev. 11:7.) Rather, it is the overcoming of individual Christians, some through martyrdom and others through repudiation of their faith. The death of believers through persecution looks like a great victory for the beast. However, the faithful are not finished when they die. They will overcome from the grave (Rev. 15:2, 6:9-11.)

At the end of the forty-two months, the beast continues to exist but is supplanted by the culmination of lawlessness—the **Man of Lawlessness**. The power of lawlessness continues to be worshipped at first when the beast out of the earth appears (Rev. 13:12.) But later, all authority is centered in the Man of Lawlessness and only a mockery of national authority remains. For this reason, the image of the beast is created and worshipped in place of the beast out of the sea. The image of the beast out of the sea is given life and the ability to speak and is called the false prophet later in Revelation.

At the time John is writing, the political power described as the beast out of the sea is centralized in Roman emperors who use emperor worship to persecute the church.

Beginning and End - [Rev. 21:6, 22:13] This title is used of God who is seated on the throne in Revelation 21:6, and also of Jesus in Revelation 22:13. See **Alpha and Omega** for an explanation of why the person speaking in the passage in Revelation 22 must be Jesus. The use of this title in Revelation affirms the deity of Jesus Christ.

Black - [Rev. 6:5,12] Black is symbolic of famine and possibly the death that results from famine in Revelation 6:5. The rider of a black horse carries a pair of scales and one of the **four living creatures** describes excessive prices for grain. The black horse presents an image of fear and doom appropriate for the suffering and hopelessness of famine.

The sun turns black in Revelation 6:12 as part of the **extreme language** of the passage. The color is not significant in any symbolic way. The point being made by the text is that the source of daylight ceases to shed light. Black is not symbolic of evil in Revelation. Scarlet or **red** are used to represent symbolically the evil nature of images.

Blue - [Rev. 9:17] It is not where the color blue appears, but where it does not appear that is significant in Revelation. The **prostitute** in Revelation 17 is dressed in purple and scarlet and is glittering with **gold**, precious stones and pearls. The text states that the prostitute is the **great city** (Rev. 17:18) and the great city has been defined in the text as the place where the Lord was crucified (Rev. 11:8.) So the prostitute is Jerusalem. If her dress is compared with the Ephod of Aaron in Exodus 39:8-14 the colors and materials are the same, with three differences. First, the Ephod also is made of **fine linen**, which in Revelation represents the righteous acts of the saints (Rev. 19:8.) Second, the Ephod does not have any pearls on it. The pearls represent the opulence of the prostitute.

Third, the Ephod contains the color blue. Blue cloths were used to cover the ark of the covenant and the furnishings of the Tabernacle (Num. 4:6-12.) Numbers 15:37-40 explains the significance of the color blue.

> *Num. 15:37-40* The Lord said to Moses, "Speak to the Israelites and say to them: 'Throughout the generations to come you are to make tassels on the corners of your garments, with a blue cord on each tassel. You will have these tassels to look at and so you will remember all the commands of the Lord, that you may obey them and not prostitute yourselves by going after the lusts of your own hearts and eyes. Then you will remember to obey all my commands and will be consecrated to your God.'"

The color blue is lacking from the prostitute's garments because it symbolized keeping the commands of the Lord designed to prevent Israel's prostitution through lust of the heart and eyes. Israel has failed to remember and so is a prostitute who does not wear blue.

The colors and materials of the Tabernacle are similar to that of the Ephod and make a similar parallel with the dress of the prostitute.

Book of Life - [Rev. 3:5, 13:8, 17:8, 20:12,15, 21:27] The book of life contains the names of the people of God. This book is first mentioned in Daniel 12:1. It is called the book rather than the **books** to distinguish it from the books that contain a record of the actions to be judged in the final judgment. To be listed in the book of life is to be saved. Anyone whose name is not listed in the book of life is thrown into the lake of fire (Rev. 20:15.)

Books - [Rev. 20:12] There are two sets of books in Revelation that are used to judge mankind. They parallel the two sets of books described in Daniel. Daniel 7:10 describes a court seated and books opened. The content of the books is not provided, but they are clearly used for judgment. Another book in Daniel 12:1 contains the names of all God's people.

In Revelation 20:12, the books which are opened contain a record of what everyone has done. The dead are judged according to what they have done as recorded in the books. Another book, the **book of life**, lists the names of the people of God. If anyone's name is not found in the book of life, he is thrown into the lake of fire.

The nature of this judgment can be seen from other passages.

> *Ezekiel 18:21ff* But if a wicked man turns away from all the sins he
> has committed and keeps all my decrees and does what is just and
> right, he will surely live; he will not die. None of the offenses he
> has committed will be remembered against him. Because of the
> righteous things he has done, he will live. Do I take any pleasure in
> the death of the wicked? declares the Sovereign Lord. Rather, am
> I not pleased when they turn from their ways and live? But if a
> righteous man turns from his righteousness and commits sin and
> does the same detestable things the wicked man does, will he live?
> None of the righteous things he has done will be remembered.
> Because of the unfaithfulness he is guilty of and because of the
> sins he has committed, he will die.

The same language is found in Ezekiel 33:12-16. A righteous man cannot
count on past good behavior to keep him from judgment.

> *Ezekiel 33:13* If I tell the righteous man that he will surely live,
> but then he trusts in his righteousness and does evil, none of the
> righteous things he has done will be remembered; he will die for
> the evil he has done.

A wicked man who changes will be redeemed.

> *Ezekiel 33:14,16* And if I say to the wicked man, 'You will surely die,'
> but he then turns away from his sin and does what is just and
> right ... None of the sins he has committed will be remembered
> against him. He has done what is just and right; he will surely live.

What is significant in Ezekiel's prophesy is the absolute differentiation
between the righteous and the wicked when they are judged. For those
who are disobedient, none of the righteous things they have done will be
remembered. For the penitent, none of the sins they have committed
will be remembered. Therefore, for a repentant man (anyone whose
name is in the book of life), the judgment of his works from the books
will be a judgment of his good works, because no offenses are
remembered against him. For a wicked man (whose name is not in the

book of life), it will be a judgment of his wickedness. None of the righteous things he has done will be remembered.

Bowls - [Rev. 5:8, 15:7, 16:1,2,3,4,8,10,12,17, 17:1, 21:9] Golden bowls hold incense (representing the prayers of the saints - Rev. 5:8) and the wrath of God.

The seven bowls of God's wrath contain the seven last plagues that complete God's wrath. From this, it appears that these are plagues poured out at the end of human history during the time of the reign of the **Man of Lawlessness**. There are a number of reasons to believe this is true. The first bowl causes painful sores to break out on those who have the mark of the beast and who worship his image. The fifth bowl plunges "his kingdom" (i.e., the kingdom of the Man of Lawlessness) into darkness. The sixth and seventh bowls are the gathering of the nations at Armageddon and the final judgment.

These plagues appear to be intensifications of the judgments pronounced by the seven **trumpets** of Revelation 8-11.

The first three plagues involve events that do not require the obvious intervention of God, so there is no comment about how the victims of the plagues refuse to repent. They may not have recognized God's wrath being poured on them. The fourth and fifth plagues are extraordinary and are recognized as God's handiwork. In spite of this, the opponents of God do not repent.

The first **bowl** is poured out on the land, just as the first trumpet caused hail and fire to be cast down to the earth. The impact of the first bowl is not on horticulture. It is assumed that the grass and trees have already been damaged to the point that they can no longer protect humanity from this plague. The bowl causes painful sores which fall only on those who participate in the activities of idolatry, called the **mark of the beast**.

There is a parallel between this passage and the plague that fell on Egypt in Exodus 9:9-11. The passages are similar in that in both God is judging a people who stand in opposition to his people, and in both, those on whom the plague falls do not repent due to hardness of heart. Additionally, there is a similarity in that the people of God are protected from the plague that is poured out on the enemies of God.

Since most of the images in Revelation are symbolic, it would not be reasonable to suggest that this image, in the midst of a section filled with non-literal imagery, is one of the few that is to be taken literally. If it were literal, the sudden appearance of sores, only on non-believers and on all non-believers would certainly be suggestive of the judgment of God. Instead, this plague is thought to be merely an unhappy circumstance by those marked by the beast. The opponents of God do not recognize God's hand in these plagues and refuse to repent until the fourth bowl is poured out.

What is suggested from the first plague is that human health is adversely impacted by the damage that has been done to the trees and vegetation on earth. How the people of God are protected from this plague is not expressed, but it is clear from the text that those marked by the beast are the only ones injured.

The second bowl turns the sea to coagulated blood and every living thing in the sea dies. The second trumpet caused the sea to turn to blood and a third of the living creatures died. This plague is an intensification of the second trumpet.

The plague of turning the Nile to blood is similar to this plague (Exodus 7:17-21), but the Nile is fresh water and this plague is much larger in scope. All of the fish in the Nile died just as they die in this plague. The results of this plague are similar in that just as Pharaoh refused to relent and hardened his heart, in the same way there is no softening of the hearts of those who are injured by this plague.

The oceans being turned to blood suggests death, bloodshed, and ruthlessness. While a comprehensive description of the results of this plague cannot be developed from such a brief passage, the intensification of the judgment proclaimed in the second trumpet does suggest disaster both for the fish of the oceans and for shipping.

The third bowl is poured out on the fresh waters, rivers and springs, and they are turned to blood. This is again an intensification of the judgment proclaimed in the third trumpet. The third trumpet proclaimed the mismanagement of fresh water by fallen humanity such that a third of the fresh water was unusable. The third bowl makes all of the waters unusable.

There is a striking similarity between the turning of the Nile to blood (Exodus 7:17-21), and this third plague. All of the waters were fouled in Egypt so that the people had to dig in the ground to find fresh water that could be used to drink. The third plague is the same except on a larger scale. All running water on the surface of the earth is polluted.

The intensification of the third trumpet suggests an intensification of the repercussions of the third bowl. In the third trumpet some die by drinking the fouled waters, so it would be expected that even more would die from drinking water after the third bowl has been poured out.

In turning the water to blood, God symbolically imposes judgment because humanity must drink the corrupted water (i.e., they must drink blood.) While God is pronouncing judgment on those who have corrupted the fresh water, he simultaneously pronounces judgment on the persecutors of the church by having them drink blood. God declares in Leviticus 17:10-14 that he will set his face against anyone who eats (or drinks) blood and they will be cut off from (his) people. So the impact of godlessness is to be its own judgment because God is in opposition and hostility toward these people who have both ruined the fresh water and shed the blood of the saints and prophets.

The fourth bowl is poured on the sun and the result is a searing heat that is recognized to be the work of God. While the problems with nature that are permitted by God in the first three plagues might not be recognized as the work of God, as a result of this fourth plague the people curse God and refuse to repent. There is an apparent awareness of God's involvement in bringing this plague.

At first glance it might be thought that there is no connection between the fourth trumpet and the fourth bowl. In the fourth trumpet, a third of the heavenly bodies are darkened while in the fourth bowl, the sun scorches people with intense heat. However, if the fourth trumpet represents the mismanagement of the air resulting in air and light pollution as has been proposed, the searing effects of the sun could result from the intensification of the effects of the polluting of the air. The reduction in the ozone layer is an example of how this could happen. That is not to say that God will do it through a thinned ozone layer. While it is sometimes interesting to theorize regarding how this could happen, it must be recognized that such considerations are merely speculation until God causes the event prophesied to occur.

Isaiah 24 contains a prophecy that is similar to the description of the fourth bowl.

Isaiah 24:4-7 The earth dries up and withers, the world languishes and withers, the exalted of the earth languish. The earth is defiled by its people; they have disobeyed the laws, violated the statutes and broken the everlasting covenant. Therefore a curse consumes the earth; its people must bear their guilt. Therefore earth's inhabitants are burned up, and very few are left. The new wine dries up and the vine withers; all the merrymakers groan.

This passage is particularly significant because it is in a section where the final judgment is described (Isaiah 24:21ff) and the scorching of the earth is in response to its defilement by evil men. The time of the beast out of the earth will be the height of lawbreaking and guilt. As a result, God's curse will lay heavily on the earth.

The fifth bowl is poured on the throne of the beast and his kingdom is plunged into darkness. The darkness is not merely dark but is a source of agony (Rev. 16:11.) The intensification of the judgment of the fifth trumpet would be expected to include both darkness and pain. When the Abyss was opened (Rev. 8:2) at the sounding of the fifth trumpet, the sun and sky were darkened by the smoke from the Abyss. The smoke from the Abyss suggests the taste and smell of the judgment to come. The locusts from the Abyss tortured those not having the **seal of God on their foreheads** causing agony (Rev. 9:5.) When the fifth bowl is poured on the throne of the beast out of the earth, his kingdom is plunged into the darkness of the smoke from the Abyss and his followers gnaw their tongues in agony. This represents an intensification of the hopelessness, sin, guilt, conflict, and isolation that belong to fallen man when he is alienated from God. Under the rule of the Man of Lawlessness, the increase in sin and rejection of God will cause an increase in the pain experienced by those who are living out the consequences of their godless practices and their movement away from relationship with God.

The darkness of the fifth bowl is similar to the plague of darkness that fell on Egypt in Exodus 10:21-23. The plague of darkness was a darkness so deep that it could be felt. The result of this plague, which occurred immediately before the final plague on the firstborn, was that Pharaoh suggested that the Israelites could leave if they left their flocks behind. When that offer was rejected, Pharaoh's heart was hardened and he refused to let them go.

The sixth bowl is poured on the river Euphrates and its water is dried up. If the previous images were being interpreted literally, there would be no water in the Euphrates, only blood.

The sixth trumpet describes four **angels** bound at the river Euphrates, who are released to kill a third of mankind. There are two hundred million mounted troops who ride horses that inflict injury both from their heads and from their tails. The description of the warriors is followed by the story of the church that bears witness, is killed, is resurrected, and ascends to heaven in a cloud.

In the sixth bowl, the **dragon**, the **beast out of the earth**, and the **false prophet** gather the nations to **Armageddon** where they will be destroyed by Jesus (Rev. 19:19-21.) The spirits of demons perform miraculous signs (Rev. 16:14) as described in Matthew 24:24, where false Christs and false prophets appear and perform great signs and miracles to deceive. False signs and miracles are also included as marks of the end in II Thessalonians 2:9. Matthew 24:29ff relates that the return of Christ will happen immediately after the distress of those days.

The false prophet appears in Revelation 16:13 for the first time without introduction or interpretation. Since the beast out of the earth always appears with the image he brought to life, it appears that the false prophet is the image of the beast out of the sea that is mentioned at the beginning of this section in Revelation 15:2.

Jesus says that he comes as a thief. This warning is repeated both in Revelation and elsewhere and advises the reader that the return of Christ is unexpected and the people of God must be prepared.

The kings are gathered against the Lord at Armageddon, the precise location of which is unknown. A Valley of Megiddo is known, but Har Megiddo (Mount Megiddo) is not. Mount Megiddo may be a fortress or stronghold near Megiddo or the Valley of Megiddo could become a mountain when the **earthquake** and splitting of the Mount of Olives occurs that is described in Zechariah 14:3-5. This gathering of the nations, by the Man of Lawlessness, to the vicinity of Jerusalem is described in Daniel 11:45, Joel 3:2,9-16, Zephaniah 3:8, and Zechariah 14:3-5,12. It is called the great day of God Almighty which is a variation of the day of the Lord (i.e., the day of judgment.)

The seventh bowl is poured out and the voice from the throne says, "It is done." In Revelation 16:18-21 there is **extreme language** describing destruction and judgment. The seventh bowl is the final judgment of God. This corresponds to the seventh trumpet which asserts that the kingdom of the world has become the kingdom of our Lord and of his Christ and that the time for judging the dead has come.

The earthquake is unlike any since man has been on earth which makes it similar to the earthquake in Zechariah 14:3-5 that splits the Mount of Olives. After that great earthquake, the Lord will come and all his holy ones with him (Zech. 14:5.)

The language of Revelation 16:20 is similar to that in Revelation 6:14, the sixth **seal**, representing the final judgment. Additionally, Revelation 16:18f is similar to Revelation 11:13, at the conclusion of the sixth trumpet, which depicts a severe earthquake that occurs after the people of God have gone up to heaven in a cloud.

Crowns - [Rev. 2:10, 3:11, 4:4,10, 6:2, 9:7, 12:1,3, 13:1, 14:14, 19:12] Crowns symbolize the authority to rule. Both good and evil characters in the book wear crowns. The crowns worn by evil characters represent authority over kingdoms in the world. The crowns promised to saints represent a kingdom received in eternity. Often, more than one crown is worn and the wearing of multiple crowns is designed to indicate rule over more than one kingdom.

In Revelation 4:4,10, **twenty-four elders** are wearing crowns and sitting on twenty-four thrones that surround the central throne where God sits. While other characters in Revelation sometimes wear more than one crown at a time, it appears that the elders are each wearing a single crown. They are ruling in heaven and have been given authority but their authority is in submission to the Lord who sits on the central throne. They lay their crowns before the throne of the Lord who later appears wearing many crowns (Rev. 19:12.)

In Revelation 9:7, the locusts which are released from the Abyss wear crowns. Their crowns represent the desire to rule that is frustrated in fallen man.

In Revelation 12:3 and 13:1, the **dragon** has seven crowns and the **beast out of the sea** has ten crowns. The beast has received his power, throne and great authority from the dragon (Rev. 13:2), so the crowns belonging to the beast out of the sea are for lesser kingdoms than those belonging to the dragon. It is likely that the seven crowns belonging to the dragon represent Satan's claim that the authority and splendor of the kingdoms of the world belong to him (Luke 4:5f.) The seven crowns represent the completeness of his presumed authority. The ten crowns belonging to the beast represent ten wicked rulers from the civilization growing out of the Roman empire.

Usually, images used to represent Jesus wear only a single crown because he is the ruler over creation, but in Revelation 19:12, he wears many crowns as **King of kings and Lord of lords**. The many crowns represent his conquering of the nations through the spread of the gospel.

Day of God Almighty - [Rev. 16:14] This term is similar to the term "day of the Lord" which is used elsewhere in Scripture. See Section One for an extensive discussion of the significance of the day of the Lord and the use of **extreme language** which sometimes accompanies it.

The day of God Almighty, like the day of the Lord, is a day of judgment. The connection of this term with the day of the Lord is strengthened by the imagery of the Lord coming like a thief in verse 15. This parallels the theme of the return of Christ being like a thief in Matthew 24:43 and Luke 12:39. It also parallels the connection between the day of the Lord and his coming like a thief that is found in I Thessalonians 5:2ff and II Peter 3:10.

The great day of God Almighty is the day of final judgment and is followed closely by extreme language (Rev. 16:18) to indicate the devastating impact of the final judgment.

Dragon - [Rev. 12:1,3,4,7,9,13,16,17, 13:1,2,4,11, 16:13, 20:2] The dragon is identified as the devil or Satan (Rev. 12:9, 20:2.) The dragon's tail sweeps a third of the **stars** out of the sky and flings them to earth. Since stars represent **angels**, this is imagery describing the casting of the angels who rebelled with Satan out of heaven (Rev. 12:9.) This is similar to the description of the **Man of Lawlessness** in Daniel 8:10, who, as the representative for Satan is described as having thrown some of the starry host to earth and trampled them.

The dragon wants to devour the child of the **woman clothed with the sun**. This child is Jesus and the images remind the reader of the effort of Satan, through Herod, to kill Jesus. However, the scope of this image is not so narrow. It is a representation of Satan's effort to frustrate Jesus' purpose in coming to earth to die for humanity. The snatching of the child to heaven is an image describing the ascension. The woman clothed with the sun is protected from the dragon for a **time, times, and half a time** also known as **1,260 days**.

The dragon makes war against the saints (Rev. 12:17) and receives worship (Rev. 13:4.) He is bound for **1000 years** in the Abyss and then is released for a short time (Rev. 20:2,3.) With the **beast out of the earth** and the **false prophet** he gathers the nations to Armageddon to be destroyed (Rev. 16:13-16.) At the end of that short time, he is thrown into the lake of fire forever (Rev. 20:7-10.)

Earthquake - [Rev. 6:12, 8:5, 11:13,19, 16:18] While earthquakes are part of extreme language reflecting the judgment of God, the Scriptures clearly teach that there will be a great earthquake at the end when Christ destroys his enemies. A great and violent earthquake is described in Old Testament passages that, within their context, must be a description of the end of human history.

Isaiah 24:18b-23 The floodgates of the heavens are opened, the foundations of the earth shake. The earth is broken up, the earth is split asunder, the earth is thoroughly shaken. The earth reels like a drunkard, it sways like a hut in the wind; so heavy upon it is the guilt of its rebellion that it falls - never to rise again. In that day the Lord will punish the powers in the heavens above and the kings on the earth below. They will be herded together like prisoners bound in a dungeon; they will be shut up in prison and be punished after many days. The moon will be abashed, the sun ashamed; for the Lord Almighty will reign on Mount Zion and in Jerusalem, and before its elders, gloriously.

Ezekiel 38:19 In my zeal and fiery wrath I declare that at that time there shall be a great earthquake in the land of Israel.

Zechariah 14:3-5 Then the Lord will go out and fight against those nations, as he fights in the day of battle. On that day his feet will stand on the Mount of Olives, east of Jerusalem, and the Mount of Olives will be split in two from east to west, forming a great valley, with half the mountain moving north and half moving south. You will flee as you fled from the earthquake in the days of Uzziah king of Judah. Then the Lord my God will come, and all the holy ones with him.

Throughout Revelation, a great earthquake is used in the places where the return of Christ and the final judgment are discussed. The opening of the sixth **seal** (Rev. 6:12) is accompanied by a great earthquake. Its opening is followed by **extreme language** after which all of mankind call on the rocks and mountains to hide them from the wrath of the Lamb.

Following the ascension of the church in Revelation 11:12, there is a severe earthquake that collapses a tenth of Jerusalem and kills seven thousand people (Rev. 11:13.) An earthquake that collapses Jerusalem fits the description of the final earthquake from other texts. In Zechariah 14, the splitting of the Mount of Olives and the reference to fleeing as they did the earthquake in the time of Uzziah, together suggest a major earthquake. The Lord's coming with his holy ones (Zech. 14:5) is the return of Christ. Jesus' statement in Matthew 24:2 that not one stone of the temple will be left on another has not yet been literally fulfilled. It easily could be literally fulfilled by a massive earthquake.

The ascension of the people of God who are told "Come up here." is the rapture at very end of history. The seven thousand who are killed in Revelation 11:13 could easily represent all of humanity who did not ascend but were left behind. If so, the survivors would be those who were taken by the angels in the rapture. They would naturally give glory to the God of heaven because they are his followers. They could properly feel terror at seeing the wrath of God poured out. The images of the ascension and destruction of the godless are followed closely by the seventh trumpet. The seventh **trumpet** proclaims the kingdom of the world has become the kingdom of our Lord and of his Christ, and he will reign forever and ever. After the twenty-four elders announce that the time has come for judging the dead ... and destroying those who destroy the earth, there is an earthquake (Rev. 11:19.)

When the seventh **bowl** is poured out, there is a severe earthquake (Rev. 16:18.) It is so severe that "No earthquake like it has ever occurred since man has been on earth." This passage must be describing the end of human history because the language of "every island fled away and the mountains could not be found" comes from the extreme language of the sixth seal in Revelation 6:14 which represents the final judgment. Additionally, if the seventh bowl has the same meaning as the seventh trumpet as has been asserted, it must refer to the final judgment.

Ephesus - [Rev. 1:11, 2:1] Ephesus is one of the **seven churches** to whom Revelation is addressed. The Ephesian church had taken action to ensure their purity in the face of difficulties like travelling preachers who claimed to be what they were not and heretical groups who did not hold to the truth. However, diligence in remaining pure had been carried to the point that purity had become an end in itself. The church had lost the love for God that had been the motivation for purity at its inception.

Extreme Language - [Rev. 6:12-17, 8:5, 11:13,19, 16:18-21] The description of extreme language, its significance and its biblical background should be read in Section One before attempting to use this definition section to interpret Revelation. Extreme language consists of imagery describing cataclysmic events on earth and in the heavens. This can include heavenly bodies being changed or falling out of heaven, earthquakes, lightning, and destructive hail. Extreme language is used to represent God's judgment on a nation or group of people. Some extreme language can be expected to be fulfilled literally; for example, the severe **earthquake** that is prophesied both in the Old Testament and in Revelation will occur as it is described. Other extreme images from the Old Testament could be literally fulfilled but their literal fulfillment is not necessary. In any event, it can be affirmed that these images represent the judgment of God that will be so devastating for those toward whom it is directed that it will be as though their world had been turned upside down.

Eyes Like Blazing Fire - [Rev. 1:14, 19:12] See "**Face Like the Sun**" for a discussion of the passage in Revelation 1. In Revelation 19, Jesus is the rider on the white horse just as he was the character in Revelation 1. He must be Jesus because his name is the **Word of God**, which is taken from the introduction to Jesus in John 1. Jesus and his army, who are dressed in white linen, defeat the beast and **false prophet** both of whom are cast into the lake of fire.

Face Like the Sun - [Rev. 1:16] This description is similar to that of the man dressed in linen in Daniel 10:6, whose face was like lightning. Other similarities include; a belt of **gold** that is like the sash of gold (Rev. 1:13, Daniel 10:5), his **eyes which are like blazing fire** (Rev. 1:14, Daniel 10:6) and body parts that look like gleaming bronze (Rev. 1:15, Daniel 10:6.) The man in Daniel is not identified, but he does describe events at the very end of history. It appears that he is the same person as the one "like a son of man" who is described in Revelation 1. The one like a son of man, in Revelation 1, is Jesus. This is seen from Revelation 1:18 where he describes himself as the living one, who was dead, and who lives forever and ever. He holds the **keys** to death and Hades, suggesting that he is divine.

False Prophet - [Rev. 16:13, 19:20, 20:10] While the false prophet is first mentioned in Revelation 16:13, the way he is included in that passage suggests that he has appeared before. He is not introduced or described and is included with two other characters who were previously introduced.

The false prophet is always seen with the **beast out of the earth** (Rev. 16:13.) Prior to the appearance of the false prophet, the beast out of the earth appears with the image of the **beast out of the sea** (Rev. 15:2.) It appears that "false prophet" is another name for the image of the beast out of the sea. As discussed above, the false prophet is the illusion of national political power that is maintained after the **Man of Lawlessness** takes power. He allows some to continue to reign and exert power in opposition to the church although they have no independent power and answer in all things to him.

The false prophet participates in gathering the nations to war against God, he is judged at the return of Jesus Christ and he is cast into the lake of fire with the beast out of the earth.

Feet Were Like Bronze - [Rev. 1:15] See "**Face Like the Sun**"

Fine Linen - [Rev. 18:12,16, 19:8,14] In the Old Testament, fine linen is included in the offerings being given for the Tabernacle (Exodus 25:4.) Fine linen was used in the Tabernacle (Exodus 35:6) and in the priestly garments including the Ephod (Exodus 28:5, 39:3.) Fine linen was used in the curtain that separated the Most Holy Place (the Holy of Holies) from the rest of the temple (II Chron. 3:14.) Those who brought the ark of the covenant to Jerusalem wore fine linen as did those who participated in the consecration of Solomon's temple (I Chron. 15:27, II Chron. 5:12.) The wife of noble character in Proverbs 31 wears fine linen. Ezekiel describes Israel as having been dressed in fine linen by God, cared for by

God and then deserting God to engage in prostitution (Ezekiel 16:10,13.)

Fine linen is used in the literal sense in Revelation 18. Merchants that traded with Jerusalem mourn that they cannot sell their cargoes to her any longer.

When it is used allegorically in Revelation 19:8, fine linen represents the righteous acts of the saints. The text states that this fine linen is given to the bride of the Lamb. This reflects the worthlessness of righteous acts unless they are cleansed by the Lord. Righteous acts are only righteous in God's sight when they are motivated by a desire to express love toward him. Isaiah describes Israel's righteousness as filthy rags (Isaiah 64:6.) In the same way, any righteousness that the bride of the Lamb (the church) could offer would have the appearance of filthy rags unless they were cleansed and purified by the Lord. It is for this reason that the bride is given fine linen, bright and clean to wear rather than having the bride buy or make her own fine linen as might have been expected. The dependence of the church on the Lord is so complete that her righteous acts are of value only as they are inspired and empowered by the Holy Spirit.

The armies of God in Revelation 19:14 are riding **white horses** and dressed in fine linen. In a passage describing a gathering for war, the weapons of the army of God are not mentioned. Only their clothing is mentioned. To some extent, this indicates that the power of the army of God is their obedience to the Lord. Primarily, the point being made is that the only power or weapon needed is the strength of the Lord, who is able to overcome without assistance.

It appears that the fine linen which is white and clean could be the same **white robes** as are described earlier in Revelation (chapters 6 and 7) as being worn by those who have come out of the **great tribulation**.

First and Last - [Rev. 1:17, 2:8, 22:13] This title belongs to the Lord God Almighty in the Old Testament.

> *Isaiah 44:6* This is what the Lord says - Israel's King and Redeemer, the Lord Almighty: I am the first and I am the last; apart from me there is no God.

> *Isaiah 48:12f* Listen to me, O Jacob, Israel, whom I have called: I am he; I am the first and I am the last. My own hands laid the

foundations of the earth, and my right hand spread out the heavens; when I summon them, they all stand up together.

In these two passages, the title is applied to the God who is Redeemer and King over Israel and the God who is the Creator of the earth. However, in all three places in Revelation where the term appears, it is a title applied to Jesus. In Revelation 1:17 and 2:8, Jesus clarifies who he is by saying that he was dead and is alive, or came to life again.

The use of a title for Jesus that is used of God Almighty in Isaiah, requires that Jesus be divine. This is reaffirmed when other titles used of God Almighty are combined with the title First and Last and are applied to Jesus in Revelation 22:13. The one who was seated on the throne in Revelation 21:5-7 uses the titles **Alpha and Omega** and **the Beginning and the End** and says that he will be God of him who overcomes (Rev. 21:7.) These titles are again used with the title First and the Last in Revelation 22:13 concerning Jesus. If Jesus uses all three titles in Revelation 22:13 for himself and if God on his throne uses the same titles in Revelation 21:5-7, the use of similar titles must suggest either that they are the same person or persons of equal dignity and authority. Jesus could not properly use these titles unless he were God the Son, the second person of the Trinity.

First Resurrection - [Rev. 20:5,6] The first resurrection is equated with coming to life and reigning with Christ a thousand years. The significance of the millenium can be understood if the term first resurrection is defined. The millenium and the first resurrection are the same thing. For there to be a first resurrection requires a first death. The word resurrection is defined as "the act or fact of coming to life again, rising from the dead." While it may seem natural to think of the first resurrection as a physical resurrection after physical death, the first death described in Scripture is not physical death. The first death in which all humanity shares is the spiritual death of those who are "dead in your transgressions and sins" (Eph. 2:1, Col. 2:13.) The first resurrection is therefore the resurrection to spiritual life.

There are several arguments that support this view. One point in favor of understanding the passage this way is John's description of the people he saw in Revelation 20:4-6. He reports that he saw the souls of those who had been beheaded. If the first resurrection was a bodily resurrection, it would be expected that John would have seen the people (their bodies.) Instead, he sees their souls, suggesting that it is their souls that are coming to life rather than their bodies. This is consistent with passages like John 3:3-8, 5:19-30, and 11:17-27 which speak of being born of the Spirit, being given life by the Son and Jesus' claim to be the resurrection and the life.

> *John 11:25f* Jesus said to her, "I am the resurrection and the life. He who believes in me will live, even though he dies; and whoever lives and believes in me will never die.

It should not be overlooked that John does not define the term first resurrection, as he does the **second death**. He must therefore have assumed that his readers already knew what the first resurrection was. The teaching of the apostles regarding the first resurrection is documented in the gospel of John:

> *John 5:21* For just as the Father raises the dead and gives them life, even so the Son gives life to whom he is pleased to give it.

> *John 5:24* I tell you the truth, whoever hears my word and believes him who sent me has eternal life and will not be condemned; he has crossed over from death to life.

The crossing over from death to life, called rebirth or regeneration, is the first resurrection. It is difficult to believe that John would not define the first resurrection if it was a partial resurrection of some believers found nowhere else in Scripture.

Another argument against the first resurrection being a physical resurrection is the description of who is resurrected. The group resurrected includes some who have been beheaded for Jesus. They have already been martyred. Why should the text give the encouragement that the second death has no power over those who have part in the first resurrection? They already died for Christ. There is no reason for them to fear the second death. It could be assumed that anyone who had died for Christ, particularly those who had been martyred, would not have any concern about the second death. It is more reasonable for the text to encourage those who have new life in Christ with the promise that they will not face the second death. Those who are spiritually resurrected (true believers) will face persecution. When they count the cost they will need to know that suffering now is less costly than suffering the second death.

The first resurrection is the rebirth of a believer through the Spirit to life eternal. This new life, also called regeneration, is available because of the sacrificial death of Jesus Christ.

The term first resurrection suggests additional resurrections. After all, if there were only one resurrection, there would be no reason to speak of a first one. The second resurrection is that which occurs after physical death, where all humanity is raised to face the final judgment (Rev. 20:12f.) This universal resurrection is not called the second resurrection in Revelation because, as a foundational element in the faith, there was nothing new to teach on the topic to the seven churches. The resurrection of all humanity to face judgment is mentioned in Revelation 20, but is not called the second resurrection.

Closely tied to the first and second resurrection are the first and second deaths. The first death is not mentioned in Revelation, but the second death is. Those made alive through Christ have no fear of the second death. They do not worship the beast or his image, neither do they receive his mark, because they are marked in the first resurrection with the **name of God on their foreheads**. The second death is defined as being cast into the lake of fire (Rev. 20:14.) Those who have part in the first resurrection need not fear the second death because it has no power over them (Rev. 20:6.) For this to be true, it is necessary that those participating in the first resurrection be completely assured of salvation. So the first resurrection must be the irrevocable work of the Holy Spirit that makes believers alive in Christ Jesus (regeneration/rebirth.)

If the first resurrection were reversible, it would be possible for the saved to become unsaved. Those who shared in the first resurrection would have reason to fear because the second death would potentially have power over them.

Since the second death has been defined as being cast into the lake of fire, the first death must be physical death. This may seem inconsistent because the first resurrection is a resurrection from spiritual death. The first death follows the first resurrection because spiritual death is assumed as a pre-existing condition in those with a fallen nature. There is no biblical support for children being born spiritually alive and then dying spiritually. In fact, the opposite is observed when David asserts that he was sinful from the time his mother conceived him (Ps. 51:5.) Since this "dead" condition is the natural state, the counting of the deaths in Revelation (first death, second death) begins with the first death that is a change of state (physical death.)

To summarize, believers experience the first resurrection (new life in Christ) before the first death (physical death.) When they die, they come to life in the second resurrection (final judgment.) For those made alive by the Spirit, there is no second death.

Those who do not believe do not experience the first resurrection (regeneration), so they do have reason to fear the second death. They participate in the first death (physical death) and the second resurrection (final judgment.) They have not been made alive in Christ, so their names are not in the book of life and they must face the second death (the lake of fire.)

Forty-Two Months - [Rev. 11:2, 13:5] This symbolic time reference describes the same period as the **1,260 days** and "**time, times, and half a time**" all of which represent a period of three and a half years. [The 1,260 days represent three years of three hundred sixty days (twelve months at thirty days per month equal 1,080 days) plus half a year (one hundred eighty days.) The forty-two months (of thirty days each) are also three and a half years.] These references to time are not intended to be taken literally. The original reference in Daniel to time, times, and half a time is too indefinite to be applied to a literal three and a half years. Instead, the similarity between the three images conveys that they refer to the same period.

The time, times, and half a time imagery comes from Daniel 12:7. In Daniel 12:1 a time of distress is prophesied as is quoted in Matthew 24:21. In Daniel 12:2f a description of the final judgment occurs which is paralleled in Matthew 24:29-31. **Extreme language** is used in Matthew to symbolize the final judgment, followed by the second coming of Christ. Then in Daniel 12:6, a question is asked, "How long will it be before these astonishing things are fulfilled?" The answer in verse 7 is that it will be for a time, times, and half a time, when the power of the holy people has been finally broken. This breaking of the power of the holy people at the end is the same thing as the death of the **lampstands/olive trees/prophets** (church) in Revelation 11.

In Revelation 11:2, the Gentiles will trample the holy city for forty-two months. This directly corresponds to Luke 21:24 which speaks of Jerusalem being trampled by the Gentiles until the times of the Gentiles are fulfilled. In Luke, the mention of the conclusion of the times of the Gentiles is immediately followed by verses 25 and 26 which use extreme language, indicating judgment. Then verse 27 goes on to describe the return of Christ. The Gentiles trample the holy city for forty-two months which is the church age. The **two witnesses** (two olive trees, two lampstands) prophecy for 1,260 days (which is the same period as the forty-two months, the church age or the time of the Gentiles.) At the end of their prophesying they go to heaven in a cloud (Rev. 11:12.) This is followed by a passage of extreme language (Rev. 11:13) and the judgment (Rev. 11:18.)

The forty-two months is the period from the death of Christ until the release of Satan and the revealing of the Man of Lawlessness. This must be true because the forty-two months is the same time as 1,260 days (forty-two thirty day months.) The 1,260 days are identical to the time, times, and half a time (see Rev. 12:6,14.) The 1,260 days covers the period from the time the child of the woman clothed in the sun is snatched up to heaven (Jesus' ascension) until the woman is no longer protected (the death of the church - Rev. 11:7.) The various terms used to represent three and a half years throughout Revelation all refer to the same period.

The second place in which forty-two months is mentioned is in Revelation 13:5 referring to the **beast out of the sea** who exercises his authority for forty-two months. The language from the early part of chapter 13 describes this beast in terms of a world power (the resemblances in verse 2 are taken from Daniel's description of world powers in Daniel 7.) The beast conquers the saints (Rev. 13:7) which shows that it is a persecuting power. The beast out of the sea is the power of lawlessness that ends when Satan is released. The power ends because its culmination, the **Man of Lawlessness** (the beast out of the earth) is revealed. Paul says that the power of lawlessness is already at work when he is writing II Thessalonians (II Thes. 2:7), so it has existed from at least the time of the ascension and will continue until the Man of Lawlessness is revealed (II Thes. 2:8.)

Gog and Magog - [Rev. 20:8] The only place that Gog and Magog are mentioned in Revelation is at Satan's gathering of the nations. The names Gog and Magog are inserted to connect the message to Gog in Ezekiel to the event occurring in Revelation 20.

Ezekiel prophecies against Gog in Ezekiel 38 and 39. Gog's attack on Israel will be after many days and in future years (Ezekiel 38:8.) It will occur when Israel is living in safety and when the cities are unwalled (Ezekiel 38:8, 11.) The attack will be against a people "gathered from many nations to the mountains of Israel, which had long been desolate" (Ezekiel 38:8.) Gog comes at the head of a numerous army called many nations, a great horde, a mighty army, and a cloud that covers the land. (Ezekiel 38:4-6, 9,15f.) Gog is not merely a powerful king who will attack Israel, he is the one God prophesied would come by his servants the prophets (Ezekiel 38:17.) It appears that the prophesies Ezekiel refers to are the destruction of the nations in Joel (830 BC) and Zephaniah (630 BC.) Both books were written prior to Ezekiel which was written (590 BC.)

Joel speaks of an army without number that is like the dawn spreading across the mountains (Joel 1:6, 2:2.) It is an army unlike any that has been seen before. The coming of that army is connected to the day of the Lord.

> *Joel 2:1f* Blow the trumpet in Zion; sound the alarm on my holy hill. Let all who live in the land tremble, for the *day of the Lord* is coming. It is close at hand—a day of darkness and gloom, a day of clouds and blackness. Like dawn spreading across the mountains a large and mighty army comes, such as never was of old nor ever will be in ages to come.

Joel 3 also refers to the gathering of nations to the Valley of Jehoshaphat. The nations come for war (Joel 3:9-12) but God brings them there to be judged (Joel 3:2,12.)

Zephaniah declares that the great day of the Lord is near and then quotes Joel regarding a day of darkness and gloom, a day of clouds and blackness (Zephaniah 1:14f.) The first chapter concludes with the whole world being consumed and the sudden end of all who live on the earth. Similar language reappears in chapter 3 where God assembles the nations and the whole world is consumed.

Gog represents the Man of Lawlessness. He is the leader of the troops that in number are like sand on the seashore (Revelation 20:8.) He and his troops gather to attack Israel but he is the one destroyed. Ezekiel describes a great earthquake, and every man's sword against his brother (Ezekiel 38:19,21.) This judgment on an army attacking Jerusalem is repeated in Zechariah 14:3-5,13. Gog (the Man of Lawlessness) will also face plague, bloodshed, torrents of rain, hailstones, and burning sulphur (Ezekiel 38:22.)

In Revelation, John points back at Ezekiel's prophecy against Gog to clarify that Ezekiel and Revelation 20 are describing the same event. The two passages provide hope to Israel when the Man of Lawlessness gathers a large multi-national army to attack Jerusalem.

Gold - [Rev. 3:18, 4:4, 9:7,20, 14:14, 17:4, 18:12,16, 21:15,18,21] Gold symbolizes wealth, glory, and beauty in Revelation. Sometimes, gold is the wealth accumulated but lost because of the coming of the judgment of God. Often, the gold is heavenly gold (e.g., gold in the new Jerusalem, and golden crowns on the heads of the twenty-four elders.) The goal for the believer is to buy, from God, gold refined in the fire so as to be rich in the world to come (Rev. 3:18.)

Great City, The - [Rev. 11:8, 16:19, 17:18, 18:10,16,18,19,21] The great city is identified in Revelation 11:8 as the place where the Lord of the **two witnesses** was crucified. This clear reference to Jesus' crucifixion requires that the great city be Jerusalem.

There is an identification of **Babylon** the Great (Rev. 16:19, 17:5,18) and the **prostitute** with the great city in Revelation 17:8. The great city, Babylon, and the prostitute dressed in scarlet all represent the same city. While some have wanted to define Babylon and the prostitute as Rome, there are several reasons why they must be symbols for unfaithful Jerusalem.

1. John clearly defines the symbol "the great city" as Jerusalem in Revelation 11. If the meaning of the symbol were to be changed later in the book, for consistency's sake, John would have to provide some clue that the meaning of the symbol had been changed.

2. The clothing worn by the prostitute bears a striking similarity to the materials that made up the Ephod and the Tabernacle. (See the article on the prostitute for an in depth analysis.)

3. The description of how the ten kings hate the prostitute and burn her and eat her flesh is more applicable to the history of Jerusalem than it is to the history of Rome (Rev. 17:16.)

4. The description of the destruction of Babylon "in one hour" (Rev. 18:10, 17, 19) and "in one day" (Rev. 18:8) is consistent with Jerusalem's destruction but not with Rome's.

5. The prostitute is an unfaithful bride, not merely a promiscuous woman. She boasts that she is not a widow, a category that would have no meaning if she had never been married (Rev. 18:7.) Throughout the Old Testament, Israel is portrayed as an unfaithful bride who turns to adultery and prostitution (Hosea 4:12,15.) The book of Hosea is an analogy comparing the unfaithfulness and prostitution of a human bride with the unfaithfulness of Israel. Israel is called a prostitute throughout Scripture, but the term is not used of Rome anywhere in Scripture (e.g., Lev. 17:7, Num. 15:38-40, Hosea 9:1, Jer. 3:1-3.)

6. The symbol of the prostitute dressed in scarlet referring to the city of Jerusalem appears in Jeremiah 4:30. It would be inconsistent to use the imagery of an unfaithful bride and prostitute dressed in scarlet of Jerusalem in Jeremiah 4 and to use it of Rome in Revelation.

7. The description of Babylon having in her the blood of the prophets and saints applies to Jerusalem but not to Rome (Rev. 18:24.) Rome may have killed some saints, but Jesus condemned Jerusalem for having killed the prophets (Matthew 23:37, Luke 11:47ff, 13:34.)

There are different reactions to the fall of the great city (Jerusalem) in Revelation 18 and 19. Some see her destruction and mourn at the loss of a trading partner. The faithful people of God rejoice on observing God's judgment of a corrupt city that killed the saints and the prophets.

Great Tribulation, The - [Rev. 7:14] Those who are in **white robes** have come out of the great tribulation (Rev. 7:13f.) The time of the great tribulation is defined by the groups who are wearing white robes. All of the martyrs in the fifth seal and millions of others in the sixth seal are given white robes to wear.

The King James Version translates Revelation 7:14, "These are they which came out of great tribulation . . . ," which could suggest a group who faced troubles in life. Most modern translations (e.g., the New King James Version, the Revised Standard Version, the New American Standard Version and the New International Version) say, these are they which have come out of the great tribulation. The Greek text contains a repeated definite article (the great the tribulation) which supports the translations by the newer versions. Abbott writes that the repetition of the definite article "adds weight and emphasis to the article." [7] The repeated articles emphasize that the vision is referring to a specific event called the great tribulation.

In Revelation 6 and 7 two groups are given white robes to wear. All of those wearing white robes lived during the great tribulation. When the fifth **seal** is opened (Rev. 6:9ff), white robes are given to all of those who have been slain because of the word of God and their testimony. These are the Christian martyrs. The description appears to include all martyrs who have died prior to John's vision. They are instructed to wait until their number is completed. So this group wearing white robes can be expected ultimately to include all of the martyrs of the church.

In Revelation 7, beginning in verse 9, a group of people wearing white robes is introduced. They are a great multitude that no one could count from every nation, tribe, people, and language. If those who have come out of the great tribulation are all of those in chapters 6 and 7 who are wearing white robes, then the great tribulation must extend through the lifetimes of all martyrs and the millions who are holding palm branches.

The number of people - too many to count - is too great for the tribulation to last only a few years (some have suggested it is seven years or less.) If the great tribulation lasted a short time at the end of human history, millions of Christians from every nation would have to be killed during that period. It is impossible that all of the martyrs wearing white robes could come out of a great tribulation that lasted a few years.

The great tribulation lasts a long time but there is an intensification for a few years at the end of history. The time of the **Man of Lawlessness** lasts for a few years before the return of Christ. It will include persecution and difficulty for the whole church. The time of the Man of Lawlessness will be an intense tribulation but it will not be the entire great tribulation. Imagine telling the Christians burned alive by Nero that they were not facing the great tribulation. The Christians who died in various ways in the Colosseum had no doubt that their death, for the entertainment of the wicked, was part of the great tribulation. The church needs to know that the great tribulation lasts until the end of history so that no one will become discouraged by persecution. Persecution is expected by those living during the great tribulation.

Support for this is found in Revelation 12. The **woman clothed with the sun** is kept safe for **1,260 days** or for a **time, times, and half a time** while Satan makes war against her offspring who obey God's commandments. Satan's war against the saints is the great tribulation.

Additionally, the **beast out of the sea** wars against the saints and conquers them (Rev. 13:7.) He exists during the forty-two months, the time of the Gentiles. This is the same period that the woman clothed with the sun is protected. The warring and conquering by the beast out of the sea is the same as the dragon's making war against those who obey God's commandments and hold to the testimony of Jesus (Rev. 12:17.) It is an attack on individuals through persecution that wounds them but is unable to harm the church of God. All of this calls for patient endurance on the part of the saints (Rev. 13:10, 14:12) who are living through the great tribulation.

Horns - [Rev. 5:6, 9:13, 12:3, 13:1,11, 17:3,7,12,16] Horns represent authority and power in the ancient world and throughout Scripture. Alexander the Great was called "The Horned One." In pagan religions horns represented the strength of gods and men. In Scripture, God is called the horn of salvation (i.e., the power of salvation.) The Psalmist calls on God to exalt his horn (i.e., strength.)

Psalm 18:2 The Lord is my rock, my fortress and my deliverer; my God is my rock, in whom I take refuge. He is my shield and the horn of my salvation.

Psalm 89:17,24 For you are their glory and strength, and by your favor you exalt our horn. My faithful love will be with him, and through my name his horn will be exalted.

Psalm 112:9 He has scattered abroad his gifts to the poor, his righteousness endures forever; his horn will be lifted high in honor.

In Revelation 5:6, the lamb has **seven** horns representing his complete authority over the world. The number seven is a number that represents completeness.

The **dragon** (Satan) has ten horns as do the **beast out of the sea** and the **scarlet beast** on which the **prostitute** sits. While seven horns represent complete authority, the ten horns of Satan represent ten political figures who serve him. The ten horns have their origin in imagery from the book of Daniel, where in the seventh chapter in verses 7, 20, and 24 a fourth beast has ten horns. The interpretation is that the four great beasts are four kingdoms that will rise from the earth (Daniel 7:17) and the ten horns are ten kings (Daniel 7:24.) The four kingdoms that arise after Daniel's vision are Babylon, Media/Persia, Greece, and Rome. The Roman empire (and the civilization that grows out of it) is the fourth kingdom referred to in Daniel's vision. After the ten kings, there is another king who will speak against the Most High, oppress his saints, and try to change the set times and the laws. The saints will be handed over to him for three and a half "times" and then he will be destroyed and the kingdom handed over to the saints forever (Daniel 7:24-27.) He is the **Man of Lawlessness** from II Thessalonians 2 who is revealed at the end, immediately prior to the return of Christ.

John interprets the sign of the ten horns by saying that they are;

Revelation 17:12-14 ten kings who have not yet received a kingdom, but who for one hour will receive authority as kings along with the beast. They have one purpose and will give their power and authority to the beast. They will make war against the Lamb....

The ten kings are rulers after the Roman empire, from the civilization that continues after of the Roman empire, who will war against the saints. That their reigns are short is seen from the fact that they receive authority as kings for only an hour each. These kings hate the prostitute and eat her flesh and burn her (Rev. 17:16.) Since the prostitute is the **great city** which is elsewhere defined as Jerusalem (Rev. 17:18, 11:8), this suggests that these rulers also will be anti-semites and will attack either the city of Jerusalem or the Jews. The ten horns\kings make war against the Lamb but are overcome by him.

In Revelation 12, the dragon (Satan) has ten horns (Rev. 12:3) and the woman clothed with the sun is protected from the dragon for **1,260 days**. This 1,260 day period is the same as forty-two, thirty day months, three and a half years or **time, times, and half a time** (Rev. 12:6,14.) The dragon (and presumably the ten horns) makes war against her offspring during that time (Rev. 12:17.)

In Revelation 13:1, the Beast out of the Sea has ten horns indicating that his authority and activity includes the work of the ten kings described above. He is the power of lawlessness from II Thessalonians 2 who uses the political and military power of the kings to persecute the church and to attack Israel.

In Revelation 17, the scarlet beast has ten horns. The text defines the ten horns as representing ten kings who will act as persecutors of the church and opponents to Israel. The scarlet beast is the **beast out of the Abyss** described in Revelation 11:7 because he "once was, now is not, and will come up out of the Abyss" (Rev. 17:8.)

The **beast out of the earth** has two horns. The horns represent Christian authority because they are the horns of a **lamb**. The lamb is the symbol for Jesus throughout Revelation so horns of a lamb require that he be a Christian religious leader.

Image in Honor of the Beast Wounded by the Sword - [Rev. 13:14,15, 15:2] The **Beast out of the earth** has an image made of the **beast out of the sea** and he gives it life. The image is not the beast out of the sea (which represents godless political authority opposing the gospel—also called the secret power of lawlessness). It is a faint imitation of the former political power that continues to exist after the **Man of Lawlessness** (the beast out of the earth) appears. The image is, like the beast out of the sea, political power in opposition to the gospel. But it has no independent power as it did before the Man of Lawlessness was revealed. All political authority has been turned over to the Man of Lawlessness who allows national political power to continue to exist under his control.

In Revelation 15, those who have been victorious over the beast and his image stand by a sea of glass mixed with fire. The sea of glass is a symbol of judgment representing the lake of fire. From Revelation 13:11-15:2, there is no mention that the beast has been defeated. Those receiving the mark of the beast have been judged in Revelation 14:9-11, but the text does not mention the defeat of the beast and his image. Those who overcome are those who have not received the mark of the beast or worshipped his image. They have not won a military or political victory, they have won by refusing to participate in idolatry (emperor worship in John's time) which would be a denial of their faith. Some have died because of their refusal and others have been injured in other ways, but they have won through their patient endurance.

The image is later called the **false prophet** in the unholy trinity of Revelation 16:13. The Lord destroys the beast out of the earth and the false prophet in Revelation 19:20.

Iron Scepter - [Rev. 2:27, 12:5, 19:15] This image comes from Psalm 2:7-9, which is a Messianic Psalm. It is mentioned in a portion of the Psalm describing the reign of the Son.

> *Psalm 2:7-9* I will proclaim the decree of the Lord:
> He said to me, "You are my Son;
> today I have become your Father.
> Ask of me,
> and I will make the nations your inheritance,
> and the ends of the earth your possession.
> You will rule them with an iron scepter;
> you will dash them to pieces like pottery."

According to Edersheim, [8] Psalm 2:7 is quoted as Messianic in the Talmud along with other passages (Talmudic Tractate Sukkah.) Additionally, the Midrash on Psalm 2:7 uses the passage Messianically.

In Revelation 2:27, the Psalm is quoted as Jesus promises to give the authority to rule to him who overcomes, just as he (Jesus) has received authority from his Father.

In the other two passages, the image joins with other images to identify a character as Jesus. In Revelation 12:5, a woman being opposed by a **red dragon** (Satan) gives birth to a male child who will rule the nations with an iron scepter. The dragon is waiting to devour the child the moment he is born. This is a reference both to Satan's use of Herod who tried to kill Jesus during his infancy and to subsequent efforts by Satan to prevent Jesus from accomplishing his task on the cross.

The passage in Revelation 19, has other images that clarify the identity of the character riding on a white horse. The other images include, **eyes like blazing fire**, his name is the **Word of God**, and on his robe and thigh are written **King of kings and Lord of lords**. This rider, called Faithful and True, is recognized as Jesus by his iron scepter. If there were any question, the other titles applied to the rider on the white horse are also applied to Jesus elsewhere in Scripture.

Key/Keys - [Rev. 1:18, 3:7, 9:1, 20:1] Jesus holds the keys to death and Hades (Rev. 1:18), the key of David (Rev. 3:7), and the key to the Abyss (Rev. 9:1, 20:1.) In Revelation he is the only one who holds any key. The keys he holds represent his control and power over individuals and events. He holds the keys to death and Hades because he was dead and is alive for ever and ever (Rev. 1:18.) He will require death and Hades to give up the dead that are in them (Rev. 20:13.) He will then cast both death and Hades (the residence of the dead) into the **lake of fire** (Rev. 20:14.)

The reference to the key of David comes from Isaiah 22:22;

> I will place on his (Eliakim's) shoulder the key to the house of David; what he opens no one can shut and what he shuts no one can open.

Eliakim was not of the house of David, but found favor in God's sight and so received the key to the house of David. Jesus claims the key as the rightful heir to the house of David. He claims the same right that what he opens no one can shut and what he shuts no one can open. It is with this power and authority that he places an open door before the church in **Philadelphia** that no one can shut.

Only Jesus has the power and authority to hold the key to the Abyss. While Michael the archangel could only say, "The Lord rebuke you" to Satan (Jude 9), the one holding the key to the Abyss throws the **dragon** into it and keeps him there for a predetermined time. At the end of that time Satan does not escape, but is released to go to his final destruction.

King of kings and Lord of lords - [Rev. 17:14, 19:16] This title is applied to Jesus in both places in Revelation where it appears. The Lamb is Lord of lords and King of kings in Revelation 17:14. The rider on the white horse, whose name is the **Word of God**, is King of kings and Lord of lords in Revelation 19:16.

In I Timothy 6:15f, this title is used of "God, the blessed and only Ruler, the King of kings and Lord of lords, who alone is immortal and who lives in unapproachable light, whom no one has seen or can see." It would be inappropriate to use a title applied to God for any other person. So the vision revealed to John must have intended to confirm, through this and other titles, that Jesus is God the Son, the second person of the Trinity.

Some titles are exclusive because they could not apply to any other person (e.g., no one else is Almighty and therefore the title cannot be used of anyone but God.) Other titles are exclusive because of the dignity of the title that has been applied to God. If the title applies to one of God's creatures it is not appropriate to insult God by applying the same title to him. If it is suitable for God, then it is blasphemous to apply it to one of his creatures. In this case, some kings have had the title king of kings attributed to them in Scripture, but no one else is called both King of kings and Lord of lords. Its use with respect to Jesus would be blasphemous if Jesus were not a member of the Godhead.

Lake of Fire - [Rev. 19:20, 20:10,14,15, 21:8] The lake of fire is also called the lake of fiery burning sulphur (Rev. 19:20, 20:10, 21:8.) It is called the **second death** and is the place of torment where those not found in the **book of life** are cast (Rev. 20:10,15.) Into it also are thrown the beast, false prophet, and the devil. They are not cast into the lake of fire to rule it, but as those deserving punishment. The lake of fiery burning sulphur is a graphic image of the suffering to be experienced by those who reject Jesus. The symbol blends the extreme pain of burning with the putrid smell of sulphur. It is a torment that involves violation of all the senses.

Lamb - [Lamb appears more than thirty times in Revelation] The lamb is a symbol representing Jesus Christ. The lamb has triumphed and so is able to open the seven **seals** on the scroll in Revelation 6-8. The lamb is given the titles, **Lion of the tribe of Judah**, **Root of David** (Rev. 5:5) and **Lord of lords and King of kings** (Rev. 17:14.)

If the description of the lamb were to be taken literally, his appearance would be quite unusual. He has seven horns and seven eyes (Rev. 5:6) which are the seven spirits of God. The seven spirits of God, which is better translated the sevenfold Spirit of God, represent the fullness of the Holy Spirit. Horns represent power and authority throughout Scripture. The seven horns represent complete power and authority since the number seven represents completeness. The seven eyes symbolize the Spirit and the lamb who are all-seeing and by implication omniscient. The lamb has the fullness of the Spirit. This suggests a very close relationship between God the Son and God the Holy Spirit.

The power of the blood of the lamb is an important theme in Revelation. The lamb is worthy to open the seals on the scroll because he purchased men for God with his blood (Rev. 5:9.) The robes of those who have come out of the great tribulation have been made white in the blood of the lamb (Rev. 7:14.) Believers overcome Satan by the blood of the lamb, by the word of their testimony and by not loving their lives so much as to shrink from death (Rev. 12:11.)

Those unprepared to face the final judgment call on the mountains, and rocks to hide them from the wrath of the lamb (Rev. 6:16.) This image is in sharp contrast with the image of Jesus proposed by some. The people of the earth are not hiding from a bland, all accepting, meek and mild Lord.

The **book of life** lists all the redeemed. It belongs to the lamb (Rev. 13:8, 21:27.) This book is important because anyone whose name is not found written in the book of life is thrown into the lake of fire (Rev. 20:15.)

The ultimate goal of human history is to attend the wedding of the lamb. The bride of the lamb is the holy city, Jerusalem, coming down out of heaven from God (Rev. 21:9.) The lamb is not marrying buildings and streets. The life of the city is its people. Everyone invited to the wedding is given fine linen to wear representing the righteous acts of the saints (Rev. 19:7f.) On the foundations of holy Jerusalem are the names of the twelve apostles of the lamb (Rev. 21:14.)

In holy Jerusalem there is no temple because God Almighty and the lamb are its temple (Rev. 21:22.) Such a connection between God and the lamb would be blasphemous if the lamb did not share in divinity. The city receives light from the glory of God and the lamb is its lamp (Rev. 21:23.) Again, the connection between the lamb as the source of light and the glory of God as the giver of light suggests that the lamb is divine.

The lamb is only one symbol representing Jesus. He is also described as an **angel**, a **star**, and as a conquering king in Revelation. The image of the lamb emphasizes the sacrificial nature of Jesus' work and the primary importance of his death on the cross. However, he is not weak or powerless. He is the lamb who is the Lion of Judah, the Lord of lords and King of kings, and the judge whose wrath is feared.

Lamps - [Rev. 4:5, 18:23, 21:23, 22:5] Lamps represent the Spirit(s) of God (Rev. 4:5.) Some translations speak of the seven spirits of God. Such a translation is questionable because nowhere else in Scripture is there more than one Spirit of God mentioned. It is preferable to translate the seven spirits as the sevenfold Spirit (as does the NIV footnote.) The sevenfold Spirit is a term used to describe the completeness of the presence of the Holy Spirit at the throne of God (Rev. 4:5.) It also is used of Jesus who sends the Spirit (John 16:7) as a reflection of the fullness of the Spirit he possesses (Rev. 3:1.) Jesus is presented to Sardis in this way because they are nearly dead and need the fullness of the Spirit.

The connection between the lamps and the **lampstands** cannot be neglected. The purpose of lampstands is to hold lamps so that they can spread light. The lampstands (churches/**witnesses**) are only repositories of the lamps (spirit.) The spirit dwells in the church.

In Revelation 18:23, 21:23 and 22:5, lamp is used in the singular and is meant to be taken literally.

Lampstands - [Rev. 1:12,13,20, 2:1,5, 11:4] Lampstands are churches. There are seven golden lampstands in Revelation 1 which are defined (Rev. 1:20) as the seven churches to whom the letter of Revelation has been written. In Revelation 11, there are two lampstands which are identified as two **witnesses** (Rev. 11:3) and two **olive trees** (Rev. 11:4.) The two lampstands stand for the Jewish and Gentile churches. (See the discussion of olive trees below for an explanation of why this is true.)

Laodicea - [Rev. 1:11, 3:14] This is one of the **seven churches** to whom the book of Revelation was addressed. Laodicea had received a letter from Paul that is mentioned in Colossians 4:16. Laodicea was a wealthy city known for their banking, industry, and a medical school that produced a well-known eye salve. The church had been corrupted by their wealth and comfort. They suffered from self-satisfaction. Jesus' warning to this church is colorful in that he suggests that their current condition could cause him to spit them out. As an alternative, he knocks on a door to invite the believers to a more intimate relationship of love with him.

Lion of Judah - [Rev. 5:5] The term Lion of Judah comes from Genesis 49:9-12 as Jacob blessed his sons. Of particular interest are verses 9 and 10 where Jacob promises:

> You are a lion's cub, O Judah;
> You return from the prey, my son.
> Like a lion he crouches and lies down,
> like a lioness - who dares to rouse him?
> The scepter will not depart from Judah,
> nor the ruler's staff from between his feet,
> until he comes to whom it belongs
> and the obedience of nations is his.

This promise of a certain one who will rule the nations is clearly Messianic and points to Jesus who in Revelation 5:5 has triumphed. His victory, accomplished through his death, fulfills the prophecy of Jacob and results in his glory, praise, and honor (Rev. 5:9-14.)

Living Creatures - [Rev. 4:6,8,9, 5:6,8,11,14, 6:1,6, 7:11, 14:3, 15:7, 19:4] These creatures are similar in some of their characteristics to the living creatures found in Ezekiel 1, and Ezekiel 10, and in other attributes they imitate the seraphs in Isaiah 6. They represent a blending of both cherubim (Ezekiel) and seraphim (Isaiah) into a unified group of four who stand in the presence of God. The seraphs in Isaiah fly above God calling out his praise (Isaiah 6:2.) The cherubim are always found below God. The glory of the Lord rises from above the cherubim (Ezekiel 10:4,19.) In many places in the Old Testament God is called the Lord Almighty who is enthroned between the cherubim (I Samuel 4:4, II Samuel 6:2, II Kings 19:15, Isaiah 37:16.) This is because his presence dwells between the cherubim on the cover of the ark of the Covenant. Cherubim were placed at the entrance to the garden of Eden to turn away Adam and Eve (Genesis 3:24.) Cherubim are associated with the power and glory of God. David praises God the deliverer in a song that describes the Lord as flying on cherubim (II Samuel 22:11.)

The four living creatures are similar to the four living creatures in Ezekiel 1 in that there are four of them, and they have the faces of a man, a lion, an ox, and an eagle. Ezekiel 10 describes the same creatures using similar terminology but additional details are provided and their appearance changes.

> *Ezekiel 10:14-15* Each of the cherubim had four faces: One face was that of a cherub, the second the face of a man, the third the face of a lion, and the fourth the face of an eagle. Then the cherubim rose upward. These were the living creatures I had seen by the Kebar river.

> *Ezekiel 10:20* These were the living creatures I had seen beneath the God of Israel by the Kebar river, and I realized that they were cherubim.

The cherubim in Ezekiel 10 do not have the face of an ox but replace that face with the face of a cherub. Yet Ezekiel says that they are the same creatures he saw in chapter one. The cherubim in Ezekiel 10 are completely covered with eyes as are the four living creatures in Revelation (Rev. 4:6-8.) Each creature has four faces and four wings, while in Revelation, the creatures have only one face per creature and have six wings. In Isaiah, the seraphs have six wings and the message they call to one another is partially quoted in the words of the creatures in Revelation, "Holy, holy, holy is the Lord Almighty." Isaiah heard them say the whole world is full of his glory, which is consistent with the Lord he sees, high and exalted. John hears them praising the God who was, and is, and is to come, the eternal God who reigns over the earth throughout the ages.

The four living creatures surround God's throne and praise him. They also speak for God at critical points such as when the riders are called forth at the opening of the first four **seals**. One of the creatures gives the seven golden **bowls** filled with the wrath of God to the seven **angels** who will pour them on the earth. The four creatures affirm the glory, power, and holiness of God and of the **lamb**, and act as worship leaders in some contexts.

Man of Lawlessness - See **Antichrist** above.

Mark of the Beast - [Rev. 13:16,17, 14:9, 16:2, 19:20] The mark of the beast is a symbolic description of the practice of idolatry. The symbol is derived from the Old Testament description of the Passover. When the people observed the Passover they were to eat certain foods and hold a festival. Moses required of the people the following:

> *Exodus 13:8,9* On that day tell your son, 'I do this because of what the Lord did for me when I came out or Egypt.' This observance will be for you like a sign on your hand and a reminder on your forehead that the law of the Lord is to be on your lips. For the Lord brought you out of Egypt with his mighty hand.

Similar language appears in Exodus 13:16. The observance of the ceremonies commanded by the Lord are like signs on the hand and forehead. It should be noted that they are not literally signs or marks on the hand and forehead. These observances remind Israel of God's faithfulness throughout history and are used as reminders to Israel of the nature of the God they serve. Similarly, the mark of the beast is symbolic of the ceremonies of those committed to opposition to God, who through their observances keep their opposition where it can be seen and not forgotten.

The mark of the beast is not a physical mark that will be required during some period in history, such as during a seven year tribulation. Theories that suggest physical marking during a brief tribulation period following a rapture will have trouble not only with the biblical background passages but also with Revelation 14:9-13 where the destruction of those who receive the mark in verses 9-11 is followed by:

> This calls for patient endurance on the part of the saints who obey God's commandments and remain faithful to Jesus.

Why would the destruction of those having the mark of the beast call for patient endurance on the part of the saints? Patient endurance is required because the saints are not removed from earth prior to the beast's marking of his people. They are present, are marked with the Father's name on their foreheads (non-physically, Rev. 14:1) and are standing against those having the (non-physical) mark of the beast throughout Christian history.

The mark of the beast is the failure to observe those ceremonies and practices that remind of God's faithfulness. It includes the replacement of God's ceremonies with pagan or imitation ceremonies and practices designed to express the elevation of human authority and rejection of God. This is the reason that those marked are not viewed in Revelation as unwitting pawns in the battle between Satan and the Lord, but as opponents to be destroyed. Those receiving the mark of the beast are the objects of God's wrath (Rev. 14:9-11.) They are cursed by having ugly and painful sores when the first of God's **bowls** of wrath (Rev. 16:2) is poured out. In contrast, those who refuse to worship the image of the beast and who do not accept the mark of the beast have the mark of the Lord (Rev. 14:1.) The **beast out of the sea** will wage war against the saints and will conquer them (Rev. 13:7.) Everyone whose name is not written in the **book of life** will worship the beast out of the sea (Rev. 13:8.) However, the saints must continue to be faithful in spite of opposition and apparent defeat because the Lamb will overcome and with him will be his faithful followers (Rev. 17:14.)

Millennium - See **1000 Years**

Morning Star - [Rev. 2:28, 22:16] Jesus identifies himself as the Morning Star (Rev. 22:16) which clarifies the reference to the morning star in Revelation 2:28. Jesus promises that he will give the morning star to him who overcomes. This is a promise that Jesus and his blessings will belong to the one who overcomes. There is a reference to the morning star in II Peter 1:19 as Peter describes the glory of the transfigured Christ in verses 16-18. Peter asserts that the words of the prophets are to be given careful attention like a light shining in a dark place until "the day" dawns. "The day" is elsewhere used (also "that day," "the day of the Lord," and "**the day of God Almighty**") of the day of judgment (see Section One in this book on the Day of the Lord.) The morning star "rising in your hearts" after "the day" is a reference to the return of Christ.

Mystery of God - [Rev. 10:7] The mystery of God is defined in Romans, Colossians, and Ephesians. The clearest statement of this mystery is found in Ephesians 3:3-9, which can be summarized as follows:

The mystery of Christ was not made known to men in other generations as it has now been revealed to God's holy apostles and prophets. This mystery is that through the gospel, the Gentiles are heirs together with Israel, members together of one body and sharers together in the promise in Christ Jesus.

Other passages which contain a similar emphasis include;

Romans 16:25f Now to him who is able to establish you by my gospel and the proclamation of Jesus Christ, according to the revelation of the mystery hidden for long ages past but now revealed and made known through the prophetic writings by the command of the eternal God, so *that all nations might believe* and obey him.

Colossians 1:26f ... the mystery that has been kept hidden for ages and generations, but is now disclosed to the saints. To them *God has chosen to make known among the Gentiles* the glorious riches of this mystery, which is Christ in you, the hope of glory.

Ephesians 1:9 And he made known to us the mystery of his will according to his good pleasure, which he purposed in Christ, to be put into effect when the times will have reached their fulfillment —to bring all things in heaven and on earth together under one head, even Christ.

Based on the passages above, the mystery of God must be the inclusion of the Gentiles with Israel as co-heirs under the headship of Christ. Since the passages above explain that this mystery has already been revealed and the Gentiles are heirs with Israel, the seventh **trumpet** is imminent.

Revelation 10:7 But in the days when the seventh angel is about to sound his trumpet, the mystery of God will be accomplished, just as he announced to his servants the prophets.

This text suggests that since the time of the early church, the seventh angel has been about to sound his trumpet. The hope that Christ's return could be at any time is consistent with the language used throughout Scripture which promises that the return of Christ is imminent. When the seventh angel sounds his trumpet Christ will reign and judge the dead (Rev. 11:15,18.)

Name of God on their Foreheads - [Rev. 14:1, 22:4] In contrast to those who have the mark of the beast are those who have been redeemed. They bear the mark of the name of the Lamb and the name of the Father on their foreheads (Rev. 14:1.) This marking is not a physical marking any more than the mark of the beast was a physical marking. It is rather an invisible mark of God to show those who belong to him and who remain under his protection. A similar mark is observed in Ezekiel 9:4 where God orders a man in linen to mark the foreheads of those who grieve over the detestable things being done in Israel. Anyone who is not marked is to be killed without pity.

In Revelation 7:3-8, **144,000** are sealed by the placing of a seal on the foreheads of those who are the servants of the Lord. In Revelation 9:4, locust/scorpions torment those people who do not have the seal of God on their foreheads. In Revelation, the choice is not will you receive a mark, but which mark will you receive. One must be marked by the beast or by the Father.

Nicolaitans - [Rev. 2:6,15] This heretical group is not known outside of the places where it is mentioned in Revelation and as a result, little is known of their beliefs. The Greek text in Revelation 2:14f is constructed to equate the teaching of Balaam and the teaching of the Nicolaitans. The comparison clarifies that the Nicolaitans taught that believers could eat food devoted to an idol and commit sexual immorality. From this it appears that the beliefs of the Nicolaitans were similar to some Gnostics who held that the spirit was pure but all matter, including the body, was corrupt. Since the body was corrupt, actions affecting the body, like sexual immorality, were irrelevant. Eating food devoted to an idol at a meal devoted to a false god could be allowed because idols are nothing.

These practices were tempting because they allowed Christians to participate in activities that most in their society considered normal and let them comfortably relate to unbelievers. It allowed Christians to get into organizations that could improve their business connections. The problem with these accommodations was that Christians must stand out from those who do not share their faith. Something about Christianity must be significantly different from other faiths if it is offered as the true faith rather than just another style of religion. The difference required by God is that Christians will not accept idols nor will they participate in sexual immorality, because these things are prohibited in Scripture.

The Ephesians are commended for hating the practices of the Nicolaitans and Jesus says that he hates those practices also. The church in Pergamum is criticized for tolerating those in their church who are Nicolaitans.

Offspring of David - [Rev. 22:16] This is a reference to Jesus' place as the son of David, the ruler in David's line who was to rule the world. It is prophesied (Isaiah 11) that the root of Jesse (David's father) will gather the nations to himself and reclaim the scattered people of Israel. It was promised to Mary (Luke 1:32f) that Jesus would have the throne of his father David and that he would reign forever. Jesus was repeatedly called the Son of David during his life (e.g., Matthew 9:27, Mark 10:47f) and it was understood that the son of David was the Messiah (Matthew 12:22ff.) Jesus also demonstrated that the Messiah is prophesied to be both David's son and his Lord in Psalm 110 (Matthew 22:41-45.)

Olive Trees - [Rev. 11:4] There are two olive trees which are also called **lampstands** and **prophets**. Since they are lampstands and lampstands represent churches throughout Revelation, it is clear that they are churches. In Zechariah 4, two olive trees are called "the two who are anointed to serve the Lord of all the earth." The identity of the olive trees is clarified in Romans 11:17-24 where the Gentiles, called a wild olive shoot, have been grafted on to the domestic olive root (Israel.) The Gentiles are not to boast because Israel, the natural olive tree, can be grafted back into their own olive tree. So, while the two lampstands clarify that these are two churches, the two olive trees clarify which two churches, the Jewish and Gentile branches of the Christian church.

Outer Court of the Gentiles - [Rev. 11:2] The outer court of the temple has been given to the Gentiles for **forty-two months**. This is the same period during which the two **witnesses** for **1,260 days** bear witness to Jesus Christ. In Romans 11:25, Paul describes the partial hardening of Israel as lasting until the full number of the Gentiles has come in. The dominance of the Gentiles that continues during Israel's hardening is reflected in the giving of the outer court to the Gentiles. Because it is given to them for forty-two months, which is the same period that the two churches are bearing witness, it appears that the dominance of the Gentile church continues until the death of both churches. The churches are killed by the **Beast from the Abyss** (Satan) after his release following the **1000 years** and they lie dead for **three and a half days** (figurative.) They are then resurrected, indicating that the visible church experiences revival. Since Israel is no longer hardened, it participates substantially in the revival. It is for this reason that the **Man of Lawlessness** surrounds Jerusalem at the end, threatening to destroy her. When things are looking most grim, Christ returns and the final judgment occurs.

Palm Branches - [Rev. 7:9] Palm branches were a sign of national victory. Cicero describes a great conqueror as a man of many palms. In Judaism, palms appeared on coins during the second Maccabean rebellion. Palms were carried into Jerusalem and into the temple when they were recaptured. The waving of palms was the welcome for a king. Jesus was welcomed into Jerusalem with palms and the people sang songs expressing hope for national victory by calling him the Son of David and the king of Israel.

In Revelation the meaning of the palm branches is the same. The sixth **seal** in Revelation 6 has concluded with the judgment of God. God has conquered and his people congregated in Revelation 7:9 are holding palm branches symbolizing national victory (of the people of God.) They wave the palm branches for the King of kings.

Pergamum - [Rev. 1:11, 2:12] This is one of the seven churches to whom the book of Revelation is addressed. Pergamum was a center for idolatry for several religious philosophies. It was a center for emperor worship and had a temple devoted to Augustus. It also had an altar for Zeus, a temple for Diana, and it was the center of worship for the serpent god of healing, Asclepios.

In such a difficult place, the church managed to endure even after one of their number was martyred. Unfortunately, they permitted some who held to the teaching of the **Nicolaitans** to be members within the church. They are to repent from this permissiveness so that God will not discipline the church and those holding to this error.

Philadelphia - [Rev. 1:11, 3:7] This is one of the **seven churches** to whom the book of Revelation is addressed. Philadelphia was located on a main geological fault line and so experienced frequent **earthquakes**. The city was named Philadelphia, which means brotherly love, not because of the character of its citizens but after King Attalus Philadelphus who reigned from 159 to 138 BC. A false rumor that his brother Eumenes II had been assassinated caused Attalus to accept the crown. When his brother returned safely from Greece, Attalus abdicated in favor of his brother. It is also reported that Rome encouraged Attalus to overthrow his brother and he refused. For these acts of faithfulness, Attalus was given the title Philadelphus, "lover of his brother." Philadelphia is a weak yet faithful church, and so will be protected from the persecutions striking some of the other churches to whom this letter is addressed.

Prophet - [Rev. 16:13, 19:20, 20:10] The term 'prophet' in the singular is used in Revelation only of the **false prophet** who is destroyed at the coming of the Lord.

Prophets - [Rev. 10:7, 11:10,18, 16:6, 18:20,24, 22:6,9] In every place but one, this term refers to the prophets of the Old and New Testaments who served the Lord and sometimes were killed. The exception is in Revelation 11:10 where the two prophets are **olive trees** and **lampstands**. These symbols clearly identify the prophets as churches and specifically as the Jewish and Gentile churches throughout the time of the Gentiles. The churches are called prophets because they proclaim the gospel of Jesus Christ. Their testimony will be completed when the gospel has been proclaimed in all the world (Matthew 24:14.)

Prostitute - [Rev. 17:1,15,16, 19:2] The prostitute is identified as the **great city** (Rev. 17:18) that rules over the kings of the earth and as **Babylon** (Rev. 17:5.) There is a tendency to think that the prostitute represents Rome. Rome was the great world power when Revelation was written, and the woman sits on a beast having seven heads that represent the seven hills of Rome. However, the great city is elsewhere identified as the place where the Lord was crucified (Rev. 11:8.)

The prostitute is an unfaithful bride who sells her favors. It is as a bride that she speaks in Revelation 18:7:

> In her heart she boasts, 'I sit as a queen; I am not a widow, and I will never mourn.'

The assertion that she is not a widow would be meaningless unless she was married. This is not true of Rome which is not the bride of the Lord but it is true of Israel. There are several places in the Old Testament where Israel is compared to an unfaithful bride who is a prostitute because of her unfaithfulness toward God. The best known examples are in Hosea (Hosea 1:2, 3:1, 4:12,15,18, 5:3, 6:10, 9:1) as Hosea lives with an unfaithful wife. She represents the unfaithfulness of Israel toward God. But this theme is also found elsewhere such as in Numbers 15:37-40: Israel is to remember the commands of God and not prostitute themselves.

Israel's prostitution involves the exchanging of devotion to the Lord for devotion to trade, commerce, and wealth. The text describes the prostitute as committing adultery with the kings of the earth (Rev. 18:9) and she is mourned by the merchants and sea captains (Rev. 18:11,17.) This idea of prostitution through trade is found in Isaiah where it is applied to Tyre.

> *Isaiah 23:17* At the end of seventy years, the Lord will deal with Tyre. She will return to her hire as a prostitute and will ply her trade with all the kingdoms on the face of the earth.

Tyre is a prostitute because she will do anything for money. While Rome could potentially fit this description, the great city has already been defined as Jerusalem (Rev. 11:8.) Additionally, there are several other reasons to believe she is Jerusalem.

The clothing the prostitute wears suggests a connection with Jerusalem. A comparison of her dress with the ephod of Aaron in Exodus 39:8-14 reveals a remarkable similarity. The ephod is made of gold, blue, purple and scarlet yarn, and of finely twisted linen. On it are mounted gold and precious stones. The tabernacle in Exodus 26:1 also is made of the same colors and materials. There are some dissimilarities, but these are for a purpose. The prostitute does not wear linen. In Revelation 19:8, fine linen represents the righteous acts of the saints. Since the prostitute behaves wickedly, she has no right to wear linen.

The prostitute does not have any blue in her clothes. In Numbers 4, the most holy things from the tabernacle including the ark of the covenant were covered with blue cloths. In Numbers 15:38-40 the significance of the color blue appears to be that of consecration and holiness:

> Speak to the Israelites and say to them: 'Throughout the generations to come you are to make tassels on the corners of your garments, with a blue cord on each tassel. You will have these tassels to look at and so you will remember all the commands of the Lord, that you may obey them and not *prostitute* yourselves by going after the lusts of your own hearts and eyes. Then you will remember to obey all my commands and will be consecrated to your God.

The prostitute is wearing pearls which do not appear on the ephod or the tabernacle. This is a sign of the wealth that the prostitute has received for her unfaithfulness.

The most compelling evidence to prove that the prostitute is Jerusalem is found in Jeremiah 4 where the same symbol, a prostitute dressed in scarlet, represents Jerusalem. Both Israel and Judah are compared to adulterous wives who live as prostitutes in Jeremiah 3.

> *Jeremiah 3:1-3* "If a man divorces his wife and she leaves him and marries another man, should he return to her again? Would not the land be completely defiled? But you have lived as a prostitute with many lovers - would you now return to me?" declares the Lord. "Look up to the barren heights and see. Is there any place where you have not been ravished? By the roadside you sat waiting for lovers, sat like a nomad in the desert. You have defiled the land with your prostitution and wickedness. Therefore the showers have been withheld, and no spring rains have fallen. Yet you have the brazen look of a prostitute; you refuse to blush with shame.

Israel and Judah are like two sisters who are married to God. Both act unfaithfully and their idolatry is like adultery against God.

Jeremiah 3:8,9 I gave faithless Israel her certificate of divorce and sent her away because of all her adulteries. Yet I saw that her unfaithful sister Judah had no fear; she also went out and committed adultery. Because Israel's immorality mattered so little to her, she defiled the land and committed adultery with stone and wood.

Jeremiah 3:20 "But like a woman unfaithful to her husband, so you have been unfaithful to me, O house of Israel," declares the Lord.

In Jeremiah 4:3 the prophecy moves on to discuss the judgment of Judah. A powerful army will come against her from the north. The Lord proclaims judgment against Jerusalem in this prophecy in Jeremiah 4:11,14, and 16. The depiction of Jerusalem as a prostitute in a scarlet dress appears at the end of Jeremiah 4.

Jeremiah 4:30-5:1 What are you doing, O devastated one? Why dress yourself in scarlet and put on jewels of gold? Why shade your eyes with paint? You adorn yourself in vain. Your lovers despise you; they seek your life. I hear a cry as of a woman in labor, a groan as of one bearing her first child - the cry of the Daughter of Zion gasping for breath, stretching out her hands and saying, "Alas! I am fainting; my life is given over to murderers." "Go up and down the streets of Jerusalem, look around and consider, search through her squares. If you can find but one person who deals honestly and seeks the truth, I will forgive this city.

The principle of interpretation called "internal consistency" applies to this text. Since the Old Testament uses the image of a prostitute dressed in scarlet to represent Jerusalem, that image should have the same meaning in Revelation.

The prostitute sits on a **scarlet beast** which represents Satan. The beast has **seven heads** which are the seven hills of Rome. Nothing about the woman represents seven hills and she sits or rests on the beast which has the seven hills, not on the heads that symbolize the seven hills. The beast has characteristics representing the city and authority Rome (the seven heads are both seven hills and seven kings.) The woman sits on the beast representing her reliance on the secular power that stands in opposition to the gospel, (i.e., Roman authority and commerce.) The beast will hate the prostitute, bring her to ruin and burn her with fire (Rev. 17:16.) This clearly foretells the hatred of Jerusalem by Satan who uses the godless power of Rome to burn and destroy and destroy Jerusalem in 70 AD. If the prostitute represented Rome, the ongoing hatred of the beast for Rome would have to be explained. There has been no historic campaign against Rome as there has been against Jerusalem.

Further evidence that the prostitute is Jerusalem is found in Revelation 18:20:

> Rejoice over her, O heaven!
> Rejoice saints and apostles and prophets!
> God has judged her for the way she treated you.

and again in Revelation 18:24:

> In her was found the blood of prophets and of the saints,
> and of all who have been killed on the earth.

While a case could be made that some New Testament **prophets** and saints would have been killed in Rome before this time, it is Jerusalem and not Rome known for killing the prophets.

> *Matt. 23:37* O Jerusalem, Jerusalem, you who kill the prophets and stone those sent to you,...

In Scripture, it is from Jerusalem that intense persecution breaks out, causing some of the saints to be killed and the church to be scattered (Acts 7:59ff, 12:2.) In John's time, it would be difficult to support the contention that Rome was a place of "all who have been killed on the earth." The evidence that the prostitute in Revelation represents Jerusalem is simply overwhelming.

Rapture - This term is not found anywhere in Scripture. Its definition is "being filled with, and completely taken up in, a feeling of delight or bliss." It is used theologically to describe the return of Christ in which he gathers his people to himself. While many hold to a silent and secret rapture of believers that precedes the visible and noisy return of Christ, this view is of recent origin and is contradicted by Scripture.

In I Thessalonians 4:15, Paul writes, "According to the Lord's own word, we tell you that we who are still alive, who are left till the coming of the Lord, will certainly not precede those who have fallen asleep." He then goes on in verses 16 and 17 to describe the visible and noisy return of Christ (loud command, voice of the archangel, trumpet call of God.) This text creates a problem for those holding to a silent rapture because, if Scripture taught that there was to be a silent rapture first, Paul would be waiting for the silent rapture rather than the noisy one he describes. By saying we who are still alive, Paul includes himself among those who could participate in the noisy and visible future return of Christ. For one to hold to a silent rapture preceding the loud, and visible return of Christ described in this text, it must be asserted that Paul, who felt he could teach the Thessalonians about this subject, did not know the truth about the return of Christ. Paul would have had to have been mistaken when he included himself among those who awaited the visible return of Christ.

While the description of angels taking one and leaving another in Matthew 24:36-42 is thought by some to be a description of the invisible and silent rapture, the context does not allow the text to be understood in that way. Just a few verses earlier, Matthew 24:26-31 described this gathering of believers and leaving of unbelievers as part of the visible and noisy rapture.

> (26) So if anyone tells you, 'There he is, out in the desert,' do not go out; or, 'Here he is, in the inner rooms,' do not believe it. (27) For as lightning that comes from the east is visible even in the west, so will be the coming of the Son of Man.

Then following the use of **extreme language** in verse 29, the text continues:

> (30) At that time the sign of the Son of Man will appear in the sky, and all the nations of the earth will mourn. They will see the Son of Man coming on the clouds of the sky, with power and great glory. (31) And he will send his angels with a loud trumpet call, and they will gather his elect from the four winds, from one end of the heavens to the other.

It is in the context of a noisy and extremely visible return of Christ that one is taken (by the **angels** from verse 31) and another left in verses 36 and following.

The promise of the angels at Jesus' ascension (Acts 1:11) was that Jesus would return "in the same way you have seen him go into heaven." If there were to be two returns, a silent one and a visible one, it would be expected that there would be some clear statement by the Lord or his angels regarding multiple returns, one silent and invisible and the other loud and visible. Instead, the Scriptures constantly speak of *the* return of the Lord or *the* coming of the Lord. There is to be only one return and the angels contribute to that understanding by saying that his return will be like his ascension.

Red - [Rev. 6:4,12 9:17 12:3 17:3,4 18:12,16] Red or scarlet is the color of wickedness and evil in Revelation when the color bears a symbolic significance. At times, the color red is used because the image in Revelation comes from another biblical source (such as the red horse, and the moon turning red - Rev. 6:4,12.) However, even in those cases, the image may be wicked. In Revelation 6:4, the **red horse** that is borrowed from Zechariah 1 is also wicked because it takes peace from the earth.

The **dragon** symbolizing Satan is red, the **prostitute** in Revelation 17 is dressed in red, and the beast she is sitting on is red.

Scarlet clothing is symbolic of wealth in some of the images in the book (Rev. 18:12,16.)

Red Horse - [Rev. 6:4] When the second **seal** is opened in Revelation 6:4, a rider on a fiery red horse comes forth to take peace from the earth. In Zechariah 1:8ff, a man riding a red horse describes the whole world as being at rest and in peace. An angel who is present reports that the Almighty is angry with the nations that feel secure and he describes how **Babylon** will be plundered by their slaves (Zech. 1:15, 2:9.)

In Revelation, it is the **Lamb** who opens the second seal, indicating that it is under his authority and control. Then the second of the **four living creatures** orders the rider to come forth. God has no love for war. War is a normal part of human existence in a fallen world. God uses the pain and sorrow that come with war to draw men's attention to their inability to live in comfort without the Almighty.

The End

Root of David - [Rev. 5:5, 22:16] The root of David in Revelation 5:5 is identified in Revelation 22:16 as Jesus. It is likely that his identity could be determined without the cross-reference. See **Offspring of David** for further information regarding the background of this title.

Sardis - [Rev. 1:11, 3:1,4] This is one of the **seven churches** to whom the book of Revelation is addressed. Sardis, like **Laodicea**, was an affluent industrial center and the city had a reputation for relaxed moral standards. Apparently, the looser morals of the culture had infected the attitudes of the church members. The church had a reputation for being alive but was not. They were a church that looked good on the outside, but they had left behind what they had heard and received when they originally came to faith. They are not absolutely dead because there is something in them that needs to be strengthened before it dies.

Scarlet - See **Red**.

Scarlet Beast - [Rev. 17:3] The scarlet beast is Satan. This can be recognized by his coming up out of the Abyss and going to his destruction (Rev. 17:8, 20:7-10.) He is described as "once was, now is not, and will come." There is no other evil character who fits the once was, now is not, and will be structure other than Satan. He is the only person in Revelation who comes up out of the Abyss. But it should be noted that the text clearly states he now is not. For this to be true he must have already been cast into the Abyss from which he will come forth as described in Revelation 11, 17, and in Revelation 20:1-10.

Since the 1000 years must have already started for Satan to be "now is not," it is impossible that the 1000 years from Revelation 20 is a literal time. If it had been, Satan would have been released from the Abyss hundreds of years ago. Satan is released so that he can deceive the nations and gather them to fight against God's people. Revelation 20:3 says that Satan will be set free for a short time. Satan is only bound once according to the text and for him to have been, "now is not" and will be, he must have been bound when John wrote Revelation.

Those who disagree with this view will have to assert that the scarlet beast is not Satan, requiring that some other beast fulfill the qualifications of this beast. The scarlet beast comes up out of the Abyss. In Revelation only the locusts that torment people (Rev. 9:3-11) and

Satan (Rev. 20:1-10) come up out of the Abyss. If the scarlet beast is some other character that comes out of the Abyss, its identity must be obvious because John does not say who he is. If the scarlet beast is not Satan, someone other than Satan must have existed before the time that John wrote, must have been in the Abyss at the time John was writing, and must be anticipated to come out of the Abyss in the future. If the scarlet beast is not Satan, there must be two characters who go into and come out of the Abyss. Additionally, the scarlet beast will go to his destruction when he comes up out of the Abyss (Rev. 17:11.) This parallels the description of Satan's fate when he is released from the Abyss (Rev. 20:10.) There are simply too many similarities for the scarlet beast to be anyone but Satan.

The scarlet beast also bears a strong resemblance to the dragon that represents Satan in Revelation. He is **red** and has **seven heads** and ten **horns** like the **dragon** (Satan) in Revelation 12. The meaning of the seven heads and ten horns in this text is the same as that for the dragon and the **beast out of the sea**.

Scroll - [Rev. 1:11, 5:1-5,7,9, 6:14, 10:2,8-10] John records what he sees in his vision on a scroll. In Revelation 5, there is a scroll with writing on both sides, sealed with seven **seals**. It is so important that the scroll be opened that John wept and wept when no one could open or even look inside of it. Based on the contents of the scroll when the seals are opened it would appear that it is similar to the scroll in Ezekiel 2:8-3:3 that had written on both sides words of lament, mourning, and woe. Certainly the message is sad in describing the dangers that will overtake so many including the Christian martyrs.

In Revelation 10, there is a little scroll which John is instructed to take and eat. It was as sweet as honey to his mouth but was sour to his stomach. The scroll tastes sweet because it bears a message of hope and deliverance. The Lord will return and the church will be delivered. This image comes from Ezekiel 2:8-3:3 where Ezekiel was given a scroll with words of lament, mourning, and woe written on both sides of it. He was instructed to eat it and when he ate it, it was as sweet as honey. Ezekiel proclaimed mourning, and woe in his time against a rebellious people. He was responsible for warning Israel of the judgment that was coming. Israel became accountable once she heard his warning. Revelation 10 has a similar message of judgment and woe. The sixth **trumpet** sounded in Revelation 9 was the second woe. John's message is a lament because it tells of the destruction of the church and the coming judgment of the world. The scroll is sweet because it bears a message of hope that God will ultimately redeem his people.

The scroll does taste sweet but it makes John sick. Its message is sickening because of the extreme evil to be revealed when the beast that comes up out of the Abyss kills the two witnesses (the Jewish and Gentile churches). John's reaction is similar to that of Daniel when he prophesied about the same events (Daniel 7:28, 8:26f, 10:2f.)

Seals - [Rev. 5:1,2,5, 6:1,3,5,7,9,12, 7:2,3, 8:1, 9:4, 10:4, 22:10] Several different things are sealed in Revelation. Of greatest prominence is the **scroll** which is sealed with seven seals. Additionally, the servants of God are sealed with God's seal for their protection. In two places, things John hears are either sealed so that they are not included in the book or he is told not to seal them so that what he has heard will be passed on.

It is so important that the scroll sealed with seven seals be opened, that John wept and wept when he thought there was no one worthy to open it (Rev. 5:4.) John clearly believed that it was important for the seals to be opened and the images and the things they symbolized to be released on the world.

When the **lamb** opens the seals he releases a series of dangers to the world. These dangers are warnings that no one can be careless about their relationship with God. At the very time that one feels safe, sudden destruction can fall unexpectedly.

The first seal is the danger of the conquering Lord. The rider on the **white horse** is seen later in Revelation 19 where he is identified as Jesus. His riding forth is a danger not to his children but to those who fight against him. The final conquest of the world by this king is recorded in Revelation 19:11-21.

The second seal is the danger of war. War is a danger not only to those who die because of it but also to those who become captives or slaves, those wounded and maimed, and to the many who are displaced. While many lose property because of war, this is not as important as the loss of loved ones who are taken away through death and captivity. War is a danger because of the Fall of man and it is a danger that will be removed by the return of Christ. War can come unexpectedly and remove the things that make a person feel secure.

The third seal is the danger of famine. Some will die of famine, but many more will suffer under its effects. The impact of famine includes the loss of goods in having to pay excessive prices for food, displacement of those who have to leave their homes to find food, and the suffering of those who experience both the pain of hunger and the sorrow of seeing those they love hunger and die.

The fourth seal is the danger of death. John is not prophesying that one-fourth of the earth will die by the sword, famine, plague, and wild beasts in one instant. He is warning that throughout history one-fourth of humanity will die in this fashion. Through this seal John warns that everyone must be prepared to stand before God because many will face the unexpected termination of their lives. This theme is also found in the parable of the rich man who wanted to build more barns (Luke 12:16-21.)

The fifth seal is the danger of martyrdom. This seal warns believers that they should not become complacent as though persecution could not come, and that they should not be fearful if they must face persecution. The martyrs are under the altar of God where they are kept safe. They are given **white robes**. The white robes represent their inclusion with those who have come out of the **great tribulation** (Rev. 7:13-17.) They are given the robes to represent the nurturing care they will receive from God who meets all their needs. Although it is not mentioned, the white robes are likely fine linen, representing the righteous acts of the saints (Rev. 19:8.) Works of righteousness are always attributed to God because he inspires them through the work of his Holy Spirit (Philippians 2:12f.) That is why the righteous acts of the saints are given to them by God (Rev. 19:8.)

The sixth seal is the danger of judgment. It is possible that this seal gives a literal description of events occurring at the end of history. Whether it does or not, the **extreme language** is similar to that found in Matthew 24 and elsewhere and represents the final judgment. The significance of this passage is not its description of signs in the heavens. The extreme language is a warning of how terrible God's judgment will be on those who are not prepared. Everyone hides in Revelation 6:15-17 because of the wrath of the one on the throne and of the lamb. Their wrath is so awful because it is so absolute. The final judgment has come.

The seventh seal, like the seventh day of creation, is a time of resting. In this case, God rests from bringing dangers. The silence in heaven reminds the believer of the warning not to be excluded from God's rest due to unbelief (see Hebrews 3:7-4:11.)

The foreheads of the servants of God are sealed in contrast to the marking of the beast on hand or forehead (Rev. 7:2,3, 9:4.) This seal protects the wearer from some of the judgments enacted against the earth. As with the **mark of the beast**, the mark is not physical, but is designed to convey the idea that God protects his own.

John is told not to seal up the words of the prophecy of this book because the time is near (Rev. 22:10.) If the intent was that the content of Revelation should be largely unintelligible, it would not make any difference whether the words were sealed up or not, because no one would understand them. The intent must be that the book be understandable and accessible.

Second Death - [Rev. 2:11, 20:6,14, 21:8] This term is defined in Revelation 20:14 and 21:8. The second death is the lake of fire. The second death has no power over those who have part in the **first resurrection**.

Some have suggested that those who reign with Christ during the millennium consist of a small select group who have been physically resurrected. The group is made up of some who were given authority to judge and others who have been beheaded because of their testimony for Jesus. If this is true, it needs to be explained why anyone would think that there was a reason to mention that these faithful people would not have to fear the second death. Those who have died serving the Lord have already had their destiny decided. The encouragement that they will not face the second death can only be understood if, as the articles above assert, the first resurrection is the spiritual resurrection of believers (regeneration) during their lifetime. It is important to believers who will face persecution to mention that the second death has no power over them. Fear of death and pain are nothing when compared with the pain of the second death. Believers who remain faithful will not face the second death. Avoiding the second death must be seen by the church as more important than any other pressure that can be brought to bear so that they will patiently endure.

Likewise, the promise written to the people in **Smyrna** as they face persecution, is that they will not be hurt by the second death if they are faithful. This encourages them to persevere in difficult trials. Some may die physically, but they need to know that the problems they are about to face are less serious than the alternative, which is the lake of fire.

Seven - [The number seven appears more than fifty times] Seven is a biblical number of completeness. The Lord created the earth in seven days. Daniel speaks of seventy 'sevens' that are decreed for Israel (Daniel 9:24.) In Revelation the number seven is very important in that it expresses the fullness or completeness of a thing or action. The book is addressed to **seven churches**. There are seven **lampstands**, seven **stars**, seven **seals**, seven **trumpets**, and seven **bowls** of God's wrath. Some translations refer to the seven spirits of God in Revelation. However, it appears a better interpretation to translate the phrase, the sevenfold spirit (i.e., the complete or fullness of the spirit), as another way of speaking of the Holy Spirit.

The **dragon** has seven heads as does the **beast out of the sea**. The dragon also has seven crowns representing his rule over this fallen world. Satan asserts in his temptation of Jesus that the authority and splendor of all the kingdoms of the earth has been given to him (Luke 4:6.) Satan's crowns and his authority are taken away at the end of human history.

Seven Churches - [Rev. 1:4,11,20, 2:7,11,17,23,29, 3:6,13,22, 22:16] The book of Revelation is addressed to seven churches in Asia; **Ephesus, Smyrna, Pergamum, Thyatira, Sardis, Philadelphia,** and **Laodicea**. While most of the references to the churches occur in the first three chapters, the churches are mentioned again in Revelation 22. Some interpreters of Revelation suggest that after chapter 3 God has finished with the seven churches. Jesus' comment in Revelation 22:16 clarifies that Jesus sent his angel to give John this testimony for the churches. Not for the church, which would emphasize the futuristic elements of this book, nor for churches, which would emphasize the universal applicability of the book. The testimony is for the churches to whom this book was addressed. The book must therefore be read with awareness that it was addressed to those churches and that it was a testimony for them.

Seven Heads -[Rev. 12:3, 13:1, 17:3,7,9] The **red dragon** from Revelation 12:3, who is later identified (Rev. 12:9) as the devil or Satan, has seven heads and the **beast out of the sea** (Rev. 13:1) has seven heads. In Revelation 17 the great **prostitute** is sitting on a **scarlet beast** that has seven heads. The interpretation of the seven heads is provided in Revelation 17:9 where the seven heads are defined as seven hills and seven kings. All of the characters having seven heads are red (the color of wickedness in Revelation) or are empowered by a character who is red. They all are wicked characters including; Satan (Rev. 12:3,9), the beast out of the sea who makes war against the saints and conquers them (Rev. 13:1,7), and the scarlet beast covered with blasphemous names and having **ten horns** which will make war against the **lamb** (Rev. 17:3,14.) The seven heads are seven hills and since Rome is famous for being located on seven hills, the seven heads symbolize Rome. The dragon and beasts that have seven heads represent authorities that use Roman power in opposition to Christ and his saints. (The great prostitute does not have seven heads, does not sit on seven heads, and is not symbolic of Rome or Roman authority. She represents Jerusalem.)

The seven heads symbolize more than the city of Rome. They symbolize the authority of Rome because they are both seven hills and seven kings. The seven kings are both past and future kings. Five have fallen indicates that five of the kings have already reigned and died. One of the kings "is", so the current emperor is one of the seven. One will be, so there will be another emperor in the current line. The seven kings are the Roman emperors from the time of the Roman conquest of Israel until the destruction of Jerusalem and the temple. The five kings who "were" are Julius Caesar, Augustus, Tiberius, Caligula, and Claudius. The one who now is, is Nero. The one who is coming is Vespasian who will be reigning when Jerusalem and the sanctuary are destroyed by Titus in 70 AD.

The year 69 AD is known as the year of the four emperors because after Nero's death a succession of three men were raised as emperors and deposed before Vespasian took control at the end of the year. Galba was the first and he reigned from the death of Nero in 68 until January of 69 when Otho bribed the Praetorian guards to murder him. Vitellius invaded Italy with his troops and defeated Otho's army in April. Otho killed himself and Vitellius reigned until December when his armies were defeated by Vespasian's troops who captured and executed him.

The three men who reigned for a few months are not included among the seven because they never consolidated their power sufficiently to reign. The text makes it clear that they are not considered when it says of the seventh ruler "the other has not yet come; but when he does come, he must remain for a little while" (Rev. 17:10.)

The **beast from the Abyss** is an eighth king who belongs to the seven. The beast from the Abyss represents Satan. This beast once was, now is not and yet will come. This reflects Satan's presence on earth prior to the coming of Christ, his binding and imprisonment in the Abyss at the time John is writing, and his future release described in Revelation 11:7 and 20:7. He comes from the Abyss and since Satan is the only character described as going into and coming out of the Abyss, the beast from the Abyss must be Satan. As has been mentioned previously, the **Man of Lawlessness** physically represents Satan in some of the activities on earth attributed to Satan. In this case, he is the eighth king who belongs to the seven because he is a world ruler. He elevates himself in an effort to be worshipped as they were. The imposition of emperor worship and the claims of the first seven emperors that they should be called gods are similar to the description in Daniel of the demands of the Man of Lawlessness. Revelation 13:4 describes Satan being worshipped as is the beast out of the sea to whom he gives his authority.

Seven Spirits of God - [Rev. 1:4, 3:1, 4:5, 5:6] Seven spirits of God are found only in Revelation. Elsewhere in Scripture, when seven spirits gather it is for the purpose of possessing someone. Jesus tells a story of a demon who, having been cast out of a man, returns with seven demons more wicked than itself to possess the man again (Matthew 12:43-45, Luke 11:24-26.) Additionally, Jesus cast seven demons out of Mary Magdalene (Luke 8:2.)

In Revelation, the seven spirits are the seven spirits of God who are before his throne. Since this is the first time that seven spirits of God appear in Scripture, it could be expected that John would explain who they are. John does not define this image and so must believe that the reader can determine their identity from the passages where they are mentioned.

In Revelation 1:4f, John delivers a greeting to the **seven churches** from three persons. The first of these persons is he who is, who was, and who is to come. He is identified in Revelation 1:8 and 4:8 as the Lord God Almighty. The third person is Jesus Christ. The second person is called the seven spirits before God Almighty's throne. This is a Trinitarian formula representing the Father, the Holy Spirit and the Son. It is therefore most appropriate to accept the translation found in the footnote in the New International Version (NIV) of the sevenfold Spirit. The number seven represents completeness in Scripture and in this context is symbolic of the fullness of the Spirit.

In Revelation 3:1, the church in Sardis hears the words of Jesus who holds the sevenfold Spirit of God. Since they are dead and need to strengthen what is about to die, they have a dramatic need for the lifegiving work of the Holy Spirit.

The sevenfold Spirit is identified with seven **lamps** blazing before the throne of God in Revelation 4:5. This image is found in Zechariah 4:2 where seven lights sit atop a golden **lampstand**. Seven lampstands have been identified as seven churches in Revelation 1:20. The sole purpose of a lampstand is to hold a lamp so that it can give light. In the same way, the role of the churches is to hold up the witness of the Holy Spirit and give light to this dark world.

The sevenfold Spirit is also called seven horns and seven eyes in Revelation 5:6. Horns are symbolic of strength throughout Scripture and the seven horns represent the strength and power of the Godhead.

The seven eyes is an image derived from Zechariah 4:10 where there are seven eyes of the Lord that range throughout the earth. The "these seven" of Zechariah 4:10 refers to seven that are mentioned earlier in the text. The only seven referred to previously are the seven lights on the gold lampstand. So Zechariah makes a connection between the lights and the eyes similar to the description of the sevenfold Spirit in Revelation 4:5 and 5:6. The word of the Lord to Zerubbabel in Zechariah seems to be providing a definition of the seven lights.

> *Zechariah 4:2-6* He asked me, "What do you see?" I answered, "I see a solid gold lampstand with a bowl at the top and seven lights on it, with seven channels to the lights. Also there are two olive trees by it, one on the right of the bowl and the other on its left." I asked the angel who talked with me, "What are these, my lord?" He answered, "Do you not know what these are?" "No, my lord," I replied. So he said to me, "This is the word of the Lord to Zerubbabel: 'Not by might nor by power, but by my Spirit,' says the Lord Almighty.

It appears that Zechariah is being told that the lampstand with the seven lights represents the Spirit of God. The seven eyes ranging throughout the world represent the Spirit of God who sees all things.

Smyrna - [Rev. 1:11, 2:8] This is one of the **seven churches** to whom the book of Revelation is addressed. The city was a center for emperor worship and had a large Jewish community that was antagonistic toward Christianity. The church had experienced persecution and is warned that there will be additional persecution for a short time that probably will include martyrdom. The church is financially poor but is spiritually rich.

Soon - [Rev. 1:1, 2:16, 3:11, 11:14, 22:6,7,12,20] While it might be thought that such a simple word could be easily passed over, it appears that some things that are going to happen soon occur significantly later than other things that happen soon. In the prologue in Revelation 1, John is writing what must soon take place. Some things described in Revelation are less than ten years away (e.g., the destruction of Jerusalem.) But John's vision does not describe only those things that will happen in the next several decades. While he begins to tell the churches about events in the next several decades, he continues to tell the story of human history up to the return of Christ. For God, the author of this vision, events a thousand years in the future also can be called soon. In Revelation 22:7, Jesus promises that he is coming soon and yet he has not returned in the 1900 years that have followed. This should not be a surprise because for the Lord a day is like a thousand years and a thousand years like a day (II Peter 3:8, Ps 90:4.) Yet, many things described in Revelation are soon even for the churches to whom this letter is addressed.

Stars - [Rev. 1:16,20, 2:1,28, 3:1, 6:13, 8:10,11,12, 9:1, 12:1,4, 22:16] Stars, when they are used as images in a vision, are **angels**. This image is defined for the reader when the seven stars in Revelation 1 are defined as the angels of the **seven churches** (Rev. 1:20.) The star described in Revelation 9:1,2 is a person/angel who was given the **key** to the shaft of the Abyss (Jesus.) The person who has the key to the Abyss in Revelation 20:1 is clearly Jesus and he is called an angel.

Jesus is called the **Morning star** and is promised to the overcomers in **Thyatira.**

Not all stars/angels in Revelation are good. The star called **Wormwood** is an angel that fouls one-third of the fresh water of the earth. When Satan is presented as a **dragon** in Revelation 12:4, his tail sweeps one-third of the stars out of heaven and flings them to earth. This represents how those angels that supported Satan were cast out of heaven when he was "hurled down" (Rev. 12:10.)

When **extreme language** is used, the stars in the heavens are described as falling to earth.

Three and a half days - [Rev. 11:9,11] This short time is the period during which the church is dead. The two **lampstands**, two **olive trees** and two **witnesses** represent the Jewish and Gentile portions of the church. These witnesses finish their testimony (Rev. 11:7) and the **beast from the Abyss** (Satan) attacks and kills them. Their bodies lay exposed for three and a half days (Rev. 11:9-10), reflecting the continuation of the externals of the church even though it is dead. It may include the regular practice of worship by churches that have repudiated the need for Jesus Christ's sacrifice. They look like a church on the outside, but there is no soul (gospel) to make the body alive. At the end of the three and a half days, the church is resurrected by the breath (Spirit) of God and ascends to heaven, leaving their enemies behind (Rev. 11:11,12.) This ascension of the church is the rapture in which the angels gather the believers (Matt 24:30,31,40,41) and leave the non-believers behind to face destruction.

The symbolic three and a half days comes from Daniel 9:27. A series of seventy 'sevens' (or weeks) are decreed for Israel (Daniel 9:24.) At the end of that period transgression will finish, sin will end, and there will be everlasting righteousness. These qualities are typical of all in the new Jerusalem who have been sanctified by the Holy Spirit. There are seven 'weeks' and sixty-two 'weeks' and then the Anointed One (Messiah) comes. The seven 'weeks' represents the time from the decree to rebuild Jerusalem until it was rebuilt. The sixty-two 'weeks' represents the period from the rebuilding of Jerusalem until the coming of the Messiah. After the sixty-two 'weeks' the Messiah is cut off and has nothing. This is a clear reference to the crucifixion of Jesus. Then the people of the ruler who will come will destroy the city and the sanctuary. This has been fulfilled in the destruction of Jerusalem and the temple in 70 AD. The ruler who will come is the **Man of Lawlessness** described in Daniel 7, 8, and 11 as well as in II Thessalonians 2 and in Revelation where he is known as the **beast out of the earth**. He confirms a covenant with many for one week but in the middle of the week (i.e., for three and a half days) he puts an end to sacrifice and offering and on a wing of the temple sets up an **abomination that causes desolation**. Daniel, mentions in other texts the Man of Lawlessness waging war with and defeating the saints (Daniel 7:21), the destruction of the holy people (Daniel 8:24) and the power of the holy people finally being broken (Daniel 12:7.) In Daniel 9:27 the Man of Lawlessness puts an end to sacrifice and offering for three and a half days that corresponds to the death of the church for the three and a half days in Revelation 11:9.

The use of three and a half days is designed to communicate that this death of the church is for a short period. It is not a literal time any more than the **forty-two months** or **1,260 days** or the **time, times, and half a time** are literal times. The time, times, and half a time in Daniel 7 is the same three and a half day period. Daniel 12:11 says there will be 1,290 days (about three and a half years) from the time that the daily sacrifice is abolished and the abomination that causes desolation is set up until the end.

The three and a half days of Revelation 11:9f occur in the middle of the final "week" of Daniel 9:27. It begins after the 1,260 days, during which the church successfully bears witness to Christ and ends immediately before the final judgment. It is during the final "week" of Daniel 9:27 that Satan is released as he was in the time before Christ (Rev. 11:7, 20:7,8.) The accommodation of the church to moralism in place of what is distinctively Christian will make it appear to the world that Satan has won and the church has lost. Those who are opposed to the church will send gifts to celebrate its death (Rev. 11:10.) But just when things look most hopeless, God intervenes to bring final victory. This will include the people of God ascending to heaven in a cloud (Rev. 11:12, I Thes. 4:17), the destruction of the enemies of God with fire (Rev. 20:9, 11:18, II Peter 3:3-10, I Thes. 5:1-3) and the casting of Satan into the fire of hell (Rev. 20:10.)

Thyatira - [Rev. 1:11, 2:18,24] This is one of the **seven churches** to whom the book of Revelation is addressed. Thyatira was a commercial city that was dominated by its trade guilds. To succeed in business it was necessary that one participate in the trade guilds. For Christians this was a problem because the trade guilds ate meals together and the meals were dedicated to one or another pagan deity. Often the meal would conclude with some kind of morally improper entertainment. The church is growing spiritually but is weakened by their tolerance of those who encourage accommodation with the culture. The accommodating group is led by a woman who claims to be a prophetess. God will judge those who accept her teaching but the rest of the church is to continue growing as they have been.

Time, Times and Half a Time - [Rev. 12:14] This terminology comes from Daniel (7:25, 12:7) where it refers to two different periods. In Daniel 7, the phrase "time, times, and half a time" refers to the period that the saints are handed over to the eleventh king who speaks against the Most High. As will be discussed elsewhere, it appears that the length of the period in Daniel 7 is approximately three and a half years. In Daniel 12, the same phrase is used to answer the question, "How long will it be before these astonishing things are fulfilled?" The time, times, and half a time refers to the period from when this question is asked (in Daniel's time) until the power of the holy people has been finally broken. The power of the holy people (church) has not yet been broken, so the period described in Daniel 12 lasts more than 2000 years.

The purpose of time, times, and half a time is to hide the precise length of the period being discussed. It can be used of any period of any length that the writer does not want to define. In both places in Daniel, events are described that define the end of the period. In Daniel 7, the time, times, and half a time ends when the saints are liberated from the power of the eleventh king. In Daniel 12, the time, times, and half a time ends when the power of the holy people is finally broken. It is important to be familiar with both passages in Daniel that use time, times, and half a time before moving on to consider how the phrase is used in Revelation.

In Daniel 7 the time, times, and half a time is a period of persecution under a king who is in opposition to the Lord.

Daniel 7:23-27 He gave me this explanation: 'The fourth beast is a fourth kingdom that will appear on earth. It will be different from all the other kingdoms and will devour the whole earth, trampling it down and crushing it. The ten horns are ten kings who will come from this kingdom. After them another king will arise, different from the earlier ones; he will subdue three kings. He will speak against the Most High and oppress his saints and try to change the set times and the laws. The saints will be handed over to him for a *time, times, and half a time.* But the court will sit, and his power will be taken away and completely destroyed forever. Then the sovereignty, power, and greatness of the kingdoms under the whole heaven will be handed over to the saints, the people of the Most High. His kingdom will be an everlasting kingdom, and all rulers will worship and obey him.

The time, times, and half a time define the period that the saints are handed over to an eleventh king. The eleventh king is the **Man of Lawlessness** from II Thessalonians 2 who is also the beast out of the earth from Revelation. There are several reasons why this figure in Daniel 7 must be the Man of Lawlessness.

1. The little **horn** is described as another king different from the other ones (the preceding ten kings), who speaks against the Most High (see II Thes. 2:4 - speaking against the Most High, also Rev. 17:12 - the ten kings who precede him.)

2. The end of his kingdom is the final judgment (compare Daniel 7:9-11 and Rev. 20:11f) and after his destruction, Christ's everlasting kingdom is established (Daniel 7:13, 21f, 27.)

3. His defeating of the saints in Daniel 7 is similar to the description of his actions elsewhere (Daniel 8:24, 12:7, Rev. 11:7.)

In Daniel 7, the time, times, and half a time represents the symbolic three and a half days from Daniel 9:27. The Man of Lawlessness puts an end to sacrifice and offering and sets up the abomination that causes desolation in the middle of the final "seven" (or week) of the seventy "sevens". The middle of the "seven" or week is three and a half days. Since each of the previous sixty-nine "sevens" or weeks lasted about seven years it should be expected that half a "seven" or three and a half days would last about three and a half years. The three and a half days of Daniel 9 is the same as the three and a half days that the church lays dead in Revelation 11:7-11.

In Daniel 12, the end of the world is described.

Daniel 12:1-7 At that time Michael, the great prince who protects your people, will arise. There will be a time of distress such as has not happened from the beginning of nations until then. But at that time your people - everyone whose name is found written in the book - will be delivered. Multitudes who sleep in the dust of the earth will awake: some to everlasting life, others to shame and everlasting contempt. Those who are wise will shine like the brightness of the heavens, and those who lead many to right-eousness, like the stars forever and ever. But you Daniel, close up and seal the words of the scroll until the time of the end. Many will go here and there to increase knowledge. Then I Daniel, looked, and there before me stood two others, one on this bank of the river and one on the opposite bank. One of them said to the man clothed in linen, who was above the waters of the river, "How long will it be before these astonishing things are fulfilled?" The man clothed in linen, who was above the waters of the river, lifted his   right hand and his left hand toward heaven, and I heard him swear by him who lives forever, saying, "It will be for a *time, times, and half a time.* When the power of the holy people has been finally broken, all these things will be completed."

Clearly the text is describing the end times. The text refers to a time of distress which Jesus quotes in his prophecy in Matthew 24:21 and Mark 13:19. The people of God, whose names are written in the book, are delivered by the resurrection of the dead and the final judgment (Daniel 12:1-3.) An unidentified man asks, how long before these things are fulfilled? He is asking for a date for the end of the world. The answer is that it will be for a time, times, and half a time and it will be when the power of the holy people has been finally broken. This answer first denies that the date when this will happen is going to be provided. The time, times, and half a time is a period of indefinite length. It should be noted that if any length of time could be determined from this phrase, Jesus would have known when he was to return. He denied that he knew in spite of his perfect familiarity with Scripture. The sign that can be looked for is the power of the holy people being broken. This will happen at the very end.

In Revelation, the time, times, and half a time are also used to describe an indefinite period. However, in Revelation it is connected to other time images. Its ties to those other images limits it to a particular period. This is unlike Daniel where time, times, and half a time refers to two different periods of different lengths. It is helpful to compare Revelation 12:6 where the **woman clothed with the sun** is to go to the desert and be cared for 1,260 days and Revelation 12:14 where the same woman flies to the desert to a place prepared for her where she will be taken care of for a time, times, and half a time. From this comparison it is clear that the 1,260 days and the time, times, and half a time are the same period. Both of these symbols are also tied to the **forty-two months** because forty-two (thirty day) months is 1,260 days. In the New Testament period all months were thirty days. In Revelation, the time, times, and half a time (and the 1,260 days or forty-two months) ends at the reign of the Man of Lawlessness. It begins at the ascension of Jesus Christ. The son of the woman clothed with the sun is snatched up to heaven (the ascension) and she is protected in the desert for 1,260 days (Rev. 12:5f.) This period is the time of the Gentiles. The Gentiles trample on the holy city for forty-two months (Rev. 11:2.) Luke also says Jerusalem will be trampled on by the Gentiles "until the times of the Gentiles are fulfilled." (Luke 21:24)

The time that the woman is kept safe is the same as the forty-two month time of the Gentiles and the 1,260 days that the two witnesses will prophecy (Rev. 11:3.) This is because all of the time symbols represent the same thing. The woman clothed with the sun and the two witnesses represent the church. At the end of the 1,260 days the witnesses are killed and after a short time are resurrected. The fate of the woman after the 1,260 days is not described but must be the same.

Trumpets - [Rev. 1:10, 4:1, 8:2,6,7,8,10,12,13, 9:1,13,14, 10:7, 11:15] In the Old Testament, a trumpet was used to sound the alarm and to prepare to go into battle. There are many examples of this in Jeremiah, Ezekiel, and elsewhere. The use of trumpets in Revelation is similar. Trumpets are used to represent the voice of God which warns the churches of what is to come. Trumpets are also blown by angels as warnings of judgments and the three woes.

In the first two places where trumpets are heard in Revelation, the voice of God sounds like a trumpet. This is similar to Isaiah 58:1 where God instructs Isaiah to raise his voice like a trumpet to warn Israel of her rebellion. The instruction to write down the message and send it to the

seven churches, precedes the individual warnings given to those churches in chapters 2 and 3. The repeated statement, "He who has an ear, let him hear..." warns the churches to remember Jesus' words not to be like those who have ears and do not hear.

Matthew 11:15 He who has ears, let him hear.

Matthew 13:14 In them is fulfilled the prophecy of Isaiah: "'You will be ever hearing but never understanding; you will be ever seeing but never perceiving. For this people's heart has become calloused; they hardly hear with their ears, and they have closed their eyes. Otherwise they might see with their eyes, hear with their ears, understand with their hearts and turn, and I would heal them.

These warnings require that the seven churches either remove some evil from their midst or that they remain faithful in the face of persecution. In Revelation 4, when the focus changes from the current situation to what must take place later, the voice of God again sounds as a trumpet because the message of the rest of Revelation is a warning to remain faithful in the face of difficulties.

In chapter 8, seven **angels** sound seven trumpets. The results of their trumpet blasts are judgments and woes. The disasters that occur after the blowing of the trumpets are not accidents or events beyond God's ability to overcome. Rather, they are events that God has caused to happen. They are initiated when his angels blow the trumpets they have been given by God. God's control is seen especially in Revelation 9:4, where after the fifth trumpet has blown, the locusts are not to harm those who have the **seal** of God on their foreheads. The trumpets act as both warnings and judgments. This is clarified by the use of **extreme language** in Revelation 8:5, which is always an indicator of judgment, and occurs right before the sounding of the first trumpet.

The first four trumpets sound a warning of God's judgment on creation. They partially destroy the works God created on days three through five. The first trumpet burns vegetation from the third day of creation. The second trumpet damages the sea (salt water) and all that lives in and on it from the fifth day of creation. A third of the sea is turned to blood which points to the judgment of God on Egypt in Exodus. The third trumpet damages fresh water and all who depend on it for life. This also was created the fifth day. The fourth trumpet damages the lights that rule the heavens which were created on the fourth day. These trumpets proclaim the damaging impact of the Fall on creation as well as fallen humanity's mismanagement of creation.

It is difficult to resist thinking that these judgments are already with us. Concerns are being expressed at this time that too much farm land is being paved for industrial uses. Forests are being removed to be replaced with housing developments. Pollution of fresh water is such a problem that a source of drinking water not requiring treatment is rare. Pollution of the seas with toxic chemicals and medical waste is an increasing problem. And how many are able to see any but the brightest stars at night from their homes? The majesty of the heavens is hidden both by streetlights (and other outdoor lighting) and by the pollution in the air.

The last three trumpets are called three woes. They are judgments specifically focused on humanity.

The fifth trumpet, the first woe, is represented by locusts, released from the Abyss by an angel (**star**) having the **key** to the Abyss. This angel is Jesus. The locusts have as king over them the angel of the Abyss (Satan.) The locusts harm only non-believers causing great pain. It appears that the locusts represent the unsatisfied desires of fallen humanity who desire the good from before the Fall but are frustrated in attaining it. This reflects the disharmony of humanity within their own souls that has occurred through the Fall. The locusts wear something like **crowns** but not crowns reflecting the desire to rule creation as Adam did. Humanity's efforts to rule are frustrated and man substitutes personal power and egotism for godly rule under God's authority. The locusts have something like human faces but not human faces reflecting the distorted image of God in man. Their teeth are like lion's teeth representing the danger and conflict of fallen mankind. They have a breastplate of iron representing the hardness of heart of fallen man. The locusts are described as looking like horses prepared for battle and the sound of their wings was like the thundering of horses and chariots rushing into battle. This is reminiscent of James 4 where James suggests that fights and quarrels among believers come from their desires that battle within them. If this is true for believers, how much more is it true for non-believers who have no hope of glory.

The sixth trumpet, the second woe, describes the killing of a third of mankind by plagues of fire, smoke, and sulphur. It appears that this is describing the death of troops in warfare. While the death of so many could cause those left to stop and consider the God who inflicts this catastrophe, those who are left do not repent. This suggests the disharmony of humanity with one another. War is the ultimate inability to get along with others. This passage is not describing a single battle that kills millions, but the warfare that has existed throughout history.

There is a parenthetical description of the history of the church in Revelation 10:1-11:13. It is in three parts. The first section describes that the **mystery of God** will be accomplished when the seventh angel is about to sound his trumpet. This mystery of God is found and defined in Ephesians 3:4-6 as the Gentiles being heirs together with Israel.

The second section involves John eating a **scroll** just as Ezekiel did (Ezekiel 2:8-3:3.) Ezekiel found the scroll to be sweet, reflecting the hope that God's promises inspired in the midst of lament, mourning, and woe. John also finds it sweet with God's promises but at the same time it makes him sick to the stomach. The reason for this is the same as Daniel's reaction at the end of Daniel 7 and 8 where he was ill for several days. John is preparing to describe in Revelation 11:1-13 the same events that Daniel described in chapters 7-12. It is what Daniel called the destruction of the holy people (Daniel 8:24) and what John will call the killing of the witnesses (the church - Rev. 11:7.)

The third section is the story of the church. The time of the Gentiles prophesied by Paul in Romans 11:25f, during which time Israel is hardened in part, is the forty-two months that the Gentiles trample on Jerusalem. This forty-two months is the church age. The two witnesses (the Jewish and Gentile portions of the church) cannot be stopped until their testimony is completed. When their testimony is completed, they are killed by the **beast out of the Abyss** (Satan.) This represents the death of the visible church through apostasy. The bodies of the churches lay exposed reflecting the continuation of externals in these dead churches even after they have neither soul nor life. The opponents of the church and of God celebrate the death of the church and even send gifts. The two **witnesses** (churches) are made alive by a breath of life from God (i.e., the Holy Spirit renews the church) and they stand up on their feet (representing revival.) After that, the voice of God says, "come up here" and the church ascends at the second coming of the Lord.

The seventh trumpet is the final judgment since "the kingdom of the world has become the kingdom of our Lord and of his Christ." The **twenty-four elders** rejoice because "the time has come for judging the dead ... rewarding your servants the prophets and your saints ... and for destroying those who destroy the earth."

Twenty-Four Elders - [Rev. 4:4,10, 5:5,6,8,11,14, 7:11,13, 11:16, 14:3, 19:4] The twenty-four elders' role in Revelation is similar to that of a Greek chorus. They complete some of what is missing in the story being told. They provide a vehicle for praising different aspects of God's glory, and they explain some of the imagery to John and to the reader. They are dressed in **white** as are all servants of the Lord in Revelation and they are rulers because they all wear **crowns**. The number of elders (twenty-four) suggests two groups of twelve, probably representing twelve Old Testament saints and twelve New Testament saints (apostles.) The songs they sing reflect both Old and New Testament themes. In chapter 4 they praise God the creator. In chapter 5 they sing a new song to him who sits on the throne, and to the Lamb, a song of redemption. In Revelation 11, they praise the Lord who reigns and announce that the time of judgment has arrived. In Revelation 19 they call on the servants of God to praise him and all the redeemed of creation praise the Lord who reigns in verses 6-8.

White - [Rev. 1:14, 2:17, 3:4,5,18, 4:4, 6:2, 6:11, 7:9,13,14, 14:14, 19:11,14, 20:11] White is symbolic of purity and holiness in the book of Revelation. White is the primary color observed near God and the godly. The **white robes** of those who have come out of the **great tribulation** have been washed in the blood of the **Lamb** and made white (Rev. 7:14.) The **fine linen** that is worn by the saints and that represents the righteous acts of the saints, is white and clean (Rev. 19:14.) The redeemed wear white and ride **white horses** (Rev. 19:14) as does their ruler (Rev. 19:11,13.) The throne on which God sits is white (Rev. 20:11.)

White Hair - [Rev. 1:14] The description of the son of man's hair in Revelation 1:14 is drawn from Daniel 7:9. The Ancient of Days has hair as white as wool and white clothing in Daniel. In Revelation, the one like a son of man has hair white like wool. It appears that a comparison is being made between the two characters. The Ancient of Days, in Daniel, is clearly God Almighty who is to judge and his judgment is based on the **books** that are opened (Daniel 7:10.) In Revelation it is the son of man who has white hair and there can be no question that he is Jesus. This comparison would be inappropriate if Jesus were not divine.

White Horse - [Rev. 6:2, 19:11,14] In Zechariah 1:7-11, there are certain ones who go through the earth on red, brown, and white horses as servants of the Lord. In Revelation, white horses are used exclusively by the Lord and his servants. The rider of the white horse in chapter 6 is not identified except that he is a conqueror who has a **crown**. His identity is made completely clear when the same rider on a white horse appears in Revelation 19 and is called Faithful and True, the **word of God**, and **King of kings and Lord of lords**. He now has many crowns (while in chapter 6 he had only one crown) because while he rode out to conquer in chapter 6 he has conquered in chapter 19 and is called King of kings.

White Robes - [Rev. 3:4,5,18, 4:4, 6:11, 7:9,13,14] The significance of the white robes is explained in Revelation 7:13 where John is asked who are these in white robes and from where did they come. The answer to these questions is that the ones wearing white robes are those who have come out of the **great tribulation**. Those wearing white robes are "a great multitude that no one could count, from every nation, tribe, people and language" (Rev. 7:9.) The statement that they have "come out" of the great tribulation (Rev. 7:13) suggests that they died during the tribulation. This does not require that they died as martyrs, because many of them may have died of natural causes.

There are theories of a seven year great tribulation and of a three and a half year great tribulation. If these theories were true, they would require that millions upon millions of believers from all nations of the world, die within a short time so as to produce a multitude that no one could count. The short time would not allow for many deaths due to advanced age and illness. Additionally, the deaths from persecution would have to be widely dispersed to include people from every nation and language. Since some of these theories suggest that believers are removed from earth prior to the tribulation, what is required by these theories is the conversion of many millions all over the world from every nation and language and their death shortly thereafter within the tribulation period.

Those who hold to a seven year or three and a half year great tribulation call the reign of the Man of Lawlessness the great tribulation. He will reign for about six and a half years and the time of his reign will be a horror. During the last three and a half years of his reign, he will put an end to true worship in the visible church and he will persecute believers. However, his reign is an intensification of the great tribulation. The church has faced persecution and trial since the death of Christ. Paul comments that everyone who wants to live a godly life will be persecuted (II Timothy 3:12.) It is important that the church recognize that the tribulation is now and serving the Lord is costly and can be painful.

When the fifth **seal** is opened (Rev. 6:9-11), John sees the souls of those who have been slain because of the **word of God** and the testimony they had maintained. From the text it appears that these are all the martyrs who have died for the Lord up to the time of John's vision. These martyrs are each given a white robe and told to wait until the number of all who were to be killed as they had been was completed. If the large number wearing white robes created a problem for those who hold to a rapture before the tribulation period, the martyrs wearing white robes makes the position completely untenable. After all, this group of martyrs must include Stephen, the apostles, and the other New Testament saints who were killed for the Lord. They are given white robes to show that they are included in those who have "come out" of the great tribulation. If the apostles have "come out" of the great tribulation, then it must have begun shortly after the death of Christ. If all of the martyrs are wearing white robes, then the great tribulation must cover the entire period during which the martyrs have died, i.e., the **forty-two months** that the Gentiles trample the holy city and the **1,260 days** that the two **witnesses** testify, which is the time before the death of the church (see the summary of Rev. 11:1-12 in Section Two of this book.) Additionally, the church in **Sardis** is promised that they will walk with the Lord dressed in white if they have not soiled their clothes. Then the promise is expanded that "he who overcomes will, like them, be dressed in white." So all who overcome, having read the promise in Revelation 3:5, can expect to be dressed in white, again suggesting that they have come out of the great tribulation. Later, speaking to church in **Laodicea**, the Lord calls on them to buy white clothes from him, suggesting that they would be dressed like the multitude in Revelation 7:9. Later in Revelation 4:4, the elders on the thrones are dressed in white, which again may suggest their inclusion in the multitude who "came out" of the great tribulation.

White Stone - [Rev. 2:17] Those who overcome in **Pergamum** are promised a white stone with their name written on it. While the meaning of this is subject to debate, it is either a reference to the white stone that would have indicated acquittal by a jury or, more likely, it is a ticket to a festival such as the wedding feast of the **lamb**. Their name is written on the stone to show that their inclusion in the festival or dinner is by invitation only.

Witnesses - [Rev. 11:3-12] The two witnesses, also called two **olive trees**, two **lampstands**, and two **prophets,** are two churches, the Gentile and Jewish churches. The identity of the two witnesses derives from the olive tree and lampstand imagery. John saw two witnesses, but in Revelation 11:4 he provides additional clues to their identity by calling them lampstands and olive trees. Without these clues the witnesses could not be identified.

John has already defined the meaning of lampstand imagery when in Revelation 1:20 the **seven lampstands** represent the **seven churches**. Since the rule of prior definition from Section One applies, the two witnesses must be two churches.

The image of the two olive trees first appears in Zechariah 4 where two olive trees represent two who are anointed to serve the Lord of all the earth. This image is further defined by Paul in Romans 11:17-24 when he compares the Gentiles, called wild olive branches, with the Jews who are called natural or domestic olive branches.

The identification of the two witnesses with the Jewish and Gentile churches fits comfortably with the images used. The Jewish and Gentile churches are witnesses. They have been set apart to serve the Lord of all the earth. They have prophesied throughout the ages and have endured against opposition.

God says that he will give power to his two witnesses and they will prophecy. The churches cannot be stopped by any opposition until they have finished their testimony (Rev. 11:7.) When they have finished their testimony, the **Beast from the Abyss** (Satan) will attack them and kill them. Their bodies will lie in the streets of Jerusalem (where their Lord was crucified - Rev. 11:8) for **three and a half days**. At the end of the three and a half days, a breath of life will enter them and they will stand on their feet. After that they ascend to heaven in a cloud.

This account describes the success of the church in the face of persecution throughout the **forty-two months** that the Gentiles are trampling the holy city (i.e., during the church age.) The church, consisting of both its Gentile and Jewish portions, bears witness to Jesus Christ, through the power given her (Rev. 11:3), until her testimony is completed.

The meaning of "finishing their testimony" is not clear from the Revelation text; however, in Matthew 24:9-14, the completion of the church's task is described in the larger context of Jesus answering the questions; when will the final and complete destruction of the temple occur, and what will be the sign of his coming and of the end of the age? (Matt. 24:1-3.)

Matthew 24:14 And this gospel of the kingdom will be preached in the whole world as a testimony to all nations, and then the end will come.

The preaching of the gospel in the whole world is the task that must be completed and when it is, the end comes. There may be individuals who have not heard, but the gospel has been preached in their region and is available.

Once the church's testimony is complete, Satan (the beast that comes up from the abyss) is released from the Abyss where he has been bound for a time (**1000 years**) and he kills the church. This release of Satan from the abyss is described in Revelation 20. Satan is cast into the abyss and bound for 1000 years. After the 1000 years, he is released and permitted to attack the church for a short time (Rev. 20:3, 7-10.)

While the attack is attributed to Satan, he is not able to act directly and physically any more than he did before he was bound. Even Job, who loses property, family, and health by Satan's explicit intervention, does not deal with Satan directly. His losses occur through military actions by local tribes and damage caused by distortion of nature (fire from heaven, high winds, illness.) Satan acts against the church through his chosen representative, the Man of Lawlessness. Throughout Revelation, there is such harmony between the thoughts and desires of Satan and the Man of Lawlessness that in some cases actions are attributed to Satan that are accomplished by the Man of Lawlessness.

The idea that the church is a powerful force that cannot be overcome until the end is found in the Old Testament. In Daniel 12:1, there is a time of distress such as has not happened from the beginning of nations until then. This language is quoted in Matthew 24 and Mark 13 in reference to the end of time and the return of Jesus Christ.

Matthew 24:21,29-31 For then there will be great distress, unequaled from the beginning of the world until now.

Immediately after the distress of those days, the sun will be darkened, and the moon will not give its light; the stars will fall from the sky, and the heavenly bodies will be shaken. At that time the sign of the Son of Man will appear in the sky, and all the nations of the earth will mourn. They will see the Son of Man coming on the clouds of the sky, with power and great glory. And he will send his angels with a loud trumpet call, and they will gather his elect from the four winds, from one end of the heavens to the other.

This **extreme language**, reflecting the devastating nature of the judgment for those who are not prepared to face it, warns of the final judgment.

Daniel 12:1 goes on to state that at that time (i.e., at the end of the time of distress), everyone whose name is found in "the **book**" is delivered. They are delivered by the return of Christ because the next verse describes the final resurrection and judgment: some to everlasting life and others to shame and everlasting contempt. Daniel looks on as an unidentified man asks how long before these things are fulfilled. The man in linen answers (Daniel 12:7) by swearing that it will be for a **time, times, and half a time**. He then adds, "When the power of the holy people has been finally broken, all these things will be completed." The time, times, and half a time as used in Revelation is the same period as the **forty-two months** and **1,260 days** (see articles below).

The death of the church described in Revelation 11:7-10 is prophesied in the Old Testament where it is called the power of the holy people being broken in Daniel 8:25 and 12:7 and the defeating and oppressing of the saints in Daniel 7:21,25. This corresponds to the release of Satan (Revelation 20:7-10, 11:7), that occurs at the end of the time of the Gentiles also known as the church age (the forty-two months that they trample

Jerusalem - Revelation 11:2, or the period of Israel's hardening until the full number of Gentiles has come in - Romans 11:25.) When Satan is released, the church dies, remains dead for a symbolic three and a half days, and then it rises from the dead (Rev. 11:7-10.) The resurrected church once again bears witness to the Lord and the time of Israel's hardening ends. The two witnesses (the church) testify for a short time before the return of Christ overcomes Satan and the Man of Lawlessness. The Lord returns to take the resurrected church to heaven.

> *Revelation 11:12* Then they heard a loud voice from heaven saying to them, "Come up here." And they went up to heaven in a cloud, while their enemies looked on.

The death of the church described in Revelation 11 is not the removal or elimination of all true believers. Rather, it is a complete compromise of the visible church such that it no longer bears witness to Jesus. There continue to be believers who participate in the resurrection of the church that occurs a non-literal three and a half days later. The church dying while individual Christians remain faithful is a reversal of the situation that has existed from the time of Christ. In the beginning of the church, individuals faced death (Rev. 2:9,10) but the church continued unhindered (Rev. 11:5,6.) The death of the church occurs through the corruption of its message and its leadership, such that it no longer focuses on glorifying God and his Christ. Nevertheless, from the beginning of human history, the Lord has always retained a remnant who remain faithful to him. It is this remnant through whom he will raise the church back to its feet. This dead church is, after the figurative three and a half days, raised to life. This would suggest a revival that reestablishes a visible church of such power that it is a source of terror to the world (Rev. 11:11.) One element in this restoration will be the revival of the Jewish church in great strength.

In Romans 11:25, Paul asserts that the Jewish church has experienced a hardening until the full number of the Gentiles comes in. This is similar to what is described in Revelation 11:2, where the Gentiles trample on the holy city for forty-two months. Since the forty-two months are the same as the 1,260 days (forty-two thirty day months) in verse 3, and since the 1,260 days are the same as the time, times, and half a time (compare Revelation 12:6 and 12:14), the time of the hardening of the Jewish church will last until the two witnesses are killed. Hosea 3:4f says that Israel will live a long time without a king or sacrifice. In the last days Israel will return and seek the Lord. When the two churches stand on their feet, the Jewish church is no longer hardened and is revived. This revival of the church takes place immediately before the return of Christ and the final judgment (see Rev. 11:12-19, Daniel 12:1-7 and Matthew 24:29-31.) The revival of the church is followed by the return of Christ where the church meets him in the clouds and after which comes the judgment. The use of **extreme language** in Revelation 11:13 points to the final judgment as does the language surrounding the sounding of the seventh **trumpet** (Rev. 11:15-18.)

Woman Clothed with the Sun - [Rev. 12:1] This woman gives birth to a son who will rule all the nations with an **iron scepter**. This son is seen in Revelation 19:15 and is called Faithful and True, the **Word of God** and wears the name **King of Kings and Lord of Lords**. These titles are clearly references to Jesus. While one might think first of Mary as the mother of Jesus, the text points to the less specific spiritual parentage of Jesus. This woman is a ruler, wearing a **crown** with twelve stars on it. The woman is to be taken care of for **1,260 days** in the desert (Rev. 12:6) and later in the chapter she flies to a place prepared for her in the desert, where she will be taken care of for a time, times, and half a time. John has thereby connected the 1,260 days and the **time, times, and half a time** to show that they are the same period. Since the woman flees to the desert after her child is snatched up to God and to his throne, the 1,260 days must begin at or after the ascension. The **dragon** (Satan), failing to kill the woman, goes off to make war against the rest of her offspring. The offspring are identified as "those who obey God's commandments and hold to the testimony of Jesus" (Rev. 12:17.) If the offspring are those who obey God's commandments, the woman must be the church. She precedes the coming of the child and so must include both the Old Testament and New Testament portions of the church. The twelve stars symbolize the twelve tribes of the Old Testament and the twelve apostles of the New Testament. The dragon is not able to attack the woman because she is protected by God, but her offspring, the individuals within the church, can be attacked. The **red** dragon's efforts to devour the child at his birth remind the reader of Herod's efforts to kill the child born king of the Jews and of Satan's efforts to tempt Jesus in the hope that he would avoid the cross and fail in his purpose.

The woman is safe for 1,260 days which is the same period during which the two **witnesses** are testifying (Rev. 11:3.) There is no mention of what happens to her after the 1,260 days. The reason for this is that the woman and the witnesses represent the same thing, the church. From the fate of the witnesses we can understand that the woman is no longer safe after the 1,260 days and if the imagery were followed further, after the 1,260 days she would be killed. Since the purpose of this book is the encouragement of the saints, the fate of the woman after the 1,260 days is not discussed. It would not be an encouragement to the church to repeat the message in Revelation 11 about the death of the church. A godly man like Daniel, who understood only a portion of the visions he saw, was appalled and made physically sick at the sight of these events (Daniel 7:28, 8:27.)

Word of God - [Rev. 1:2,9, 6:9, 19:13, 20:4] In the gospels the term "word of God" is used only of Scripture. However, in John's gospel Jesus is called "the Word" and later in John's first epistle, Jesus is called the "Word of Life" (I John 1:1.) These prior usages provide the background for the title given Jesus (Rev. 19:13) "the Word of God."

Throughout Revelation, the term "word of God" is connected to the phrase "the testimony of Jesus" in every instance except where the term is used as a title for Jesus. These phrases are connected because they represent the fullness of the message in the New Testament church. The word of God is needed because at the time John is writing, the Old Testament Scriptures provide the background for understanding the person and work of Christ. The testimony of Jesus is necessary because he has fulfilled and interpreted the Old Testament, and his words, in whatever oral or written forms existed at the time Revelation was written, are necessary for the church.

In his prologue, John describes everything he saw as the word of God and the testimony of Jesus (Rev. 1:2.) So John holds that his vision, recorded in Revelation, is God's word and can be called Scripture.

In Revelation 1:9, he reports that he was on the island of Patmos because of the word of God (i.e., he was imprisoned on Patmos because of his faith.) Similarly, in Revelation 6:9, John saw the souls of those who had been slain because of the word of God (i.e., those who died as Christian martyrs.) In Revelation 20:4, John saw the souls of those who had been beheaded because of the word of God.

The connection between Scripture, and persecution and martyrdom in Revelation demonstrates the importance of the Scriptures to John and the early church. According to John, Christians were persecuted and martyred during the early history of the church not for lofty principles or ideas but for their faithfulness to the Scriptures as the word of God.

Wormwood - [Rev. 8:11] Wormwood is the name of a **star** that falls on the fresh waters and fouls them. Since stars are **angels** in Revelation, this is an angel who is participating in God's judgment. While the angels who sound the **trumpets** of judgment are good, this angel is not good. He is evil just as the locusts released from the abyss at the fifth trumpet are evil. The angel shares his name with a mildly poisonous plant found in Palestine whose name is synonymous with bitterness. He lives up to his name by making the waters bitter, so that many who drink from the waters die.

[1] For a more complete discussion see Before Jerusalem Fell, Kenneth L. Gentry, Jr. Institute for Christian Economics, Tyler, Texas, 1989.

[2] G.W. Butterworth, Clement of Alexandria (London: Heinemann, 1919) pp. 356ff. Quoted in Before Jerusalem Fell, Kenneth L. Gentry, Jr. Institute for Christian Economics, Tyler, Texas, 1989. From Clement's Quis Salvus Dives, Section 42.

[3] For more information see Redating the New Testament, John A. T. Robinson, Philadelphia: Westminster, 1976.

[4] Abbott, E. A., Clue. Johannine Grammar, 1906, quoted in A Grammar of the Greek New Testament, A. T. Robertson, Broadman Press, Nashville, TN, 1934, page 762.

[5] The Ante-Nicene Fathers, Alexander Roberts and James Donaldson, eds., Grand Rapids, Eerdmans, 1975, Volume 1 pp. 559-560.

[6] Quoted by Eusebius, 5:8:5-6. Cited from Philip Schaff and Henry Wace, eds., A Select Library of Nicene and Post-Nicene Fathers of the Christian Church: Second Series, 14 Volumes (Grand Rapids:Eerdmans, [1890] 1986) 1:222

[7] Abbott, E. A., Clue. Johannine Grammar, 1906, quoted in A Grammar of the Greek New Testament, A. T. Robertson, Broadman Press, Nashville, TN, 1934, page 762.

[8] The Life and Times of Jesus the Messiah, Wm. B. Eerdmans Publishing Co., Grand Rapids, Michigan, page 716.

Outline/Timeline of the Book of Revelation

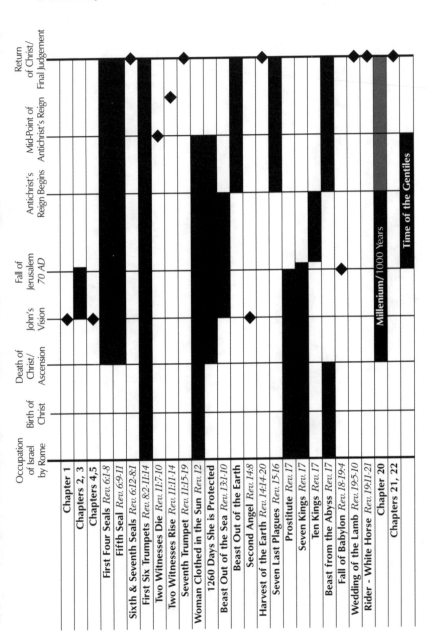

Square Halo Books

In Christian art, the square halo identified a living person presumed to be a saint. Square Halo Books is devoted to publishing works that present contextually sensitive biblical studies, and practical instruction consistent with the Doctrines of the Reformation. The goal of Square Halo Books is to provide materials useful for encouraging and equipping the saints.